ONE OF US

ONE OF US

Officers of Marines—Their Training, Traditions, and Values

Jack Ruppert

Foreword by
Major General (Ret.) O.K. Steele, USMC

Westport, Connecticut
London

Library of Congress Cataloging-in-Publication Data

Ruppert, Jack, 1934–
One of us : officers of Marines : their training, traditions, and values / Jack Ruppert ; foreword by O.K. Steele.
p. cm.
Includes bibliographical references and index.
ISBN 0–275–97222–4 (alk. paper)
1. United States. Marine Corps—Officers—Training of. 2. United States. Marine Corps—Officers. 3. Ruppert, Jack, 1934– I. Title.
VE23.R88 2003
359.9′6332′0973—dc21 2002029772

British Library Cataloguing in Publication Data is available.

Library of Congress Catalog Card Number: 2002029772
ISBN: 0-275-97222-4

First published in 2003

Praeger Publishers, 88 Post Road West, Westport, CT 06881
An imprint of Greenwood Publishing Group, Inc.
www.praeger.com

Printed in the United States of America

The paper used in this book complies with the Permanent Paper Standard issued by the National Information Standards Organization (Z39.48-1984).

10 9 8 7 6 5 4 3 2

To every man and woman who has earned the right to wear the eagle, globe, and anchor, especially the 557 men of the 3-56 Basic School Class. May courage, honor, and commitment guide our path until the last trumpet sounds.

Contents

Acknowledgments

The act of authoring a book creates myriad material and intangible debts, due and payable from the writer's emotional bank account to the order of family, friends, and a number of total strangers. It would be difficult to recount the acts of kindness, generosity, and beyond-the-call-of-duty assistance that came my way during the three years it took me to complete this work. A mention in the acknowledgments section of a book is small recompense to those to whom large debts of gratitude are owed.

In 1998 a friend sent me an article from a Savannah newspaper which recounted the experience of a former Marine corporal, one Melvin Tuten of Sea Island, Georgia. While attending a reunion of the Seventh Marine Regiment in Hawaii, Tuten told his former company commander, Colonel Paul B. Goodwin, USMC (Ret.) that he had never received the Silver Star he was told he had earned 26 years earlier for his valorous actions at Mutter's Ridge in Vietnam. Goodwin said he would look into it, and Tuten forgot about the conversation. A few weeks later Tuten received a call from Headquarters, USMC. He was told that he would be awarded his Silver Star on the parade grounds of the Parris Island Recruit Depot. Paul Goodwin did what Marine officers are supposed to do. When he discovered that one of his people had been failed by the system, he took it upon himself to intercede with the Commandant's office. No matter that the issue was a quarter of a century old—it needed fixing. As an old Marine myself, this story intrigued but did not surprise me. It took place at the same time an Assistant Secretary of the Army was describing the Marine Corps as "extremist" to a gathering at an eastern university. Based on my own experience, Paul Goodwin's actions were in keeping with the loyalty expected of an officer of Marines. I called Colonel Goodwin and we agreed to meet to talk about leadership and the Marine Corps. Over the next few weeks Colonel Goodwin's willingness to share his broad knowledge of the modern Marine Corps spurred my own interest in further exploring the Marine leadership ethic and examining how the Marines manage to maintain it from one generation to another. Colonel Goodwin's invaluable help in getting this project off the ground in its early stages is deeply appreciated.

From the day in June 1956 when I first met Orlo K. "Ort" Steele, it was obvious that he would, in all likelihood, end up a general. He didn't disappoint us; he retired in 1990 as a two-star general, the highest permanent rank attainable in the Marine Corps, after 35 years of service. Seventeen of those years were spent in command of troops, from platoon commander to command of the Second Marine Division. Ort Steele fulfilled our predictions, and never lost the modest, gentlemanly air of leadership that made him a standout among the members of the 3-56 Basic School Class. His help in reintroducing me to the Marine Corps, coupled with the high regard in which he is held by that institution, made my job much easier. His willingness to share his time, experience, and perspectives throughout the course of writing the book reflects the selflessness that identifies the best in leaders.

Randy Brooks is a Vietnam vet, the son of a Marine, and an occasional golf partner of mine. He and I first discussed this book in 1998. His suggestions, particularly regarding the use of market research techniques to explore the attitudes and opinions of two generations of officers, convinced me that the project might hold broad interest. I value his expertise and generous friendship.

Lieutenant Colonel Harvey J. Morgan, USMC (Ret.) and Clifford G. Fox, a former major who spent 14 years on active duty in the Corps, are also 3-56 classmates. This book would never have been attempted without their groundwork. They tracked down all but ten of our surviving classmates and had created a class roster long before this book was started. I benefitted from their work in many ways, not the least being the ability to communicate directly with almost 200 classmates through e-mail. Communication with the balance of the class was a bit slower, but their cooperation and interest in the project were underpinned by the work performed by these two gentlemen. I am humbled by the assistance provided by these two men, as well as by the rest of our classmates, when I sought input through hundreds of electronic messages and through the mail. Without my classmates there would be no book.

I cannot repay the hospitality extended to me by Colonel George J. Flynn, USMC, Commanding Officer of Officer Candidates School and Colonel John R. Allen, USMC, Commanding Officer of The Basic School. Both Colonel Flynn and Colonel Allen were accessible to me whenever I sought input or perspective. Their unbounded willingness to assist was mirrored by their staffs, and I can honestly say that no request I made was denied by these two officers. To have the opportunity to discuss, in depth, many issues that affect the Marine Corps and its officer selection and training processes with men of their intelligence and broad experience was as pleasurable as it was educational.

I must extend my gratitude to my old classmate, Colonel Tom Reis, USMCR (Ret.) who had sufficient faith in the idea behind the book to direct me to John Harney of Book Consultants of Boston. And, to John Harney whose patience, experience, intellect, encouragement and blue pencil were major factors in getting this author through the inevitable low points in such a project. May every author find two such solid friends.

There are so many Marines who freely shared their time and thoughts with me over a three-year period that it would be impossible to list them all. Here are some to whom I offer my sincere thanks:

Major General James C. Conway

Lieutenant Colonel Steve Cooperider

Majors James C. Brennan, Patrick Kelleher, Rick Spooner, USMC (Ret.)

Captains Tim Bairstow, Kevin Burton, Yolanda Davis, Jonathan Farley, Trent Gibson, John Hackel, Doug Hanley, Emily Howell, Tom Jarman, Ricardo Martinez, Keith Parry, Brad Pennella, Tim Powledge, Michael Samarov, and William Shuell

First Sergeants Tim Campbell and Paul McKenna

Gunnery Sergeant Charles Jackson

Staff Sergeants Tyrone Horton and Bradley Newton

The hundreds of OCS candidates and TBS lieutenants who are the subject of this book.

Special thanks go to Captain David L. Parks and Captain Anita L. Weissflach, two of the Corps' most helpful and accommodating Officer Selection Officers. Captain Parks furnished me with a basic understanding of today's Marine Corps officer selection process. He was my go-to guy for just about everything before he retired from the Marine Corps a few months ago. Captain Weissflach, a very squared-away Marine, and her motivated pool of candidates and recently commissioned lieutenants provided me with OCS anecdotes and memories, and patiently answered my unending stream of questions and requests for information. This old Marine is most grateful to you.

Finally, to my wife of 45 years, Maureen Harrington Ruppert, my deepest appreciation. I would never have finished this work without her support, patience, understanding, and motivation. She is the love of my life, an intelligent critic, and my closest friend.

Foreword

Outsiders sometimes view United States Marines as a rather strange breed of cat to be in anybody's alley. To civilians we may appear intimidating, cultist, and even a tad abnormal. Other services often scoff that we are nonconformist, overly concerned about image, and paranoid about the possibility that the Corps may one day be declared irrelevant and therefore eliminated. While these may not be the most flattering of descriptions, there are few of us who would deny them. Nor should we. We are, in fact, a different breed from the vast majority of men and women who make up the Armed Forces of the United States. Indeed, in many respects, one can find more commonality between the U.S. Marines and several foreign military organizations than between the Marines and our sister services. The fact that a traditional Marine Birthday Cake Cutting Ceremony leads off with a drum and bugle corps playing "The Foreign Legion March," for instance, is not just happenstance.

But even as Marines own up to these unmistakable differences, these should not be a cause for alarm to American citizens. Nor should Americans necessarily conclude that their Marines are out of step with the society they serve. Rather, it should be taken as a simple recognition that Marines are who they are because of their unique mission and history and because each succeeding generation has striven to preserve the Corps' most cherished values and traditions, as inconsequential and outmoded as these may appear to others.

If there is a single underlying factor that distinguishes the Marine Corps from the nation's other armed forces, I believe it is simply this: Marines do not have the luxury to rest on past laurels, or take themselves for granted. Five times in its 226-year history, the U.S. Marine Corps has been brought to the threshold of extinction. In its last battle for survival, during the aftermath of World War II, the Eighteenth Commandant of the Marine Corps, General Alexander A. Vandegrift, appeared before the Senate Naval Affairs Committee and said, "We have pride in ourselves and in our past, but we do not rest our case on any presumed ground of gratitude owing us from the nation. The bended knee is not a tradition of our Corps. If the Marine as a fighting man has not made the case for himself after 170 years of service, he must go."

As all Marines know, thanks mainly to the will of the 80th Congress, we successfully overcame that assault, and the Corps was not absorbed by the other services. Nevertheless, General Vandegrift's words ring just as clearly in the psyche of every Marine today as they did when he first uttered them over 50 years ago. Implicit in his remarks was the message he was also sending to the future, as well as present, members of his own Corps. That message was simple and direct: There can be no room for complacency in our ranks. Either each succeeding generation will make the case that the U.S. Marine Corps is, and always will be, the best and most effective fighting force in the nation, or it must go. Even today, that admonishment seldom fails to engender an extraordinary sense of duty, commitment, and fidelity which manifests itself daily among every rank and file. Briefly put, to wear the eagle, globe, and anchor carries the solemn obligation never to let down those Marines who have gone before. Being a Marine, therefore, means to share an ethos once imbued in the minds of ancient Greek warriors when going off to battle: Either return carrying your shield with honor, or be carried on it.

I believe it is this same fear of complacency that has inspired creativity and has kept the Marine Corps institutionally on its toes. Except for a brief time during the mid-1970s, when it came under criticism for its outdated structure and operational practices, the Corps has received high marks from most defense analysts for being not only tenacious in combat, but also a remarkably innovative, flexible, and adaptable force. This is especially evident whenever the Marine Corps has perceived the need to modify its seaborne amphibious doctrine—to exploit changes in technology, to counter some future battlefield threat, or to satisfy a requirement imposed by cuts in defense spending. Moreover, it has consistently managed to make these transformations without compromising its primary mission: to be ready to deploy and fight whenever and wherever a crisis may arise. In this regard, the projection of a 1,200-man Marine air-ground task force over 300 miles from the Arabian Sea to seize and secure a forward expeditionary base inside a hostile, landlocked Afghanistan was unquestionably a remarkable operational feat. Clearly, today's soldiers of the sea have not lost their flair for staying both combat ready and extraordinarily flexible.

Nevertheless, preserving our time-honored values and a warrior spirit has not always come easily, or without cost. During times of peace, for example, the Corps has often found itself crossways and alone in its resistance to fall in step with some new political expedient or social trend. I recall a case in point in the early 1960s when I was a lieutenant. It was then the sense of the Congress that all members of the Armed Forces of the United States should receive indoctrination training on the evils of communism. Later, when the Service Chiefs were testifying before one of the Congressional committees, each was asked to describe what his service was doing to comply with this requirement. After receiving testimony on all the positive steps being taken by the three other services, the chairman turned his attention to General David M. Shoup, who was then the Commandant, and asked him what the Marines were doing in this regard. General Shoup responded, "Frankly, Mr. Chairman we are doing nothing. Marines are taught to fight against whatever enemy the President may direct. And in my view, that is all they need to know." Those of us who were serving in the Fleet Marine Force cheered, but, needless to say, this was not the response the politicians expected or wanted to hear. Doubtless, some good will was probably lost with that committee. Nonetheless, whenever the Marine leadership has decided to stand firm on a controversial issue, such as not mixing the sexes while undergoing recruit training, or allowing women Marines to serve in the combat arms, more often than not they have ultimately come to be praised in the court of public opinion for remaining faithful to their principles.

It has been more than 45 years since we of the 3-56 Basic Class first convened at the outdoor theater of Camp Upshur and were formally welcomed to The Basic School by our commanding officer, Colonel Lew Walt. As my good friend and former messmate Jack Ruppert has so faithfully recorded in this book, the intervening years ushered in a number of momentous events which have affected both the nation and its Corps of Marines. The 1960s brought a protracted war in Southeast Asia, dividing our country right down the middle. The 1970s saw an increase in social permissiveness and an end to conscription in favor of an all-volunteer military establishment. The decade of the 1980s culminated with an end to the East-West Cold War. Although the 1990s started with a swift, victorious military campaign against Iraq, emerging on its heels has come the more shadowy, but just as deadly and menacing, threat of global terrorism. Each of these potent forces has in some way brought inevitable change to the Marine Corps. Assimilating some of those changes has not always made for a smooth ride, and the fortunes of the Corps have alternately waxed and waned in the process.

In *One of Us,* Jack Ruppert compares the many changes that have taken place in the Marine Corps' officer selection, screening, and training processes over the last half century. He takes us through the prospective officer's initial contacts with a Marine Officer Selection Officer, describes the chaos and challenges that mark Officer Candidates School, and reviews the basic education of a new lieutenant at The Basic School. Much has changed since the days when Basic School Class 3-56 sweated up and down the pole-line roads of Quantico in herringbone twill dungarees. Today's lieutenants march those same hills in camouflage utilities, carrying modern packs and weapons. The distinctions are manifold and obvious, but, while the uniforms and equipment may be different, the hearts and souls inside those uniforms are much the same today as they were 50 years ago. Furthermore, as Jack concludes in his final chapters, despite profound dissimilarities in the societies under which the two generations were reared, the attraction and appeal that motivated both groups toward becoming a Marine are almost indistinguishable. Today, he reflects, the Corps continues to be the ultimate proving ground for American youth, a beacon for those who believe that personal integrity and character still count. So long as that beacon continues to shine brightly and attract the few and the proud, I am confident that the health of the Leatherneck Corps will remain as vibrant in the future as it has in the past.

Major General (Ret.) O.K. Steele, USMC
Grass Valley, California

A Note to the Reader

This book contains two elements of information that require comment. First are the recollections of my classmates, as well as my own, of events that occurred 50 years ago and are recounted in this book. Although memories dim over time, I am confident that these stories are accurate, with few embellishments. We were all involved in some of the same, or similar, unforgettable experiences, and I assure the reader that these memories reflect the realities of that time.

The second type of information includes descriptions of the events that I witnessed and the people whom I observed over the two years in which I made periodic visits to the Officer Candidates School (OCS) and The Basic School (TBS). Because of the time span covered by this book, it was not feasible for me to follow an OCS class through its full ten weeks of training and a five-month TBS course. In order to provide continuity, I have written about events witnessed over a series of weeks or months as if these happened to a single OCS company or a single TBS class. A similar approach was used with the OCS staff personnel who appear in the book. Because some of these Marines are assigned to OCS only for a single summer, Sergeant Instructors who appear in the book as members of "the company" may not have served concurrently at OCS. Apart from these caveats, the events that I have reported in the book unfolded as I describe them.

Introduction

> No one of us exists for himself alone, but one part of us belongs to our country.
>
> Plato, 385 B.C.

It was late July 1956, and the 189 second lieutenants of G Company, 3-56 Class, Marine Officers Basic School had spent seemingly endless, steamy days on the rifle range at Quantico. To the uninitiated, rifle qualification in the Corps is akin to a priest saying his first Mass or a pilot making a solo flight. Rifle marksmanship is the base-rock requirement to be a Marine. If you cannot fire a rifle with a reasonable degree of expertise you will not be a Marine. Rifle qualification is a major event and the men of Golf Company had just fired for record, determining who would receive the expert, sharpshooter, or marksman badges.

As we lined up for noon chow in front of the field kitchen, a jeep pulled into the area. Out of the jeep leapt a solid, bull-necked man, Colonel Lewis J. Walt. Colonel Walt was a genuine hero, having won the Navy Cross in 1942 on Guadalcanal, the first offensive action undertaken by American forces in the Pacific. Guadalcanal was the opening act of the island-hopping campaign that would, by the end of World War II, take Marines across the vast expanse of the Pacific to Okinawa, a scant 400 miles from the Japanese homeland. Colonel Walt, who would command all Marine forces in Vietnam and later be named Assistant Commandant of the Marine Corps, was, at the time, the Commanding Officer of The Basic School (TBS). He had come to share noon chow with us on this day. He would troop the line, congratulating each officer who had qualified that day, underscoring the importance he placed on his lieutenants' rifle qualification.

The entire company was in the chow line and, as Colonel Walt approached, we began to make room for him at the front of the chow line. Of course, we knew that officers always eat after their troops are fed in the Marine Corps. That principle is preached to officer candidates from day one of Officer Candidates School (OCS). We had heard that song many times. We believed it but, seeing those eagles on the colonel's collar, we were not quite sure how it related to bird colonels and second lieutenants. So we opted for what we thought was a safe approach and tried a bit of "managing up." We found out quickly that it did not work with Colonel Walt. He glowered at us, and it was obvious that he would enjoy this teaching opportunity. As an experienced craftsman shares a trade secret with some apprentices, he gathered us around him. "Gentlemen, I am here to eat good Marine chow with you. You have been doing important work since early this morning while I have been in my office. I will not eat until every one of you has been fed. If there's anything left over, *then* I will eat." With a menacing smile, he continued, "And if I ever see any of you eat before your troops are fed, I will personally do you bodily harm." He smiled and his comment was met with some nervous laughter but not one of us missed his point or his ability to do a person bodily harm. We clearly understood that we *would* be more concerned for our Marines' welfare than our own. Only after the troops were taken care of would we be concerned about our own needs. That moment is etched as clearly in my mind as if it happened yesterday. And it says something about the lasting effect of the Marine leadership experience.

"It ain't like the old Corps" is an age-old complaint, most often uttered by some senior Marine as the first sergeants and gunnery sergeants gather over their beers at the Staff Noncommissioned Officer (NCO) Club or some other watering hole. Over the 260 years of the Corps' existence, career Marines have bewailed the inevitable changes that technology, as well as social and political pressures, force on their Corps. Such railings about the "Old Corps" are part of Marine culture. Over the last half century, the Marine Corps has demonstrated an uncanny ability to adjust its strategies, tactics, and training procedures to the vast technological, political, and social changes that have so swiftly and dramatically changed the face of the world and the society that the Corps is called upon to defend. The Marines have worked their way through the bad times following the Ribbon Creek incident in 1956, post-Vietnam drug problems, and racial conflicts and appear to have come out stronger. And the Marines have made these adjustments and adaptations without compromising their bedrock principles and traditions. This ability to adjust and survive is, in this writer's opinion, the result of two institutional characteristics. First, without the luxury of large budget allocations, the Corps has developed a singular ability to innovate. Second, the Marine Corps is driven by an unbending, overarching devotion to the development of principled, innovative, and selfless leadership at every level.

The original intent of this book was to compare the training of today's young officers with the training of the 1950s. However, as I spent time with more and more Marines, observing them and their activities, the focus changed. The story is not in the differences in training techniques, or in the differences that separate two groups of officers. The most revealing aspect of the story is the remarkable consistency of backgrounds, values, and beliefs found in two groups of Marines separated by 50 years.

In a world where principles like courage, honor, and commitment are sometimes viewed as outdated, the Marine Corps stands apart in the demands it makes on its potential leaders, just as it did five decades ago when this writer arrived at Quantico, Virginia, for officer candidate training. By the mid-1950s the Corps had changed. In 1956 Drill Instructor Staff Sergeant Matthew McKeon marched his platoon of recruits into the sinkholes of Ribbon Creek at the Parris Island Recruit Depot. Six young lives were lost, and the Marines came under the guns of the media, Congress, and public opinion. The Corps was forced to review its training policies, particularly the selection and training of drill instructors. Additional commissioned officers were assigned to oversee recruit platoons, and the brutality, previously a common hallmark of boot camp, all but disappeared. More African Americans and Hispanics were enlisting and making careers in the Corps as it slowly, but surely, began to reflect America's changing racial attitudes.

Some things changed; however, throughout the 1950s, the Corps remained very much like the "old Corps." Names had changed since the close of World War II in 1945, but the Korean War, with the notable exceptions of the helicopter and jet aircraft, was fought with essentially the same weapons and tactics used in the bloody Pacific engagements from Guadalcanal to Okinawa. The C Rations the troops ate in the field, as well as the ammunition crates they humped up and down the world's hills, often carried packing dates from the 1940s. Even the distinctive canvas leggings worn over the tops of their boondockers up until the 1950s were vestiges of the early twentieth-century banana wars. All were part and parcel of a shoestring, make-do, find-a-way-and-fix-it Marine tradition, a result of the Corps' being at the bottom of the food chain when budget time for the Department of Defense came around. The new and the exotic flowed to the nuclear age Air Force and, to a lesser extent, the Army and Navy. What was left over from the Navy budget filtered down to the Marines. And it was a point of Corps pride that it could make do with what was left and still do the job better than any other fighting force in the world. It is this in-your-face attitude that has played a large role in the formation of a brotherhood of men (and today, women) who have demonstrated, throughout history, a willingness to take on any task and make any sacrifice for country, Corps and each other.

This book, in part, focuses on the 557 newly commissioned second lieutenants who arrived at Marine Corps Schools, Quantico, Virginia, in June 1956 for eight months of officer training at TBS. What motivated them to join the Marine Corps in the first place? Certainly there were easier paths to follow than serving in one of the world's most demanding combat arms. Did the Corps change these men and the manner in which they would conduct themselves personally and professionally? How have nearly 50 years of living changed their attitudes? We will compare the attitudes and motivations of that generation with those of the second lieutenants currently attending TBS. How different are the backgrounds, attitudes, and motivations of these two groups? Is there some combination of upbringing, family, economic, or religious background that predicts an individual's predilection toward "Marinehood"? Was there such a predictor in 1956, and is there one today? We will explore all these questions.

THE SILENT GENERATION OF THE 1950s

To understand the 3-56 Class, one needs to understand the America of World War II and post-World War II in which the "silent generation" grew up. In the election of 1952, Dwight David Eisenhower ended a Democratic presidential reign that extended back to 1932. Americans had whipped the Great Depression, won a world war at great cost and sacrifice, and begun the rebuilding of Europe and Japan. It was time for a change.

Eisenhower's monumental achievement in organizing and managing the complex conglomerate of forces, clashing personalities, and political agendas of a multinational war machine in Europe underpinned one facet of the electorate's decision. Another was simply that Ike's straightforward honesty; his sometimes painful syntax reflected the common person. Never glib or flashy, Ike did not look like a matinee idol. He was a Midwesterner, a man of the people, who had achieved great things. Compared to the intellectual, urbane Adlai Stevenson, Ike was a plain, commonsense man. He promised to go to Korea, to bring an end to the fighting there, which had settled into a savage struggle for small pieces of real estate along the thirty-eighth parallel. Americans believed and put their trust in Ike.

In the generation that grew up during the war years, the average young American male sincerely believed in the ultimate goodness of America and its cause. Raised on radio, newspaper, and newsreel reports of their fathers', brothers', cousins', and neighbors' sacrifices across a world that was much larger than today, young American men of the 1950s were not sophisticates. There was little moralizing about intruding ourselves into the affairs of the two Koreas or any other trouble spot. If our nation's leaders said it was needed, we believed it was so.

The Age of Aquarius, marijuana, protests, and noncommunication between the generations were somewhere out in the future. One did what one's country asked. And what America asked was a man's help in fighting the spread of communism. Despite the 20–20 hindsight of some modern-day analysts, despite revisionist historians' minimization of the threat, it was very real to those of us who lived it. Two of the world's most powerful and populous countries, the Soviet Union and China, were arrayed against us. All of Eastern Europe was under the Kremlin's thumb. China, mysterious, backward, and technologically impaired, held nearly a billion people and posed a threat to every country in Southeast Asia. We couldn't know that the Soviet behemoth would, in time, fall of its own weight, pushed over the edge by the productive capacity, economic strength, and determination of capitalist America. Young America was willing to hitch up its trousers, roll up its sleeves and wade in whenever events threatened America or its friends.

Of course, not every young man shared this mind-set. Some found doctors who provided them with a way out of military service, sometimes due to alleged back problems or asthma. But most of us felt that we owed something to the nation for which our neighbors and family members had fought and bled. We didn't like the idea of giving a couple of years to the defense of the country, but we believed it was necessary.

Our generation was formed in the 1940s, a time of total war when the schools fostered a brand of patriotism that we eagerly accepted. Adolf Hitler, Benito Mussolini, and Hideki Tōjō, who led the Axis powers, were perfect villains, made more so by the nationalistic propaganda generated by our wartime government. Hitler, evil personified, led one of the world's most educated and cultured nations down into a maelstrom of police state genocide which was fully comprehended only after the war neared its conclusion. Pictures of thousands of corpses, stacked like cordwood in the stark snows of Poland and Germany, were forever etched in blood in our generation's hearts and minds. It was obvious that the blackest sort of evil was roaming the world and needed to be eliminated.

World War II and the extraordinary cooperative effort made by every level of society fed a boy's sense of duty. Paper drives; aluminum foil drives; the collection of cooking fats; gas, oil, and food rationing; and War Bond drives were a part of everyday life as America plunged headlong into a death struggle with villainous forces from across the seas. Blue stars on small flags in the windows of our neighborhoods reminded us of the men and women who were missing from family tables at suppertime. A gold star reminded us that some neighbor would never come home. Every family with a blue star in its window dreaded the arrival of a telegram that began, "We regret to inform you . . ."

Our radio heroes, including Captain Midnight, Jack Armstrong, the Green Hornet, and Little Orphan Annie, joined the effort across the airwaves, struggling with and always overcoming Axis plots to thwart our ultimate victory. Even before America entered the conflict, our parents gathered around the family radio to listen as Edward R. Murrow described our English cousins' courage when Hitler's Luftwaffe hammered the population centers of that country. As the war wore on, we devoured Ernie Pyle's columns from the front and laughed at Bill Mauldin's "Willie and Joe" cartoons. It was clear that the Germans, Italians, and Japanese were fighting for something that was repugnant to good people. That's all a kid understood. And we felt it was our job to see that they didn't get away with it.

It was an age of acceptance. We accepted what our government, the local cop, the teacher, and parents told us. They represented rightful authority—an authority handed to them by a just God. One might not like it but one accepted it. It was hard to wait to reach an age when we, like the generations before us, could go forth to serve a country blessed by the Almighty himself, in its role as protector of liberty, freedom, and justice.

That world, those attitudes, that acceptance are largely gone. The world remains a dangerous place, but military operations no longer take on the appearance of a crusade, which is exactly how we viewed World War II. The heroes of our youth, Thomas Jefferson, George Washington, Abraham Lincoln, and Eisenhower, unable to defend themselves from the grave, are cited as examples of leaders who have succumbed to sins of the flesh. And, one in my generation wonders, for what purpose? We live in an age of cynicism, relieved by flick-of-a-switch gratification. No more do young boys dream of heroic deeds accompanied by muted bugles and rolling drums. No more do children go to sleep to the haunting call of the steam locomotive in the distance, sending a message of wonder about the world outside their farm, town, or city. American youth gets its kicks electronically now. A simple click of the remote control transports the young to Japan, Peru, or Samoa, and technology produces a sophistication in the young that too often erases wonder from their eyes, too soon. The generation of the 1950s has been described as hokey, corny, too easily manipulated, and too trusting of the people and institutions we had been raised to hold in almost sacred awe. Whether the destruction of our icons is a good thing is subject to debate. The worldly sophistication of twenty-first-century America, measured by the yardsticks of incivility, cynicism, and self-possession has not, thus far at least, translated to meaningful human progress. That analysis will be left to future historians.

If the criticisms of my generation are valid, so be it. But across the rivers of time, we had a focus that was sharp and crystal clear. Certainly, there were dark sides to American life. Despite the desegregation of the armed services a few years earlier, racial prejudice was all too common, both in civilian life and in the military. There were other imperfections in the fabric of everyday American life, obvious from the perfect hindsight that 50 years provides. Nevertheless, we believed America's fundamental cause was right, and we believed that God was on our side. We were men and we understood that a man did his duty simply because it was expected of him. That is just the way it was.

The members of the 3-56 Basic School Class and those who pass through today's Basic School are products of completely different worlds. Beneath the surface differences, beneath the changes in American life brought about by the upheavals of the past half century, however, something bonds these officers together, something good and lasting, which certainly includes, but goes beyond, the high honor of leading Marines. We will search for it in the pages that follow.

1
A Few Good Men and Women

> My Dad was more nervous and apprehensive about this venture than I was. I started telling him facts about the Marine Corps, things that impressed me. That the Corps is the only service that consistently meets its recruiting goals without lowering standards. That among all the armed services it has the highest ratio of enlisted personnel to officers and that it has only 500 female officers. At that point, for some reason, I started crying. It was impossible to describe how I was feeling. I already had so much pride and respect for the Marine Corps that it wasn't a question of whether or not I'd like it. I knew I'd love it. The question was whether or not I'd make it. It was that untested challenge that lay ahead. I already had such pride and passion for this organization that it is difficult to explain the emotional surge of trying to prove you are worthy of its ranks.
>
> E-mail from a female Platoon Leader Class (PLC) member to her officer selection officer (OSO)

It is a long, sweat-drenched, chaotic, out-of-your-comfort-zone road from the college dorm or sorority or fraternity house to a commission as a second lieutenant of Marines. I wonder what it is that, through good and bad economic times, propels a select few college students to pursue the hard life of an officer of Marines. Even in the best of economic times and, without a Selective Service board breathing down one's neck as they did in the 1950s, the Corps consistently meets its needs for officer talent.

While watching NFL or college games on television I am occasionally exposed to one of the Marine Corps' recent officer recruitment commercials. In it a young man survives the perils of a surreal, "Dungeons and Dragons"-like set of traps and obstacles, at the conclusion slaying a computer-generated dragon with his two-handed sword. The young man is transformed into a Marine lieutenant, resplendent in dress blues, complete with the Mameluke officer's sword. The tag line is, "The few. The proud. The Marines. Maybe you can become one of us."

Slaying a dragon? I assume this appeals to this generation of college students. I wonder how and why today's college student is drawn to the difficult road that leads to a Marine commission. After all, a large percentage of today's students take more than four years to complete their degrees. Only the highly motivated or the unlucky ones schedule themselves into Friday classes. For many, it is a four-day week in which a regimen of staying up late and sleeping in is widely accepted. Then, too, there are the college administrators, quite a number of whom were, if not actually involved in protesting the Vietnam War, at least were never particularly disposed to think kindly about the military. Why, then, is it that the Marine Corps, the most rigid and traditional of our armed services, is able to recruit more officer candidates than it needs, wash out 20 percent who cannot or will not measure up to Marine standards, and continue to fill its requirement for 1,400–1,500 new second lieutenants each year?

The rigors of Marine training can't be a mystery even to a generation far removed from the all-out war efforts of World War II and the societal upheavals surrounding our involvement in Vietnam. Movies, television, video stores, libraries, and bookstore shelves are replete with descriptions of rugged and relentless Corps training. Why would a young person opt for all this? Who are these people, what motivates them, and how does the Corps continue to identify them and bring them on board?

To answer these questions, I needed to obtain some firsthand experience by observing the recruiting and selection process. I contacted the OSO in Columbus, Ohio, and we made arrangements to meet. Over a beer, the captain was very open to my request for information, even more so when he learned about my Marine background. He stated, "Sir, the Marine Corps has nothing to hide. Come along on a visit to one of my campuses and see for yourself what we do—and how we do it." We agreed on a date. I'm intrigued by the chance to learn what it is that attracts students to become "one of us."

On an October morning in southern Ohio, I drove east to Ohio University, located in Athens, Ohio. The drive took me through some parts of Ohio unreached by prosperity. The rolling terrain was splashed with the vivid reds and golds of autumn, despite an extreme summer drought. This farm country is interspersed with small towns, places like Georgetown, Wellston, and Jackson, which beckon to travelers on the Appalachian Highway, inviting them to visit the local McDonald's or Burger King.

My appointment was with Captain David L. Parks, USMC, an OSO. Captain Parks, who works out of Columbus, must recruit 32 Marine officer candidates this year from the universities and colleges of central and southern Ohio. His campus sources range from Ohio State University, with its 48,000 students, to Oberlin College, with a student population of 2,800.

Old Marines have memories of their own reasons for joining the Corps and, as the miles went by, I reflected on my own experience. I thought back to the winter of 1952 and South Hall at Xavier University in Cincinnati. When I walked into the white frame building that served as the student union for XU's 2,000 males, the Marine Corps was the furthest thing from my mind. Just inside the entry I was confronted by an erect, young first lieutenant in his dress blues. His ribbons told me he had served in Korea, where he had earned the Bronze Star for valor and a Purple Heart.

I was wearing my freshman football numeral sweater, and he asked, "You play football?" When I answered in the affirmative, he slipped easily into his presentation. He was recruiting a company of athletes for a Platoon Leaders Class (PLC) which he personally would command through a six-week training period at Quantico, Virginia, in the coming summer. He was looking for athletes because the physical demands of Marine training were tough. He outlined the program to me, explaining that I would attend two summer sessions of PLC training. Then, if I successfully completed both summer sessions, I would earn a commission upon graduation and begin my two-year tour of duty. In a matter-of-fact manner, he laid out the program and the demands it would make of me as well as the benefits I would receive. His attitude was, "If you're man enough to handle it, this may be for you."

I signed up the next day. Why? In the early 1950s the Korean War was still being waged. Every able-bodied college man had three choices. He could serve as an officer in one of the services, take his chances with his local Selective Service Board, or join a reserve outfit. Neither the draft nor the reserves held any interest for me. I wanted to be an officer. Besides, I had been thinking about the Marines since World War II. My brother-in-law had served in the Seabees alongside the Marines on Iwo Jima, and one of my many cousins had survived Guadalcanal. Their stories about the Corps stirred something in me that was undefined, yet compelling. Movies like *Wake Island, Pride of the Marines,* and *Sands of Iwo Jima* had their intended effect on me. At 18 years of age I simply knew that I wanted to be a part of it. I wanted to prove that I could handle the rough treatment and training for which the Corps was noted. It was a test of manhood, and I wanted to prove something to myself. In retrospect, I was an easy mark for that lieutenant.

As I came out of my reverie, I speculated on how the Corps' approach to officer recruitment might have changed in the last 47 years. I found the exit for Ohio University and then expended an inordinate amount of time finding a place to park. Parking must be one of the worst aspects of college life these days. I finally located a space about a half-mile from the Convocation Center where the Ohio University Job Fair was being held. I grabbed my briefcase and walked toward the center through a polyglot subsociety that exists on most campuses of any size today. I passed a young man with long orange and black hair dressed in combat boots, a black vest, and yellow and white striped tights, the kind worn by the Munchkins in *The Wizard of Oz.* He was accompanied by a young woman whose lips, eyebrows, and ears were pierced with rings, jewels, and other devices. I doubted very much that these pilgrims would be spending time at the Marine Corps booth.

The job fair was a sea of people. Over 100 exhibitors were participating, including large corporations, banks of every description, and high-technology firms seeking the computer talent needed to compete in the new millennium. I quickly found the U.S. Marine Corps Officer Selection booth. Captain Parks was engaged in an animated conversation with a student, and Staff Sergeant

Lawrence Bowman was keeping a watchful eye out for any student who might linger in front of the exhibit.

Captain Parks, a man of average height, trim physique, and excellent physical shape, exuded energy and urgency. Parks, from Louisville, Kentucky, was an 18-year-old, first-semester freshman at Bellarmine College in Louisville when he first considered the armed forces as a career.

I didn't know what I wanted to do with myself. I only knew I didn't want to be in college, so I quit. I worked at a bank, then as a Domino's Pizza Parlor manager while managing the apartment building I was living in. After a year or so, I knew there was something missing from my life. So, one day, I walked into the Air Force Recruiting Office in Louisville, fully intending to join.

I told the Air Force recruiter that I wanted to be proud of myself. I wanted to be a part of a something bigger than myself. I wanted to change the way I was living.

The NCO listened patiently. When I finished, he surprised me. "You're in the wrong place. You need to go across the hall to the Marines. They're in the life-changing business and frankly, we're not."

So, I did what he told me. I walked into the Marine Corps Recruiting Office and there, behind his desk, stood a bull-shouldered Master Sergeant with his hands on his hips. He took one look at me and said, "And just why the f—k do you think you could be a Marine?"

Parks signed his enlistment papers on the spot, and 28 days later he was on his way to the Parris Island Recruit Training Depot. He spent ten years as an enlisted Marine, achieving the rank of staff sergeant. At that point he was recommended for Officer Candidates School (OCS) on the MECEP program (Marine Enlisted Commissioning Education Program). Upon completion of OCS he attended The Basic School (TBS) and was assigned to a Marine Air Wing as an aircraft maintenance officer. For the last five years, Parks has been involved in recruiting, first as the Operations Officer and then as the Executive Officer of the Recruiting Station, Cincinnati, Ohio. Ten months ago, he was assigned as the OSO for Southern Ohio in the fourth Marine Corps Recruiting District.

Parks is one of the few Marine officers I have met who appears to thrive on the challenges of recruiting duty and successfully manages its professional and personal dislocations. Several officers, from captains to lieutenant colonels, told me, "Recruiting duty is the worst job in the Marine Corps." Reasons include stress on marriages and intense pressure to produce. This assignment also takes Marines away from the people with whom they feel most comfortable—other Marines.

Recruiting duty takes its toll on family life. The hours are long, and travel, particularly in the less densely populated areas of the country, is frequently five days a week. While Marine families generally bear up well under the separations caused by deployments to places like Somalia, Bosnia, or Afghanistan, they do not do as well when separated from the support system provided by families who are sharing the same separation experience. Although the Marine Corps does its best to accommodate family life in a civilian venue, the conventional wisdom is that divorce is too often the result of a recruiting tour.

Parks and his wife, Jenny, appear to have adapted themselves to living in the civilian world very well. Parks attributes this to several things, but most of all to Jenny. He believes that recruiting duty simply has an amplifying effect on marriages and relationships in general. Weaknesses are magnified, and bonds grow stronger. Parks was straightforward about the impact that recruiting duty has had on his family time as well as the personal financial burden he has incurred to make it easier for his family. He has spent almost $20,000 on nonreimbursed expenses to make the duty more comfortable for him and his family. He considers this an investment in his marriage and family. For example, since his work required long days and time on weekends away from the family, he used his own funds and purchased a cell phone long before these were authorized for OSOs. This provided him with an additional two or three productive hours per day while driving, allowing him to spend more time with his family when he was at home.

Parks stated, "We made a decision to come to recruiting duty and finish my career. Whatever it took to make that work was simply the cost of that decision." He and his family have no regrets, although he admits this is a price some are not willing to pay.

Jenny Parks is also very busy with her career as an accountant and raising their two children. While she would like the support that more time with her husband would bring, she said, "When you are as busy as I am, you don't have much time to sit around and feel sorry for yourself." Parks added that he had observed that many of the marriages that fail on recruiting duty are those in which the spouse was not very active. Parks, who feels strongly about this, advises Marines coming on board recruiting stations to encourage their spouses to work or to take some college courses.

Jenny has never taken the demands of recruiting duty personally. "I know how hard the duty is. David really needs to work hard to do the job well. He needs to work this hard to be as successful as he wants to be. Some spouses resent the long hours and time apart, but some of that stems from the attitude of the Marine. It is hard to be supportive if a Marine comes home whining or complaining about the long hours and hard work." The Parkses feel that their success as a couple and their success in their careers stem from the fact that their positive, supportive attitudes feed on each other.

A significant pressure point associated with recruiting duty is the Corps' absolute insistence that its recruiters and OSOs achieve their "mission." In civilian sales work the term "mission" is synonymous with "quota," but the Corps does not use that word in any of its activities. Call it a quota or a mission, careers have been sidetracked by failure to meet the recruiting mission. To attain the mission Marines work extremely long hours and log many miles on the road.

The OSO's mission is clear. Captain Parks is required to submit the files of 32 "qualified candidates" to the Officer Candidate Selection Board (OCSB) this fiscal year. (Approximately 70 OSOs spread throughout the United States must select 2,100 candidates per year in order to fill 1,200–1,300 OCS slots.) Just two months into the recruiting year, Parks has 32 candidates lined up. He has set a personal goal of 50 candidates and is confident that he'll reach it. The biggest challenge is to ensure that the candidates submitted to the OCSB are "qualified."

A qualified candidate must

- Be a U.S. citizen
- Upon commissioning, be from 18 to 29 years of age (ground officers); 18 to 26 years of age (air officers); or 18 to 32 years of age (lawyers)
- Achieve a 1000+ combined score on the SAT, or 45+ combined score on the ACT, or score 115+ on the electronics portion of the Armed Services Vocational Aptitude Battery
- Have achieved a 2.0 GPA for the most recent semester of school and carry a 2.0 cumulative GPA overall
- Be 60–78 inches tall (male) or 58–72 inches tall (female) and not exceed weight limits assigned to each height
- Not use drugs; not have been arrested; have less than five speeding tickets; and must not have been fined more than $130 for any offense
- Have no tattoos.

A candidate who meets these requirements is qualified and requires no waivers. The OSO may request that a requirement be waived for a candidate who does not meet the parameters described. OSOs often seek waivers for candidates who bring many positives to the table overall, but who may have made a youthful mistake.

Tattoos are an interesting subject in this time when body decoration is in vogue. While the requirement for a candidate is "no tattoos," the Marines take a reasonable and practical approach. Captain Anita Weissflach, the OSO in Hyattsville, Maryland, explains how she handles the question of tattoos.

The first concern is if the tattoo is visible in the short sleeve "C" uniform shirt. If it is, then receiving a waiver is a long shot. The applicant must be highly qualified, have glowing recommendations from high ranking officers, be prior enlisted or be a Fulbright Scholar. You get the idea. The second concern is if the tattoo is gang related, racist, or sexist. We actually have a packet of tattoos that we are able to reference. If the tattoo is questionable it's up to the OSO to make the decision whether or not to ask for the waiver.

Here are a couple of examples. If a man has a picture of an unclothed woman on his arm I tell him to either get a bikini tattooed on her or hit the road, since he won't receive a waiver with that tattoo as it is. Having an unclothed female on your arm isn't the most gentlemanly thing you could do, but I don't think it necessarily reflects bad character. Machismo or stupidity, maybe, but not necessarily bad character. On the other hand, if an applicant has a Nazi symbol on his arm I would not submit him. He can cover it up or have it removed but it doesn't erase his racism. These are decisions that OSOs make every day. We are under no obligation to submit a package if an applicant requires a waiver. We must make the decision to fight for the applicant or not.

Once accepted, if candidates are to stand any chance of making it through OCS, they are required to embark upon a demanding physical conditioning program. This is laid out in a letter from the Commanding Officer of OCS. The twelve-week regimen is designed to prepare candidates to meet the standards required in the Physical Fitness Test (PFT) prior to their arrival at Quantico (see Table 1.1).

To meet these standards, candidates are directed to engage in a circuit exercise program which includes tricep dips, half sit-ups, mountain climbers, push-ups (diamond), crunches, bends and thrusts, push-ups (wide), sit-ups (USMC), chair squats, and push-ups (USMC). Of course, a running program is absolutely essential. By the end of the twelve-week conditioning period, candidates are expected to be running between six and ten miles per day, four days per week.

These standards are not suggestions. The CO's letter states, "It is imperative that you arrive at OCS in good physical condition and within the Marine Corps' height, weight and body fat standards. Although your physical conditioning and physical appearance will improve as a result of the training you receive, this is not the time or place to get in shape or lose weight."

Captain Parks thus looks for Ohio University students who may not fit the mold for the average college student. He and his people are looking for men and women who are willing to pay the steep price demanded if they are to wear the gold bars of a second lieutenant of Marines.

From morning through late afternoon, Parks and Bowman engage in conversation with a number of young people who are simply looking for information—"tire kickers" in recruiter's jargon. Eight hours of chatting, answering

Table 1.1
Officer Candidates School Physical Fitness Standards

	Male Standards	
Event	Minimum Standard	Maximum Standard
Pull-ups	10	20
Abdominal Crunches (in 2 mins.)	80	100
3-Mile Run	24:00 mins.	18:00 mins.
	Female Standards	
Event	Minimum Standard	Maximum Standard
Flexed Arm Hang	40 seconds	70 seconds
Abdominal Crunches (in 2 mins.)	80	100
3-Mile Run	27:00 mins.	21:00 mins.

questions, separating the inquirers from the truly interested, and conducting short initial interviews result in an in-depth interview schedule with eight people considered "possibles."

These interviews are held in classic, professional sales fashion. The captain asks leading questions to determine the student's interests and goals. When this is done he tells the Marine Corps story in a persuasive, interesting manner, placing emphasis on the prospect's areas of interest. One candidate has an interest in completing a law degree after graduation, and Parks describes three different methods in which attorneys may enter the Corps. He then lays out the duties of an adjutant's billet in a Marine battalion or regiment, describing the challenges an attorney will encounter in that position.

Another candidate is interested in the more traditional life of an infantry, artillery, or tank officer. Parks tells him about the variety of programs open to candidates, but he finishes his description by saying, "And, of course, there are those who want to become Marines because they like to blow s—t up!" The prospect and the captain have found common ground. Parks then takes the prospect through a day in the life of an infantry platoon commander.

The next prospect is interested in aviation. Parks determines that the young man is a "possible" and offers him the opportunity to join two other prospects who will be picked up in Athens, driven to Columbus, and have the opportunity to talk with a Marine helicopter (CH-53) pilot about Marine aviation and perhaps take a hop in the aircraft. The student jumps at the chance. I am impressed by the lengths to which the Corps goes to bring young prospects on board. I restrain myself and don't say, "This ain't like the old Corps."

Through every interview Captain Parks makes it crystal clear that every Marine officer is first and foremost trained to lead an infantry platoon in combat. Whether a student aspires to become a pilot, lawyer, or engineer, he or she must first demonstrate an ability to lead a platoon of Marines on any basic mission.

Ask Parks what the secret to recruiting success is, and he gives a terse answer, "Hard work, long hours, and working smart." The aggressiveness with which Parks and Bowman approach their jobs is evident in an episode that occurred during the late afternoon.

A tall, athletic, young African American woman walked by the USMC exhibit and headed for the exit from the convention center. Parks, who was engaged in a discussion with another candidate, excused himself and walked quickly to catch up with the young woman. After a few moments of conversation, the woman and Parks returned to the exhibit.

Parks escorted the freshman from Steubenville, Ohio, to an interview area behind his exhibit. There, he explained the PLC program and answered her questions. A major obstacle to her entry in the program was a metal pin in one tibia, the result of an athletic injury suffered during her senior year in high school. She was concerned this would disqualify her from the PLC program, and Parks shared her concern. Rather than waiting to see if the young woman was ineligible because of her injury. Parks immediately called the Fourth District Corpsman, Navy Chief Petty Officer Wilson, who informed him that this injury, while subject to medical board review, did not necessarily disqualify her from the program. The student, obviously interested in the Marines, signed up for an in-depth interview the next morning.

I asked Parks why he picked her out of the crowd for special effort. He explained that she passed his table four times and, in true sales fashion, he was not going to let this one get away. He explained,

> Sometimes a person is teetering on the brink of talking with us. For whatever reasons, shyness or indecision, they are reluctant to step up and talk to someone in a uniform. I take the first step and alleviate their fears about talking to a Marine. That's what I did in this case . . . I simply made it easy for her to talk about something that, deep inside, she wanted to explore.

It was 4:30 P.M., and Parks and Bowman had been working since 6:00 A.M. when they left Columbus. The crowd at the job fair had thinned considerably, and Parks packed up his gear and invited me to grab a bagel and some coffee, since we had not had lunch. He mentioned, "After we grab something to eat I've got two possibles I need to interview." I decided to accompany him. By the time these interviews were concluded it was 6:15 P.M. We drove to our motel and checked in. Parks then informed me that we had a dinner appointment with two students: one a young woman, who attended PLC training last summer, and the other, a male friend of hers she was trying to convince to enter the Marine program.

Dinner was a pleasant affair, and Captain Parks discussed the PLC program with the young man, who was a member of the Marine Reserve. Having experienced Marine boot camp, he was leery of going through it all again to become an officer. Two hours of lively conversation did not change his mind. I was energized by this contact with two young people who exhibited intelligence and respect for the opinions of others, even people from my generation. We left the students and made our way back to the motel.

I asked the captain how he competes with the companies who were on campus in a fairly competitive hiring environment. I was surprised to learn that a second lieutenant's total compensation package (pay, food and housing allowances) can amount to $35,000–$40,000 per year, depending on years of service and marital status. The food and housing allowances amount to over 20 percent of the package and are not taxable. Parks concluded, "I offer a very competitive package."

I asked the captain how he felt the day had gone. He replied that he wanted to build his pool of qualified Ohio University candidates from one to seven by the end of the year, and he believed that the effort made today will start him toward his goal. He had made fifteen contacts and will have conducted eight in-depth interviews by the time he leaves the campus the next afternoon. We agreed to meet the next morning in order to conduct two more interviews. As we drove into the motel parking lot, I looked at my watch. It was 10:30 P.M. and it was obvious to me that Captain Parks had earned his money from the American taxpayer.

Early the next day, while I was leaving the motel parking lot at 6:30 A.M. to find some breakfast, I saw two people stretching, preparing for a run in the rain and early morning fog: It was Captain Parks and the female PLC we had dined with last night. Parks later explained that these early morning runs with candidates keep him up-to-date on their physical training progress and give candidates an opportunity to discuss things that may be on their minds.

After two morning interviews, I left Ohio University and Captain Parks. On the drive back home I reviewed my impressions of the modern-day officer selection process.

First, not much has fundamentally changed in how the Corps presents itself to potential candidates. No pressure is exerted. It is a process in which the requirements of the Corps are matched with the interests and abilities of the student. If there is a mutual interest, the recruiter launches into his presentation mode. This is the way good corporate recruiters operate.

Second, there is an undeniable mystique that surrounds the Marine Corps, and this plays a role in student interest. The hard life of the Marine Corps, the challenge of the "Are you man or woman enough to make it?" approach appeals to some in this generation of students, sometimes regarded as self-absorbed and physically soft. Again, this approach is not much different than it was 50 years ago.

Third, today's Marine Corps makes a stronger effort to accommodate the potential candidate who is somewhat interested in its programs but isn't completely committed. Transporting students from Athens to Columbus in order for them to meet and fly with a Marine pilot indicates the length to which OSOs will go to court good prospects. To my knowledge, this didn't happen in the days when the Selective Service system was in place.

Captain Parks and his people believe strongly in the product they sell, and they are prepared to expend the time and effort it takes to do the job thoroughly. These men and women work hard, long hours to achieve their mission, but at no time did I hear complaints about the requirements of the job.

Providing the Marine Corps with its future leaders is an important responsibility which the OSO and his people do not take lightly. How well they do their jobs is terribly important to the Marines who someday will be led by the people recruited by the OSOs. That's why the Corps doesn't recruit Marine officers; it recruits officers of Marines. There's a huge difference in emphasis here. The title, officer, implies privileges not attributable to enlisted personnel. When one becomes an officer of Marines, it's obvious where the emphasis is placed. It is placed on the privilege of leading and bearing responsibility for the well-being of those one leads. Captain Parks, in his own small part of the Marine world, is the first in a series of "gatekeepers" who ensure that the people brought in to lead Marines fully understand their job. They will focus on the well-being of the Marines who perform the difficult and dangerous jobs required of them in defending the nation's interests. The process of identifying young men and women who are interested in, and capable of, shouldering that responsibility begins at hundreds of colleges and universities across the United States.

Identifying and running "possibles" through a series of interviews and medical examinations and obtaining selection board approval is just the beginning for the OSO. There is much to be accomplished between the time a candidate signs on to the program and the day he or she reports to OCS. Parks stays in frequent contact with each of his candidates by phone, e-mail, and campus visits. He must ensure that each candidate follows the physical fitness program required to prepare for the rigors of training. Some have second thoughts about their decision; if the candidates need a friendly ear, Parks provides one. Others have significant others or parents who are not totally supportive of a candidate's decision to enter the Marine Corps program. Parks acts as friend, counselor, confidant, even foster parent at times, for those he believes possess the leadership potential required but whose commitment needs strengthening.

Additionally, he conducts a number of Marine-related events at his campuses which provide contact with his candidates as well as broadened exposure for the Marine Corps with students on a campus. At Ohio University he has scheduled a Marine Corps Birthday Run on November 10, which will showcase his candidates, introduce more students to his program, and provide him with an opportunity to assess his Ohio University candidates' physical fitness progress. Elsewhere, a wall-climbing exhibition and competition will be held. At another college a series of exercise stations that duplicate those that candidates are expected to perform is an excellent way to get other students interested in the Corps. Parks prides himself not only on exceeding his assigned mission, but on his attrition record, which is lower than the national OSO average. Nationally, about 12 percent of candidates submitted to the selection board drop out before they are shipped for training; Parks loses about 8 percent.

He can accomplish this because his team leaves no detail to chance. Because a negative remark made by a classmate or relative might weaken a candidate's commitment, he stays close to his people, answering questions, bolstering their resolve, and helping them finish what they have begun. When the school year ends, it is the OSO's responsibility to get his or her candidates to OCS on the mandated schedule.

I was invited to attend the Columbus OSO Station's "shippers party" on a typical, sultry Saturday in July. The "shippers" are the students who are to travel to OCS the next day. The party, held in the office complex that houses the Marine Officer Selection station in southeastern Columbus, is a social event, but it is also a final check and information-sharing session. A banner on the side of an automobile at the parking lot entrance contains this message in bold letters, "Here's Where Your Marine Corps Summer Internship Begins."

The event provides the Marines in the OSO office with a chance to demonstrate to the candidates, their friends, and families that, even though these young folks are headed for a tough six-week program, they have some friends in the Corps: Parks and the two sergeants who assist him, Staff Sergeant Bowman and Sergeant Gibson. Eight of the attending students will report to OCS in Quantico, Virginia, on Sunday afternoon. This requires an early morning flight and, leaving nothing to chance, Parks has put them up at a Columbus hotel for the night. On Sunday morning, one of the sergeants will transport the students to the airport and see to it that no one misses that plane.

There are fifteen students in attendance. Three have completed their first year of PLC training, and one has received her commission but has not yet reported for duty. There are two male students in attendance who were injured during PLC training the previous summer. These experienced candidates are present to answer the shippers' questions and concerns. Several parents are in attendance as well as friends of candidates who may be interested in the program and who have come to observe.

After making the rounds of candidates, parents, and other visitors, Captain Parks took his position at the front of the meeting room. His role is to transmit helpful information, and the atmosphere was open, free, and easy. He laced his presentation with humor and with concern for the success of each candidate. He covered a number of important details which could make the difference between success and failure at OCS.

- He handed out an assortment of plastic bags, advising, "At OCS you'll get really wet and muddy. Pack everything you need including extra socks and uniforms in plastic bags. Then when you need them they'll be dry."
- He held up a pad of material and asked, "Does anyone know what this is? This is probably the most important item you can take with you." Someone in the crowd identified it as moleskin. "Right! Remember this. Feet *break down* at OCS. If you'll take this moleskin and pre-cut it into four different sizes and keep it in a plastic bag, then, when you get a blister you won't be out of action."
- He advised them that Skin So Soft is certainly worth having to keep the mosquitoes and other biting insects under control.

He listed the items they could not have, under any circumstances, at OCS: any kind of weapon, cortico-steroids, pills of any kind. If a candidate was taking a prescription drug, he or she was to advise the medical staff at Quantico who would decide whether to authorize its use.

Captain Parks then led the group in a discussion about how to succeed at OCS. "OCS is not about training you. OCS is about screening out the unqualified." Then, he asked a question of the group, "How do you react when you're really bad at something?"

One of the students, who had completed the course last year, spoke up, "I never felt as incompetent as I did in my first three weeks at OCS."

Parks jumped in. "OCS is to screen and evaluate. And your goal is to survive, to get through the process. That means you're a fool if you try to give 110% on the obstacle course. Your goal is to give 99% and not get injured. Don't try to overachieve. Just focus on technique and achieve the objective. Remember, there's no waiting for you to recover from an injury. If you're injured you're on the next plane home."

He went on, "I'll let you in on a secret. Everybody struggles with the feeling that 'I'm not in the right place' at some time in OCS. That's because the OCS staff will push you until that happens. For example, if you're a world-class athlete you'd better perform at a world-class level. Anything less and you'll feel their pressure. Or, they may load responsibility on you in the form of incompetent people over you or under you to test your loyalty, your reaction under this added pressure. They'll figure out a way, poke at your weaknesses until you'll feel you're in the wrong place. Try to remember this conversation when that happens to you. Just survive. Just get through."

Finally, Parks got into one of the Marine Corps' favorite subjects. "There is one sure way for you to be bounced from the program. And that is an integrity issue. Here are some real-life examples from OCS. A candidate was bounced because he hid some candy in his locker. When asked about it, he denied it. He was booted, not because he had the candy, but because he lied about it. Another was disqualified for talking to another candidate, then denying that he did it. Again, it wasn't the act that was important, it was the lack of integrity on the part of the individual that caused his failure. Integrity isn't so much about behavior, as it is how you react. If you make a mistake, don't lie or try to hide it because that's your fastest ticket home."

When the meeting ended, the attendees were treated to burgers and hot dogs grilled by the Marines along with potato salad and soft drinks. Parents said their good-byes to their sons and daughters, and Parks and I headed south toward Cincinnati in his pickup.

For the eight candidates heading to OCS, the next six weeks would present them with challenges they never expected to encounter, and most of them would meet them successfully. They would make more mistakes in the next six weeks than they had made in several years, perhaps in their entire lives. That's the way this screening system works. Here in Middle America, and in other regions across the United States, there are young people who are willing to stare this challenge in the face and come out as stronger people on the other side.

Finding the raw human resources to feed this process is a time-intensive, demanding job. Nobody does it better than the Marine OSO and his people. That is evident in the results they achieve when compared to the other armed services. I have gained new insights into, and respect for, those Marines and their families who live outside the confines of the traditional Corps. It takes a special breed to thrive in this environment, and Captain David Parks and his people are some of the best.

2

The First 72 Hours—1953

Our chief want in life is somebody who will make us do what we can.

Ralph Waldo Emerson

The chaos, confusion, and disorientation of the first few days of any Marine's training are forever etched in memory. The 3-56 Basic School Class was no exception. This chapter includes a variety of recollections about Officer Candidates School (OCS) provided by members of the 3-56 class with special focus on their first few days at Quantico. Those memories are as vivid today as the experiences were when we lived them. To understand how Marine officer training has changed since the early 1950s, the reader should understand the events surrounding what is known in the Corps as the Ribbon Creek incident, a watershed event which impacted Marine training from that time on. This tragic event occurred after most of the 3-56 Class had completed OCS.

Any Marine who underwent boot camp in the early 1950s will tell you that officers played a minor role in recruit training. The Drill Instructor (DI) did what he needed to do, using whatever methods he felt would be effective, including group punishment and "thumping," which included slaps or punches to shape up recalcitrant or slow recruits.

On the night of April 8, 1956, Drill Instructor Staff Sergeant Matthew McKeon marched the 75 members of Recruit Platoon 71 into the murky, tide-swept waters of Ribbon Creek, which flows behind the rifle range at the Parris Island Marine Recruit Depot. McKeon was an experienced, respected staff noncommissioned officer (SNCO). He had seen combat in World War II at Okinawa while serving in the Navy. After the war, he joined the Marines, where he saw action in Korea as a machine gun platoon sergeant. McKeon graduated from DI school and was assigned to Parris Island in February 1956. Platoon 71 was his first recruit platoon. In what McKeon described as a night march designed to "improve platoon discipline and morale," six recruits drowned. McKeon made every effort to find and save his people in the blackness of that fateful night as soon as he realized that they were in trouble. Nevertheless, six young men, unable to cope with strong tides and sinkholes, sank to their death.

McKeon immediately came under fire from the media, and, in one of its less attractive leadership moments, Marine Corps top brass apparently decided that the NCO would be on his own. "When asked if Sergeant McKeon was guilty of breaking regulations, Marine Corps Commandant Randolph McColl Pate responded, 'It would appear so.' He also told the press that Sergeant McKeon had no authority for disciplinary action or for scheduling such a march" (John C. Stevens III, *Court-Martial at Parris Island: The Ribbon Creek Incident*, Naval Institute Press, 1999: p. 37). This response must have come as a surprise to thousands of Marines who had passed through the gates at Parris Island over the years. Furthermore, less than 24 hours had elapsed since the tragic event, and no investigative report was yet available on which to base this early judgment.

McKeon, who had not yet faced a court of inquiry, was set adrift. Senior leadership circled the wagons while a media feeding frenzy and the resultant public outrage were deflected toward a DI who had made a terrible mistake, and, by implication, toward all DIs. For understandable reasons, General Pate, caught in a difficult public relations bind, was determined to avoid a Congressional investigation of the incident. That aside, senior leadership's treatment of McKeon was not in keeping with what a Marine private would expect from his platoon sergeant when the facts of a charge were not yet known. The leadership abandoned, very early in the game, a man whose actions were not prohibited by any written regulation and were, in fact, not an uncommon practice at Parris Island. A number of retired and former Marines offered to testify to that effect during McKeon's court-martial proceedings. The press, however, smelled blood and portrayed McKeon as a brutal, oppressive alcoholic.

A seven-member panel of officers found McKeon guilty of two charges: involuntary manslaughter and drinking in an enlisted barracks. The court ruled that the two most serious charges, manslaughter by culpable negligence and oppression, were not proven; however, the sentence was severe. McKeon was sentenced to a "reduction to the rank of private, nine months of hard labor, thirty dollars per month forfeiture of pay, and, the toughest blow of all, termination from the Marine Corps with the disgrace of a bad-conduct discharge" (Stevens 1999, 151). Later, in his review of the court's sentence, Secretary of the Navy Charles S. Thomas reduced the sentence to demotion to private and three months of confinement at hard labor. McKeon served honorably until he was discharged owing to a physical disability in 1959. Commandant Pate, whose actions during the case have been widely criticized, was a sick man during these proceedings and died less than two years after his retirement in 1959.

The Ribbon Creek case was more about the media's perceptions of Marine training methods than it was about one staff sergeant who was, arguably, more a victim of bad luck than he was guilty of felonious misconduct. After the Ribbon Creek incident, significant changes were introduced into Marine training procedures. Aspiring DIs were required to pass rigorous psychological screening and undergo additional training. Series Officers were assigned to the recruit depots with specific responsibility to oversee recruit training. Corporal punishment and other physically dangerous, punitive practices were banned.

Ribbon Creek, accordingly, altered the Corps' training methods, including those at OCS.

Prior to 1956, however, when many of the 3-56 Basic School class arrived at Quantico for their Platoon Leader Class (PLC) training, a sergeant, backed up by two assistant DIs, generally corporals, was the supreme authority in administering the day-to-day indoctrination and training of a platoon of college students who aspired to become officers of Marines.

Prior to Ribbon Creek, officer candidates were trained using essentially the same people, procedures, and techniques used with enlisted recruits at Parris Island and San Diego. PLC training was conducted over two summer sessions of six weeks each. The first session was comparable to enlisted recruit training while the second session was a bit more oriented toward educating candidates about weapons, small-unit tactics, and general military subjects and involved noticeably less harassment. During the first summer training session, there was very little oversight by officers. The only officer a candidate would occasionally see was his company commander, generally a first lieutenant. The second session provided more exposure to the platoon commander, again generally a first lieutenant, while the platoon's lead DI was generally a technical sergeant (the 1950-equivalent of a gunnery sergeant) or staff sergeant.

Many DIs of that time had seen combat in Korea. They believed, based on their own hard experiences, that warriors are not molded with a mother's kindness, a brother's love, or the idiom of polite society. They had come from the farms, small towns, and the streets of urban America. Some were reservists who had been called up early in the Korean War and, often with minimal training, were shipped to the rugged mountains and fetid rice paddies of the Korean peninsula and quickly thrown into that conflict. They had bloodied, and had been bloodied by, the North Korean Peoples Army (NKPA) in the Pusan perimeter. General Douglas MacArthur had used them to flank the enemy in a brilliant amphibious operation at Inchon, driving the NKPA to the Chosin Reservoir, hard by the border of the People's Republic of China. They had participated in a fighting withdrawal when the Chinese unleashed eight divisions against the 1st Marine Division in one of the Corps' most torturous, but proud, moments. They had helped consolidate the United Nations lines near the thirty-eighth parallel as the war settled into a bloody struggle for hills that had more political significance than military importance. These difficult, expensive lessons had taught the DIs their warrior trade.

The typical 1950s DI was a master in the art of painting pictures with profanity, using blue language to a degree unimaginable to America's mothers of that time. Candidates returning home needed to watch their language at the family dinner table. DIs used corporal punishment with recalcitrant or slow candidates, or any candidate they unilaterally decided was not officer material. Candidates doing push-ups to exhaustion, candidates running in place with buckets over their heads shouting, "I'm a shitbird! I'm a shitbird!," platoons performing runs while holding their footlockers over their heads were all common sights in the company streets of Camp Upshur. In their platoon fiefdoms, very few DIs crossed the line separating harassment and brutality. There were, nevertheless, reports of over-the-line conduct by DIs. While I never personally observed a DI strike a candidate, some of my classmates saw this happen or were on the receiving end of such actions. For the most part, DIs were simply hard men who believed that only the most demanding training experience would mold college-age civilians into leaders. For the most part, too, we candidates understood and accepted that. Our older brothers, cousins, or neighbors had been there before us and told us what to expect.

It is understandable that most of these men who had high school educations, at best, would exert extra effort to make life difficult for those in the privileged minority who were attending college. They rubbed our noses in our comparatively easy lives. From the perspective of time, it is obvious that the DIs were performing a long-established, tradition-filled task of the enlisted Marine. They were screening out candidates whom they would not be willing to follow into combat. In effect, it was these enlisted Marines who determined who would lead them in the future. That simple, effective system remains in place today, and it is a major source of strength in the Marine officer training system.

The men with whom I corresponded and conversed, who underwent this hard-nosed treatment, believe that the experience greatly benefited them when they assumed command responsibilities in the Corps or, later on, in leadership positions in the civilian world. There is genuine fondness, respect, and humor in the words of the Class of 3-56 when they recall their DIs. Their flagrant, frequent use of obscenities and profanities probably was unnecessary, but such language was a way of life in the Corps and the other armed services of those days. It certainly was memorable. The DIs' bizarre humor and their ability to get their point across instantly became the stuff of memory when we assumed responsibility for the well-being of Marines just like them.

What follows are reflections, mostly on the first few days at OCS in the 1950s, from a cross-section of the 3-56 Class. Although we are almost 50 years removed from that time, it is apparent that the DIs made lifelong impressions on us all. The rank of Drill Instructor and the involvement of officers with candidates varied from one OCS program to another. For example, NROTC candidates attended only one six-week "cruise," which was comparable to the second summer session for PLCs. NROTC candidates had more exposure to staff NCOs and officers early in training than those attending PLC or Officer Candidate Course (OCC) training.

> We arrived by train in Quantico about midnight. Off we went to board the bus for a ride to Camp Upshur where we were met by our DI's. "Get off the f—g bus! Line up over there!" Off to the mess hall we went for a meal of ham with raisin sauce (which I still cannot eat to this day). It's now about 1:30 A.M. Back on the bus with some guy with two stripes screaming at us in a high pitched voice, "Welcome to the Marine Corps you college c—ts!" Into the barracks we

go. We pick out a rack to sleep in. I don't remember who got the bottom bunk but I made mine in a half-ass way, placed my bag in the wall locker. Before jumping up to the top bunk I put on these brand new yellow pajamas my mother had packed for me. The DI's were watching for some jerk to do something dumb like that. And the next thing I remember is that all hell broke loose. Both DI's were screaming, "Will the f—g woman who has the pajamas on get out of the rack!" Naturally, I looked around to see how many other guys had any pajamas on, much less yellow pajamas—and just as naturally there were none. I tried to take my pajamas off under the blanket but it was too late. Sgt. Carter stood by the rack and waited for me to climb down. He commenced screaming, "Take those f—g things off!!" The next thing I remember is a can of lighter fluid dousing my new pajamas and being set on fire as he made me do an Indian war dance around them, the hair on my legs disappearing from the heat. Scared shitless? You bet!

Gene Jaczko (PLC, Iona College)

Upon reaching Quantico we were marched around Mainside picking up equipment, uniforms, bedding. Then we were marched to the chow hall, marched to the barracks where we had to clean up the building, set up beds and foot lockers. At 12:30 A.M. we were finished. I went to the pay phone in the hall and called home. I told my Dad I was quitting. My Dad said, "You can quit but don't come home!"

Bill Cheadle (NROTC, Oklahoma University)

If we were looking for sympathy, it could be found in the dictionary between shit and syphilis. DI's were not constrained by "everything in writing" as they must be today. They drew upon their own boot camp experiences as well as stories they had heard about other boot experiences. As a result, we really got the flavor of boot camp that existed before the Ribbon Creek incident. While it was not amusing then, recollections of that time are truly funny—and were certainly learning experiences. We didn't have access to newspapers. One candidate found a newspaper and climbed into a dumpster to read it. He was discovered by the DI who locked the dumpster doors and had the platoon beat on the side of the dumpster with their entrenching tools. It was the most God-awful racket I ever heard.

Don Nichols (PLC, University of Virginia)

I can't forget Sgt. McAllister, my first DI, who named me "Candidate Realize It" after I once said that "I didn't realize" I was moving in ranks. I was "Candidate Realize It" for the next six weeks. Then there was Cpl. Owens, just back from action in Korea, who enjoyed letting the sand fleas eat your face while you stood at attention because "they need to eat, too."

I also recall those wonderful phrases:

"Forty inches back to breast, the guide is right, the guide is right, you dumb son-of-a-bitch!"

"You peeeeeple are twelve fathoms below whale shit!"

"Candidate, you are the only case in medical history where the baby died and the afterbirth lived!"

"I hate all civilians! I hate my mother because she's a civilian and not a Marine!"

Tony Hodge (PLC, Stanford University)

One of my funniest memories was the first day when they took us to the PX and said, "Stock up on soap, toothpaste, shaving cream, cigarettes and anything else you might need. You may not get back here again!" The next day, during our first inspection, they announced, "Cigarettes and pogey bait [candy, snack food] are off limits for you candidates! Drop those items in the box the corporal is holding." The DI's confiscated a ton of cigarettes that they enjoyed for the next six weeks.

Each night there was a "fly patrol" in the DI's quarters. They lived in DI Country at the end of the Quonset hut, with a sheet separating their quarters from the squad bay. Each night a lucky candidate was assigned to patrol their area with a fly swatter while the DI's played cards, smoked our cigarettes and drank beer.

Bill Sheridan (PLC, Mount Saint Mary's College)

I've reflected many times since those days at Quantico about the concept of toughness, something we men seem to think about a lot. The toughest men I ever met were the Marines holding the firebase at Con Thien in the summer of 1967. I was the CBS News Saigon bureau chief. My days in the Corps were long over. As a journalist I was never in the field for long. When night fell I could always get on a dust-off or re-supply helicopter or C-130 headed for Saigon or Danang and be sure of sleeping in a clean bed with a full stomach. But for the men at Con Thien, in the northern sector of I Corps, another night meant another mortar attack, another nerve-jangling night of "Marine you die!" screams from out beyond the wire, of short, lethal, crazy firefights with tracers arcing across a pitch black sky.

The men who endured those nights were men whose toughness was forged in boot camp at the hands of the same kind of DI's who showed me how tough I could be. One quality I think all of us who survived boot camp and those who survived places like Con Thien have, is a self knowledge and a self confidence I find lacking in many men who did not serve. Some substitute a kind of phony toughness, a swaggering, foul-mouthed macho that we know is not even close to the real thing. Boot camp taught us who we are, what we can endure, what real toughness means.

Ed Fouhy (PLC, University of Massachusetts)

About the third day of the OCC course, SSgt Taggert was instructing us on the proper way to mark our newly issued clothing. He was using two footlockers as his lectern, one of them mine. At the conclusion of his lecture he ordered us to "get squared away and fall in in one minute." I quickly retrieved my footlocker and found Joe Maciocco's glove on top of it. In the confusion I saw Joe standing nearby and said, "Hey, Joe! Here's your glove" and I threw it to him. I failed to notice that Joe was standing face-to-face with SSgt Taggert. The glove sailed wide and hit our DI in the face! Well, he made me try to eat the glove for several hours while pressing the eight foot, sand-filled pipe . . . About lights out he had me spit-shining a GI can.

Ed Galleher (OCC, University of Virginia)

The platoon was lined up in front of their bunks for its first night's check and harassment—air raid drills, flood drills, etc. The DI entered the barracks and started his strut down the aisle, carefully reviewing his charges in their "sack out" attire. After his strut he returned to the door, turned around and informed us, "I am turning out the lights. I will turn them back on again in thirty seconds, at which time I better not see any pajamas in this hut or it is going to be a very long night!" A quick glance around the hut revealed one poor soul standing in his pretty blue, striped pajamas, probably packed by Mom. The lights went off and all you could hear was the ripping of cloth. When the lights went back on, there stood the poor soul in the middle of a pile of rags. The platoon, of course, had a month's supply of spit-shine rags.

Bob Patane (PLC, Virginia Military Institute)

All was pleasant and relaxed until we finally approached the officer we all eventually came to know as 1st Lt. "Whitey" Johnson. Abruptly, the pleasantries ended and the screaming began. At the barracks, we practiced falling in and falling out, but never moved quickly enough. After the third or fourth try the assistant DI locked the screen door. We took it off at the hinges as we scrambled to get out of the squad bay. The first man to hit the locked door had footprints right up his back! As part of our orientation we were quickly made to understand that no "shit" was to go in the "shitcans." No cigarette butts were to be placed in the buttcans. A more useful bit of advice was to fill our boots with water and wear them until they were dry. Those who did this didn't get blisters.

Despite all we'd been through that first day, one poor soul remained enthusiastic, repeatedly remarking, "I've found a home in the Marine Corps!" Being especially conscientious he set to cleaning his 782 gear and somehow managed to stab himself in the nose with his bayonet! There he was, his very first day in the Corps, forced to report to the First Sergeant, "I stabbed byself in the nodze!"

Frank Messersmith (NROTC, Oregon State University)

My first, and probably most searing, memory of becoming a Marine is the day I reported to Quantico as a PLC. We reported to the MP office near the bus station just outside the town of Quantico. The flags were at half-mast. I asked the MP at the counter why the flags were lowered. He replied, "They're in honor of the two PLC's who died last week." Since my recruiters had mentioned nothing about the potentially life-threatening nature of boot camp, I was shocked by this news. Of course, nothing of the sort had happened but I'm sure the MP had a good laugh at my expense.

In our first formation I was asked where I was from. I said, "South Dakota." The DI said, "Do you know that there are more virgins among whores than there are Marines from South Dakota?"

I never in my life laughed so hard and so long over situations created by great DI's with a terrific sense of humor. And I'll never forget the tears in my DI's eyes the day he sent us back to what he described as our "panty-raiding campuses" to continue our education.

Don Mikkelson (PLC, Augustana College)

I recall Sgt. Victor Tunilla admonishing me about wearing "fruit boots" [white buck shoes] and berating me for bringing golf clubs in the trunk of my '48 Chevy. First Lt. "Whitey" Johnson was the funniest man I encountered in my USMC career and Sgt. Tunilla was the most sincere. He pushed me to come out of my shell. That young sergeant motivated me to be an over-achiever that summer and at other times in my later life. I served with "Whitey" at Pendleton. A letter I sent to Sgt. Tunilla after I left the Corps came back marked "Deceased."

Jim Rosser (NROTC, Auburn University)

I believe we had a greater respect for authority in those days. We were in the middle of Korea and subject to the draft or being activated with the reserves, so we were possibly more receptive to getting prepared through training. I had been advised by an older brother to "keep your eyes open, your bowels open and don't volunteer for a damned thing!" I expected it to be hard physically but had no idea about the mental game. When we first arrived at Mainside, Quantico, we were soon herded onto USMC busses for transport to Camp Upshur. As soon as we got off that bus, our first DI, Cpl. Carroll, told us, "I am your mother, father and your God for the next six weeks—if you last that long. Now get those horrible, f—g civilian clothes out of my sight!" He was not shy about using profanity. I doubt any sentence was completed without it. We ran around the parade ground with our footlockers on our heads that first evening.

One of the things that helped me understand such physical and mental abuse was thinking of the hardships we heard about in WWII and Korea and the deaths caused by hesitating before obeying an order. We were psychologically receptive to being torn down physically and mentally before being built into a team with pride in our accomplishments and the ultimate *esprit de corps* that has stayed with most of us.

Todd Hannah (PLC, Central College)

Lt. Parker was a tough dude—mean is a better word. We would work our butts off to show him that his disdain for us wasn't warranted. "Heels! Heels! Heels!," he would shout as we marched, and we would dig them in so hard it hurt. But, you know, we were the honor platoon when the summer ended. At the final farewell party at the "O Club" he turned out to be a nice guy. I asked him why he was such a SOB during our training. He said, "To build you into a team.

Because you all focused on me, you were pulling together to show me up." That is what he wanted and he got it. I never forgot that summer.

Steve Hall (NROTC, Cornell University)

I traveled by train to Quantico. There were several of us NROTC types and one PLC who was in the reserves and was wearing his Marine uniform, complete with corporal's stripes. [While PLC's received corporal's pay, they certainly weren't viewed as deserving of corporal's respect by any Marine, much less a DI.] This PLC was telling us what training would be like, talking very tough. On the platform in Quantico the DI's were waiting for us. The PLC headed for his formation. When he got there the DI's saw the corporal's stripes on his arm and were livid with rage. They ripped his stripes off and abused him unmercifully. That's when I thought, "Oh, shit!"

John Roush (NROTC, Miami University-Ohio)

I learned very quickly that no matter what question the DI asked, there was no correct answer. I knew I was in a different world and was going to have to learn how to survive. Interestingly enough, by the time I left base the first time in eleven weeks, I felt as if the civilian world was not "squared away" at all.

The one expression that tickled me the most that one of the DI's used was, "You people look like a monkey f—g a football!"

I quickly learned that there are several ways to do things but only *one* way that would suit the Marine Corps. I also learned that I was not paid to *think*—I was paid to *do* what I was told.

Nolan Adams (OCC, Kansas State University)

A memory embedded in my soul forever happened during the first six hours of my first summer as a PLC. I traveled to Quantico with three of my college friends. One, Tony Hodge, had already completed one summer of PLC so he was scheduled for his senior session. When we arrived at Mainside and showed our orders we were steered toward a reception area where all new candidates were issued uniforms. Since Tony was my experienced "leader" and was going to show me the ropes, I followed him rather than getting in the uniform issuing line. This was mistake #1. Somehow I got on the wrong bus [the bus] to Camp Upshur—with a bus full of *second year* PLC's! When we reached camp everyone hopped off the bus and seemed to have some idea what they were doing with the exception of me. This was a poor way to start, being in the wrong camp!

After realizing that I had made a monumental error I told the sergeant my plight. Some way, I'm not sure exactly how, I was sent to the proper camp (Camp Goettge) and I reported in. Of course, I didn't have any uniforms since I missed the issue at Mainside. So, here I am in my civvies while everyone else is in utilities. Man, this was not a propitious beginning. They were ready to wash me out in that first hour. I was addressed in such colorful terms that I forgot my real name. "Shitbird" was the most complimentary name I was called. There were many references to my mother and to the legitimacy of my birth and where my head was located and what substance made up my brain. I learned how to do push-ups while apologizing to the lawn that I disgraced with my civilian presence. Some other niceties I have purposely forgotten.

Later, Tony Hodge brought my civilian gear to me and he started laughing. That is, until the DI kicked him in the shins and told him, "Get your ass out of here!" I laugh at this now but, at the time, I was in total shock. I stayed in the same civilian clothes that I was wearing when I arrived at Quantico for two-and-a-half days.

The only thing that saved me were some of the dumb things several of the other candidates did which took the heat off me. One was the Good Humor truck and haircut incident. The day was hot. We were all scared, in shock and standing in the midday sun, waiting for our appointed time with the barber who asked us how we liked our hair cut—then buzzed us. After receiving our new look, we were waiting for the rest of the platoon to finish their haircuts. A Good Humor ice cream truck appeared with the familiar bells and whistles! Our very thoughtful DI asked if any of us would like some ice cream. Well, you know the story. There's always one. This kid raised his hand and was told to get a chocolate-coated ice cream bar. He did what he was told. The DI then had him peel the chocolate off the bar and drop the chocolate on the ground. He then ordered the candidate to put the remaining ice cream on his head, under his helmet liner.

Tony Holzhauer (PLC, Central College)

I got off the train and the DI said, "Y'all drop your bags on your left side." My bag was in my right hand and the next thing I feel is a swift kick in the butt and the DI saying, "College boy, the Marine Corps is going to teach you left from right." When I got to Camp Upshur I asked the DI which bunk was mine. He roared, "The Corps is not the Hilton Hotel! Take a bunk or sleep outside!"

George Maciag (PLC, Seton Hall)

With a German name like Vogelsinger, I became the target for our DI. His name was Sgt. Rother who had been in the German Army and he spoke with a heavy German accent. He was fond of shouting, "Fogelsinger! Gets up here!" He would then berate me from top to bottom in his German accent. By the time we graduated everyone in the platoon could mimic, "Fogelsinger! Gets up here!"

Bruce Vogelsinger (OCC, Penn State)

Another squad had to hold a funeral for a bumblebee that had been swatted to death by one of the guys during a lecture on stealth and the importance of self-control regarding noise-generating irritants such as bugs. The hapless candidate had to bury the bee, formally laid out in a cotton-filled matchbox in a foxhole he had to dig. His fellow squad members, who had laughed when they heard about the prospect of this object lesson, were ordered to don their ponchos and lead the cortege to the burial site. Following the interment, the bee killer was asked by the DI, "What was the sex of that bee?" Whereupon, the candidate had to exhume the body to check it out.

John Alexander (PLC, University of Pennsylvania)

One day, in the fight to get out of the hut, I lost my wristwatch. Our DI, SSgt. Armando C. Araque spotted the watch and demanded to know whose watch it was. I admitted to owning the watch and was chewed up, down and sideways as one who would never, ever, ever, ever be acceptable to the Corps. He demanded that I quit right there. When I remained silent, he dismissed the platoon, explained to me that he was going to break me one way or the other and, using his fist, knocked me flat on my ass. His final comment was, "You little shit! I guarantee that you will never make it through this program. Get out of my sight!" . . . Years later, I included SSgt. Araque in my book, *Force Recon Command,* pointing out that my lifelong belief in high stress training began with his leadership as my drill instructor.

Alex Lee (OCC, Stanford University)

That first day was the longest day of my life. The first night in a Quonset hut practicing "get in the hut, get out of the hut" until the sergeant was satisfied. This was followed by "get in the rack, get out of the rack" drill. There must have been other drills but they all became one giant obstacle to getting some sleep. When sleep did come it was short. I can't forget the sweet music of a swagger stick rattling around in a trash can and the melodious, gentle sounds of the DI suggesting that we might like to come feast in the dining room set up for us. Many of the PLC's decided civilian life wasn't so bad and were trucked off to return home. We who stayed are better for the experiences and opportunities that those six weeks and the years we were to spend in the Corps afforded us. No regrets here.

Bob McGlynn (PLC, Brockport State Teachers College)

In June 1953 I got off the train and a fat Navy doc came out and asked if any of us had played football in college. He asked them to take one step forward. It seemed to me that the biggest and best of us stepped forward. He then asked those football players who had ever injured a knee to step forward. Over half of them stepped forward. They were then told to get back on the train and go home. The Marine Corps did not want them. They were draft bait. Fortunately, no one asked about my sport—judo.

Richard Muller (PLC, Reed College)

In Milwaukee [while in college] I was a member of a Reserve unit that contained WWII and Korean War Marines. When I arrived at Quantico I realized how good my veteran marines had been to me. Before reporting to Quantico they had me stencil my name and fold and pack all my gear in accordance with *The Marine's Guidebook.* Actually, they weren't being kind—they were trying to indoctrinate me so I could become an officer, worthy to lead Marines. I had all my gear in good shape because of these Inchon and Chosin Reservoir Marines.

We arrived at beautiful Camp Upshur, were issued bedding and ordered to make ourselves comfortable. Being allowed to sleep atop a USMC rack for a few hours was most welcome. Next day we were allowed to attend Mass in the movie amphitheater. I don't know what accommodations were made for Jay Goldburg.

Jim Goham (PLC, Marquette University)

Our battalion had its first church call on Sunday. The DI pointed left and screamed, "All Protestants, on the double to that chapel!" He then pointed right and screamed, "All Catholics, on the double to that building!" Bob Goldstein and I were left standing at attention in the middle of the street all by ourselves. The DI came up to us (the only Jews in the battalion) and said, sarcastically, "Are you trying to be wise guys?" We told him we were neither Protestant nor Catholic. We were Jewish. The DI was a young corporal, not particularly worldly wise. Completely flummoxed he pointed right and blurted out, "Jews are like Catholics! On the double to the Catholic chapel!"

Jay Goldburg (NROTC, University of North Carolina)

There was a great deal of apprehension as we rode the train from Washington to Quantico. It didn't seem to affect one guy who held court telling all who would listen that this was going to be a piece of cake because his brother had done it last year and he didn't take any bullshit from the DI's. When we arrived the DI's herded us off the train with swagger sticks and words of "encouragement"—some of which I was hearing for the first time. We arrived in a wild thunderstorm. The last time I saw the guy who was doing all the talking he was down on the ground in his white bucks and sport coat covered with mud, doing push-ups and yelling at the top of his voice, "Yessir! Yessir! Yessir!"

Tom Toomey (PLC, Notre Dame University)

I recall my classmate, Don O'Shea, had the misfortune to ask Gunnery Sgt. Kreuger where he was supposed to "put his gun" (referring to his rifle). Krueger said, "Keep it in your trousers, shitferbrains and stick it where it will do some good when you have the chance if you ever become a man!"

This is where I learned the lessons all Marines learn. You *can* do it. You *will* do it. *Never* give up. *Always* take care of your people. *Get it done—do it best—Hits count.* You can bitch about the weather, the chow but *never* complain about how you feel or who was not nice to you. Looking back, I wish I had been as good to and for the Corps as it was to and for me.

Lou Kuttner (NROTC, Holy Cross University)

The day we were to report to OCC I picked up my college roommate, Bob Haidinger, at the DC train station. I was driving my red 1953 Ford convertible. As we turned off the highway, with the top down (get the picture?), and headed toward Quantico's main gate, our conversation slowed and my heartbeat began to pick up a bit. As we pulled up to the gate we noticed a gunnery sergeant standing somewhat back from the sentry. The gunny stepped forward, looked us over and politely asked if he could help. I responded by asking for directions to the Officer Candidate School. At that moment a terrible thing happened to gunny—his face turned red and his voice turned from normal into a scream. Spit flew as he shouted, "You goddam shitbirds park that goddam car over there and get your silly asses back here with your goddam gear! Don't sit there looking at me, goddam it, MOVE, MOVE, MOVE!" My memory is that things went downhill from there for the rest of the day.

Jim Reno (OCC, Notre Dame University)

Just before shipping out to Quantico I had taken the tough Missouri Bar exam. It was just a few days before my birthday and my mother wanted me to be home with her. I spent my birthday with her and showed up about ten days late for OCC. I thought this was no big deal for, after all, the Corps would be glad to have a hard-charging and well-trained lawyer in its ranks.

You can imagine what happened. From the time of my arrival I got the third degree. Finally, I was issued a footlocker with all my gear and I headed to my barracks. Upon entering the hallway I met my platoon DI. Of course he was dressed meticulously with a sparkling spit shine on a new pair of shoes. Upon seeing him I immediately braced against the bulkhead. He stopped in front of me to berate and castigate me for my many shortcomings and failures. At this moment of insecurity and fear I dropped my stuffed footlocker which proceeded downward—and caved in his shoe tips! For the remainder of boot camp my existence was virtually unbearable.

Bill Burlison (OCC, Southeast Missouri State College)

Driving into Quantico I was told at the gate to park in a 20 minute parking zone. As I got out of the car I was ordered into a truck. As you recall, we were not allowed to speak until we learned how to approach a DI. "Candidate Steely requests permission to speak, etc. . . ." had to be said perfectly. That afternoon I finally made it inside the DI office after pounding hard enough on the doorframe. Of course, I was chewed out for parking where I'd been told to park. My DI, a short German, ordered me to report behind the barracks after we left the mess hall. My imagination was carried away with what might be going to happen to me. The DI ordered me into his personal car and nothing was said. I picked up my car and followed him back to a long term parking area. As we drove back to barracks in his car, he offered me a cigarette and I said, "Yes sir." As I got out of his car I made another mistake by thanking him. He yelled, "This is not a personal favor! You are just like anybody else!"

Carl Steely (OCC, Centre College)

One event was the famous "bucket issue." I couldn't figure out why they were giving us buckets, but soon learned that the DI's had all kinds of devious and ingenious ways to use them. Placing one on your head and smoking five cigarettes at a time comes to mind, as does placing one on your head and standing on the street corner yelling just how f—d up you were when you made a mistake, which seemed to happen with regularity.

And then they were used as the final insult for the poor devils who decided they did not want to be U.S. Marines and opted out of the program. I can recall two guys from Utah who both quit about ten days after we started. The DI's marched those guys up and down every street in Camp Upshur with buckets on their heads and yelling at the top of their lungs just what non-humans they were. Those guys, and many like them, didn't know what they would miss in the future when all was said and done and we all pinned those gold bars on.

Harv Morgan (PLC, Regis College)

I am a lowly with the rest, but my father is a decorated Navy Lt. Commander and that info is in my file. For five and one-half weeks my life was miserable as the Platoon Commander and Platoon Sergeant tore me up. At long last I graduated with a high ranking and my Platoon Sergeant paid me some most welcome compliments and took me to his Staff NCO club and bought me a couple of beers. Then, at graduation from Syracuse, those wonderful gold bars were on my collar—still the height of what has been, and remains, a great life.

Roy Place (PLC, Syracuse University)

One particularly hot day we were all packed into the chowhall for the noon meal. One midshipman got up and, with virtually all his salad remaining on his tray, headed for the GI can. When he was about to scrap the salad a 1st lieutenant, the Officer of the Day, pounced on him about the need to consume all the food he takes. The midshipman calmly grabbed a piece of lettuce and told the OD that the lettuce contained bacteria of some sort. He made up a very scientific sounding name and explained that to consume the salad would result in a serious case of abnormal and frequent bowel movements. The O.D. bought the story and had all the salad removed from the serving line. We all enjoyed the fact the OD had been had.

Frank Whitton (NROTC, Notre Dame University)

Toward the end of our first six weeks of PLC we had occasion to go to the Officer's Club at Mainside. Ellery Johnson and I were leaving the club and, as we opened the door, a general and his wife came through that door. Up to that point in our lives, a junior lieutenant was God and we were somewhat confused about what to do. We were uncovered [Marines don't wear hats indoors and don't salute when "uncovered"] so a salute was out of the question. Ellery, having opened the door, smartly clicked his heels and bowed! I split a gut all the way back to Camp Upshur.

Todd Hannah (PLC, Central College)

Dressed in carefully pressed summer dress NROTC uniform, complete with shoulder boards, my classmate and I checked into the Mainside office. We were instructed to proceed to the barracks located at the far side of the base. Although the base was relatively quiet because of the weekend, we unexpectedly encountered a tall, lean and obviously unfriendly corporal. The corporal proceeded to comment unfavorably on our white dress NROTC uniforms, our status as students with college deferments and he offered several comments about our ancestry. He observed that our mere existence was a contradiction against the natural order and, much worse, by our presence we were desecrating the sacred ground of his beloved Marine Corps.

He then marched us into a nearby building from which he extracted two large push brooms. He handed each of us a broom and directed us to sweep the street around the chow hall! There, in the hot Virginia sun, attired in full dress uniform, we swept the entire street. Our NROTC uniforms were soaked with sweat and we both sported blisters on both hands. While we didn't please the corporal, he unceremoniously dismissed us and ordered us to double time to the barracks area.

The six weeks that followed was a regimen of arduous physical and emotional training under the unsympathetic eyes of the ever-present NCO's. No one who reported to Quantico that summer could possibly have fully appreciated that Marine Corps training would be the unique experience that evolved. As I reflect back to those six weeks in the summer of 1955, I have a new appreciation for the level of immaturity that all of us exhibited when we reported. The almost surreal introduction to Quantico and the six weeks of training that followed was a revealing new experience. It certainly transformed all who survived its rigors into significantly more mature and unquestionably more focused candidates for the Basic School training we would receive starting in June 1956. Importantly, the shared misery of that summer developed an enduring bond among all the members of that training class. Today, almost forty-five years later, that summer remains vivid in my memory.

Jim Sales (NROTC, University of Texas)

We arrived in DC in the early morning. After a layover of a couple of hours in Washington we caught the bus and after an hour's ride we arrived at Quantico's main gate. It was a short ride from there along the shady, tree-lined road to the Mainside area. Waiting for us there was a Master Sergeant in crisp khaki uniform, glistening dress shoes, rows of ribbons adorning his chest. Even we sophisticated college boys looked at that large man with undisguised awe. To our surprise, he didn't shout or raise his voice. He firmly, but politely, directed us to our first stop where we began a round of administrative checks as we signed our names on countless forms.

The next stop was the barbershop. Our heads weren't shaved. The barbers left us with about one quarter of an inch of hair on top of our heads while the sides of our heads were given the "white sidewall" treatment. I particularly remember watching the "duck tails" which were in style in some colleges fall to the floor, as this semblance of college cool disappeared. After haircuts, we were issued dress and utility uniforms, "boondockers" (field shoes), dress shoes, skivvies (underwear) and a seabag into which all the above were stuffed. As we went through this process, there was not a lot of yelling, although we were encouraged to do whatever we were doing silently and with speed. "Quickly, quickly, people," was a phrase we would hear hundreds of times in the coming weeks. In the Marine Corps, you never, ever do anything fast enough. We waited for the shoe to drop.

The platoon was boarded onto our first "cattle car," a semi tractor attached to a bus-like trailer containing hard benches along the sides and center of the vehicle. We would become familiar with this mode of transportation over the next six weeks. We were told that we were going to Camp Upshur. There was some nervous chatter as we headed through the rolling forest that borders the Potomac basin, thick and green in the early afternoon sun.

In about thirty minutes, we got our first look at Camp Upshur, or "Silver City" as it would become known. It was a collection of silver painted Quonset huts and other assorted metal buildings, bounded on the south by a parking lot and on the west by a large drill field, or what would come to be known as the "grinder." In the distance we could see the obstacle course. Beyond that there was nothing but thick forest on all four sides. We now knew, by our surroundings and our long bus ride, the meaning of isolation. Our bus dropped us off at the far end of the parking lot. We were about a quarter of a mile from the Quonset huts that were to become our homes.

As we disembarked from the bus a smallish, wiry, steely-eyed man in starched cotton khakis met us. He wore a permanent, evil grin and he had two chevrons on his sleeve. We were soon to learn that those two stripes made him God, or at least God's assistant. His name was Corporal Libby and he was the assistant DI for our platoon. As we hurried off the bus he screamed, "Fall in! Quickly, quickly!" We shuffled about, not knowing exactly what to do. After being referred to as "idiots" and "shitbirds" several times we got into some semblance of order and he shouted, "As I call your name, answer 'here' and raise your right hand." Of course someone raised his left hand and was met with a tirade of abuse. "You don't even know your right hand from your left! Where the f—k do you go to college?" The offender smiled and gave an answer, without ending his response with "sir." The corporal placed his face six inches in front of the offending party screaming, "Do you think I'm funny! Do you?"

"No."

"No? No-o—o! See these stripes on my arm? To you anybody with any stripes on his arms is 'sir'. You will say 'sir' whenever you speak to me—and don't you ever speak to me unless I tell you to speak to me! Do you understand me?"

"Yes, sir!"

"By God, I've got your name, Jones. You are on my list! You'd better get your shit together!"

The corporal was red-faced with obvious disgust for the poor specimens he'd been given to train. After a few moments of shaking his head and pacing back and forth in front of the formation, he composed himself, the sweat pouring off our backs as we stood at attention in the summer heat of Virginia.

"Right hace . . . double time . . . harch!" Which we did in our college boy, seersucker suits, button down shirts and tassel loafers, doing our best to run with heavy seabags slung over our shoulders, some trailing extra suitcases and other paraphernalia. Luckily, I had packed lightly, so I was able to make the run without dropping anything. Others weren't so lucky.

"You there! You! Yes you, you f—k-stick! Get back here and pick up this garbage! You're dirtying my parking lot! Do you think you're going to the prom with all that civilian shit?" Then, in a sinister tone, "You and I are going to have a long, hot summer, college boy."

When we arrived sweating and panting at our platoon hut, the Corporal screamed, "I want to see you out in this company street in five minutes in utilities and boondockers. And I don't want to see one f—king sticker on any part of your uniforms! Now get in that hatch!" Of course, we didn't move fast enough, so he had us run through our Quonset hut hatch (door) five more times. He kept shouting, "I don't want to see anything but eighty-eight elbows and forty-four assholes when I say 'get into that hatch!'" Finally, we were inside the hut, finding our racks (beds) and lockers. We scurried about, frantically searching seabags, for our skivvies, utility jackets, trousers (not pants), gung-ho caps or covers (not hats), green wool socks and boondockers.

We moved as fast as we could, as the corporal impatiently paced up and down the center aisle of the platoon hut, murmuring loudly, "College men, huh? Look like a bunch of shitbirds to me. You people are taking too much time! Hurry! Hurry, people! You people are beginning to piss me off!"

Then we went through the hatch drill once again. Again, we weren't moving fast enough so we did this drill several more times, at last breaking the screen door from its hinges. Of course, we then were berated about "destruction of Marine Corps property" and "you people can't even get through a hatch without breaking it. You're f—king hopeless." We were beginning to believe him.

Finally, we were into the street and the Corporal showed us how to get into platoon formation. Then he began to search for "tags." In the '50's every piece of cloth that went into a utility jacket or trousers was tagged with a small piece of white paper glued to the component by the manufacturer. The tags on pockets, or flaps were obvious. Under time pressure, what weren't so obvious were the tags in the crotch of the trousers or the collars of the dungaree jackets. It was here that Corporal Libby found his mother lode of "tag perpetrators."

"What's the matter with you people? I tell you I don't want to see any tags and you come out and all I see is tags! You're f—king numb-nuts! You are not going to make it, I guarantee you! Now, get back in that hut and get rid of those tags! Move! Move!"

Back in the hut, again after these unsuccessful attempts to meet the Corporal's expectations, we figured out that the way to ensure all tags were removed would be to help one another. We began to search each other's bodies like sweat-soaked mother baboons picking insects from the hides of their young. This was the only way to minimize the wrath of that little bastard with two stripes on his starched sleeve.

In retrospect, this was our first lesson of survival in our training to become Marines. The only way we would all survive this was to help one another. For, when one man screwed up, we were all punished for his error. The way to avoid punishment was to make sure your buddy didn't screw up and you did what you could to help him get "squared away." Over the next few days we began to take those first steps to develop a team attitude that pitted "us" against "them." We began to understand that none of us would get through this unless every man in the platoon carried his share of the workload. We couldn't afford to have one man who couldn't clean his rifle or make his rack correctly, because we all paid in sweat and sleep deprivation for one man's failings. Comprehension of our situation began with that first, small step; the simple act of helping one another find and remove those little tags. It was the beginning of a journey in which the individual egos we arrived with would be sublimated to the general good, a first step on the journey toward becoming a Marine and, someday, an officer of Marines.

About 1730, as hunger began to stir in our bellies, we met Sergeant Walsh, our senior drill instructor. He was a square-rigged Bostonian, a wounded Korean War veteran and a firm, fair NCO. He stood before us in starched khakis, a poster Marine. He could use profanity with the best of them but used it sparingly. He demanded your best and was an excellent teacher. He was the perfect counter-balance to Corporal Libby's constant harassment. Their "good cop, bad cop" routine played well as time passed and we deciphered each man's role.

It had been several hours since we had eaten and we assumed we would be marched to the chow hall. We were marched all right but not to the chow hall. We headed for the "grinder" (parade ground) for our first lesson in platoon drill. As the late afternoon sun beat down on the steaming, macadam drill field, Sgt. Walsh began calling cadence in his own unique style. We were to discover that every DI had his own cadence style, salty and rhythmic, a primitive beat that has directed the feet of untold legions of marching troops since time began. "Le-ulft, hup, rip, hore ya le-ulft, hup, rip, hore. Dig 'em in!" We were directed to dig in our heels in order to produce a single "tromp" sound, forty-four men marching as one body. We would wear out the heels of our first pair of boondockers in a month of drill.

PLC Jones was out of step. "Jones, do you know your right foot from your left?" Jones looks at the sergeant and begins to answer. "Goddamit! Jones! Don't you look at me! You keep your eyeballs on the man's neck in front of you! You look at me and I'll think you love me. And, by God, I'll kick your ass out of this program right now if I think you love me! Do you love me, Jones?"

"No, sir!"

"Le-ulft, hup, rip, hore ya le-ulft, hup, rip, hore."

And so it went for seemingly endless hours before we were marched to the chow hall, a large metal building on the north side of Upshur. Chow was typical Marine Corps. You could take all you wanted but you could not throw any food away. If you didn't clean your tray you would experience the wrath of your DI. And then you would sit down and finish all your food. You learned that you didn't waste anything in the Corps. You could have milk to drink—or bug juice, a Kool-Aid type drink which, after a time, we suspected of being laced with saltpeter. The chow hall was not air conditioned, so you ate and sweated in your tray.

We were given thirty minutes to eat then were reformed for our march back to the huts. When we arrived, Cpl. Libby announced that we would hold a "field day." A field day is a top to bottom scrub down of the platoon hut and "head" (toilet/showers). Squad leaders were assigned, one squad in charge of sweeping, then swabbing, the deck. Another squad was given the task of ensuring that every speck of dust was removed from racks, doors, lights, lockers, etc. Another work party was assigned to the head to scrub down the toilets, showers and wash basins.

We thought we'd finished the task, when Cpl. Libby arrived to inspect our work. He walked to one hatch, ran his finger over the top of the door and, allegedly, found some dust. And so we did it all over again—re-scrubbing, re-dusting and re-cleaning the head. By this time it was midnight and we were given thirty minutes to shower and be in our racks at lights out. Reveille at 0500 would come far too soon.

I lay on my back as Corporal Libby turned out the hut's lights. I'd like to say that I pondered the events of the day and what tomorrow would bring, but I immediately fell into a black hole of exhausted slumber. Thus began our initiation into the fraternity of the Corps in July 1953. It would be six hard weeks of sweating, grinding, thirst-filled training. In those days, "water discipline" was Marine Corps policy. You were taught not to give in to thirst. On long hikes the DI's would harass any man drinking too much water. We were taught to be macho and pour out the contents of our canteens. "You don't need it," said the DI's. The next summer, in 1954, after some cases of heat stroke occurred, the Corps directed that candidates and recruits were to drink as much water as they wanted. This all seems so crazy now, almost fifty years later. But that's the way it was—the Marine Corps way.

We gained a lot from that first summer's experiences—learning to handle confusion, stress and adversity—learning to push ourselves beyond self-imposed physical limitations—learning personal discipline—learning how important it is not to let your buddies down. From the perspective of time I see now that this experience was a fast, forced march from our teenage years to a raw, unrefined Marine Corps definition of manhood.

Jack Ruppert (PLC, Xavier University)

3

OCS—Transition—2000

> We must remember that one man is much the same as another, and that he is best who trained in the severest of schools.
>
> Thucydides, 404 B.C.

These words are prominently posted on the bulletin board of the S-3 (Operations and Training) Office at Officer Candidates School (OCS). In the two and one-half millennia since Thucydides wrote his *History of the Peloponnesian War,* his conclusion about the importance of rigorous training remains unchallenged by history. All of the world's elite military organizations use mental, physical, and emotional stress to screen out the unqualified and to test the resolve, intellectual processes, and character of those who aspire to membership. The Marine Corps prides itself on the fact that its recruits earn the title of Marine only after completing the most demanding recruit training conducted by our nation's conventional armed forces. Thucydides would find comfort in the severity of OCS.

Prior to 1934 the Marines had no officially designated officer candidate school. Up to that time officers came to the Corps either from the U.S. Naval Academy, Naval ROTC units, or from the ranks of enlisted personnel. Newly commissioned Annapolis graduates and former enlisted Marines received their officer training at the predecessors of what is now The Basic School (TBS). In 1934 the Marine Corps established the Platoon Leaders Course (PLC), drawing students from colleges that did not offer ROTC. The first PLC classes were held in the summer of 1935 at both Quantico and San Diego.

In 1940, as World War II approached, the Corps faced a growing demand for officers and established an Officer Candidate Course at Quantico. In 1943 Commandant Thomas Holcomb approved two additional, temporary officer candidate training detachments, one at Camp Eliot, California, and the other at Camp LeJeune, North Carolina. These were needed to accommodate the needs of a Corps that would reach a manpower level of 450,000 by the war's end. World War II brought women Marine officers to the Corps where they underwent training at Mount Holyoke and Smith Colleges, both located in western Massachusetts. In 1944 the Officer Candidates Class was officially designated the Officer Candidates School and was located at the Marine Corps Base, Quantico, Virginia.

By 1947 TBS had assumed responsibility for training all officer candidates as well as newly commissioned second lieutenants. In 1955 TBS moved to Camp Upshur, a remote camp on the Quantico reservation, where all officer and officer candidate training was conducted except for the Officer Candidates Class (OCC) which became the responsibility of the Training and Test Regiment, located in Mainside, Quantico. The Training and Test Regiment was officially designated as the Officer Candidates School in 1963. Finally, in 1977, training of women Marine officers was also placed under the command of OCS. OCS continues to operate in the Mainside area at Quantico where, like all of Quantico's schools, it operates under the aegis of the Marine Corps University.

Any comparison of candidate training today versus 40-odd years ago will tend to be colored by the experience of the writer and his contemporaries. The biases, recollections, and an inclination on the part of the older generation to believe that the old ways were the best ways can produce a slanted view of the subject matter. In order to reduce such bias and bring objectivity to this work, the writer observed current training practices; interviewed officers, staff non-commissional officers (SNCOs), and officer candidates; and conducted related research over a three-year period.

While there are significant differences between today's training techniques and procedures and those of five decades ago, the fundamental thrusts of officer training are very similar. There are substantive differences as well as shifts in emphasis today that are generally considered to produce a more professional and intellectually flexible final product than was the case with my generation. As American society has evolved since the Korean War so have the training methods at OCS.

The first area of difference one witnesses today is a consistent level of professionalism in the modern officer candidate training that was not apparent in my generation. The SNCOs assigned to OCS are experienced, professional soldiers who, while no less formidable and demanding than their predecessors, get the maximum out of their charges without the profanity, group punishment, or the threat of physical abuse that characterized the training of the early 1950s. Arbitrary dismissal of candidates is gone from the process, and officers are more visible and active at today's OCS, even though the vast majority of training is administered by the SNCOs. Another factor that distinguishes today's OCS from the 1950s is an unabashed moral/ethical indoctrination that is arguably more heavily weighted in candidate evaluations than proficiency in the performance of strictly military duties. A candidate may survive one poor grade in a military subject and still get a second chance, but let a candidate be caught in a lie about anything and he or she won't survive the course. There are no second chances where integrity issues are involved.

The OCS of the 1950s was nearly a photocopy of enlisted Marine boot camp. The school was run at an accelerated pace relative to the recruit depots because candidates were nearly all college students or graduates. They were required to grasp things more quickly. As we have noted, the human raw material of the officer training programs was, in large measure, composed of students who chose the Marine Corps rather than take their chances with their local draft boards. All were volunteers, but it is a fact that the Corps represented one option for fulfilling a military obligation to the country. As such, the large majority of lieutenants (about 75 percent in the 3-56 Basic School Class) would serve a two- or three-year active duty obligation and then return to civilian life. Many would continue their connection to the Corps through participation in the Active Marine Reserve.

The 1950s OCS was designed to accomplish the same ends as today although there was less emphasis on leadership development and assessment. The OCS of the 1950s transformed individuals into team members who would sublimate their individual wants, needs, and desires to the needs of the organization. The focus was on the organization's mission. The more outlandish methods of training and motivation, detailed in the recollections of the 3-56 Class, have, in more recent times, disappeared. These have been replaced by a more logical, but no less arduous and effective, method of identifying candidates who possess the qualities required to lead Marines. Gone are the platoon burials of insects and buckets on candidates' heads. Gone, too, is group punishment for individual sins. (Peer pressure, however, is definitely a factor, and candidates quickly recognize that one slow or unmotivated candidate can cause an entire platoon a great deal of time and trouble.) The consistently profane language and sexist humor of yesteryear's DI have disappeared. Those methods worked well in an earlier time when the American people, with World War II and the Korean War fresh in their minds, for the most part turned deaf ears to complaints about the Marine DI's hard-bitten training methods. "Hell, I went through that and we won the war," was the typical reaction of America's veterans. Surviving those aspects of training was considered part of a young man's maturation process, and the DI was viewed as *in loco parentis* by many Americans.

Today's OCS is only secondarily about training. The school's most important function is to screen out candidates who are unable or unwilling to demonstrate the leadership qualities the Corps considers essential. OCS focuses on those elements that will produce officers who are not only examples of military effectiveness, but who will serve as role models for their troops in areas of conduct that go well beyond the scope of military proficiency.

The OCS Mission Statement reads, "To train, evaluate and screen officer candidates to ensure that they possess the moral, intellectual and physical qualities for commissioning and the leadership potential to serve successfully as company grade officers in the Fleet Marine Force." The elevation of the moral side of leadership to equal status with intellectual and physical qualities didn't exist at the OCS of the mid-twentieth century. Based on conversations with a number of retired and current Marines, this recognition of the need to focus on the moral and ethical side of leadership probably started at the time that drug usage and racial strife rocked the Marine Corps as well as the other armed services after the Vietnam War.

Then, too, the perceived changes in American society's values since Vietnam have led a succession of Commandants to the conclusion that, if the Marine Corps is to fulfill its mission, it should represent a way of life that insists on certain standards for its Marines and does not tolerate the societal weaknesses and failings that fill America's media. Let's be clear. Marines at all levels will admit that dishonesty, corruption, infidelity, lack of commitment, racial prejudice—all those failings that afflict mankind in general—can be found in the Marine Corps. It is a human institution and is not immune from the darker side of American culture, but it disputes these influences and aspires to other behavior.

By establishing proper standards of conduct for Marines, the frequency and severity of the societal ills that infect the Corps will be significantly reduced. Marines are expected to live by a set of Core Values: *courage, honor,* and *commitment* and all that these words imply. Situational ethics, excuses for nonperformance, self-centeredness, intellectual dishonesty, and failure to accept responsibility are to be replaced by principled, selfless honesty in all aspects of a Marine's life, not just during working hours. Those are lofty ideals, but few who are exposed to today's Marine Corps would deny that the organization has succeeded in this effort to a far greater degree than most civilians can comprehend. In part, this emphasis on principles and high expectations may, in part, explain the criticism leveled at the Marines that the Corps does not reflect the society it is responsible for protecting.

As we will discuss later, there are some who believe that the Marines have estranged themselves from American society and its culture; that Marines believe their culture to be superior to the one they are charged to defend. If the allegation is that belief that their culture is a superior one, then the Marines are guilty as charged, as are the best of the world's military organizations. It certainly is not a new phenomenon, and it has been a hallmark of elite military organizations throughout history.

Discussion of Marine culture is a valid area of investigation and exploration, but the suggestion that a military organization should mirror its civilian culture ignores the history and the realities of life in such organizations. Does it makes sense to expect or require a person who has chosen a career in a warfighting organization to look like, act like, or think like his or her civilian counterpart? It seems logical to ask, "Just how closely can a military organization be expected to reflect its civilian culture before it ceases to be an effective military organization?" We will revisit these questions in more depth in a later chapter.

Another change between current-day OCS and that of the 1950s is that candidates today must arrive at OCS in excellent physical condition. The earlier generation, in large degree, was worked into physical condition during the course of training. Today's candidates must also do some mental conditioning work prior to reporting. They are instructed as to what will be expected of them at OCS. They are advised that being a Marine requires the candidate to

- Place others above self
- Dedicate self to the Corps
- Understand that Marine leadership is a profession
- Understand that it is a privilege to be a Marine
- Understand that it is an honor to *lead* Marines
- Be the best.

Those are tall orders, but the 2,000 or so candidates in any given year who accept them ultimately make their way to northern Virginia and begin their journey to a Marine commission.

> The lessons learned in those first few days were invaluable keys to success throughout the course. Was OCS hard? Definitely, but no one chose the Marine Corps because it was easy. The standards were high, the challenge daunting, the failure real. But the experience was unforgettable. Although the price was great, the reward is absolute.
>
> E-mail from female PLC to the author

The OCS training schedule calls it "Transition," but the staff generally refers to it as "Pickup." Candidates report on Sunday and for two and one-half days undergo a head-to-toe physical screening to determine their readiness for OCS. By the time Tuesday afternoon rolls around, all of the required administrative and medical details have been completed. Candidates have undergone urinalysis, body fat tests, and dental and physical examinations. Particular attention is focused on potential knee, ankle, and foot problems since most of the candidates who are dropped from the program for physical reasons suffer leg and foot injuries. The Navy doctors, nurses, and corpsmen are very thorough, examining all candidates in extreme detail, ensuring that they are physically ready to undergo the demands of OCS.

Candidates are again examined for tattoos. Any tattoo on the hand, wrist, or lower arm, as well as any judged inappropriate, may disqualify the candidate. The final decision as to whether a tattoo disqualifies a candidate lies with the commanding officer of OCS.

Candidates have been issued uniforms but are dressed in civilian khaki trousers and, depending on the weather, Marine-issue sweatshirts or T-shirts with their names stenciled on the back. The majority sport civilian haircuts although there is a sprinkling of prior enlisted Marines in the class whose "high and tight" haircuts separate them from the rest. Even the regulation haircuts will disappear the next day when male candidates have their heads shaved. (Females are provided with guidelines for practical hair length and style.) The administrative process has been fairly low-key except for an occasional reprimand for too much conversation between candidates.

Candidates have taken a fast trip through the small PX (Marine Corps Exchange) and have purchased the toiletries and other items that the Hats tell them they need. It will be a while before the candidates again see the inside of the PX.

Time has been provided for candidates to write a required letter to their parents to advise them of their safe arrival. Prior to this Transition session, all the candidates' gear, including suitcases and the large plastic bags containing their newly issued uniforms, has been stacked outside the classroom. To this point, candidates have learned how to move from one point to the next, but there has been no hint of the chaos and confusion that are about to envelop their lives.

There is a fog-like tension in the classroom. These young people, drawn from all quarters of the country, are about to be turned over to the company's SNCOs who will be their unrelenting taskmasters, constant critics, and teachers during the demanding, pressurized weeks ahead.

The majority of this company consists of recent college graduates, but about 10 percent of the company are prior enlisted personnel, which is average for OCS. This is an OCC, and its members will spend ten weeks in screening and training before earning a second lieutenant's gold bars.

On average, 23 percent of them will not make it. Some will not be able to handle the physical aspects of the training, and others will fail academically. A few will be disqualified for integrity violations, and others will fail to demonstrate the leadership capacity required of officers. There are also candidates who will drop on request (DOR), leaving the program voluntarily, unable to adjust to the pressure or the physical and mental demands made on them.

At the front of the classroom, Colonel George J. Flynn, Commanding Officer, OCS, is telling the candidates what the Marine Corps expects from them—and what they can expect from the OCS experience.

The OCS staff promises to

- Do what's best for the Marine Corps.
- Provide a level playing field.
- Provide candidates with a fair evaluation and maximize their opportunity to succeed by:
  a. Providing the candidate with required tools.
  b. Evaluating whether candidates have ability to apply them.
  c. Allowing for "Progressive Failure." (This is a process used by the OCS staff to communicate to candidates that they will be given every opportunity to succeed. They will be allowed to make mistakes and will be given feedback to enable them to improve. Then the candidate will be evaluated on how well the feedback is applied. Problem candidates will be placed on progressively higher levels of probation before being disenrolled.)
- Look for character and potential in candidates, not necessarily current ability.

Candidates are specifically advised that they will be evaluated and screened

- In an environment characterized by chaos, uncertainty, and stress
- To determine how each candidate reacts and identify those who have the potential to be successful company grade officers in the Marine Corps
- Both by those who lead (officers) and those that successful candidates will lead in the future (enlisted Marines).

Candidates are told that they can expect

- Firmness
- Fairness
- Respect
- To progress from self to team
- An opportunity to demonstrate leadership potential.

They are told that OCS will expect candidates to demonstrate

- Honor, including integrity, responsibility, accountability. "I am accountable for my professional and personal behavior. I will be mindful of the privilege I have to serve my fellow Americans."
- Courage to do the right thing. "Courage is the value that gives me the moral and mental strength to do what is right, with confidence and resolution, even in the face of temptation or adversity."
- Commitment, through devotion to the Corps and to my fellow Marines. "The day-to-day duty of every man and woman in the Department of the Navy is to join together as a team to improve the quality of our work, our people and ourselves."

The product of OCS is a graduate who

- Is a person of character who intuitively adheres to Marine Corps Core Values
- Is confident but unselfish
- Is physically fit
- Has a basic understanding of the ethos and legacy of the Marine Corps
- Is dedicated to being a professional, with a willingness and aptitude to learn
- Understands the magnitude of the responsibilities of being an Officer of Marines.

The colonel continues, "You will be judged as follows: twenty-five percent of your performance grade will be based on your Physical Fitness Test results, twenty-five percent on Academics and fifty percent on your Leadership performance." He concludes, "I will tell you this right now. Over the next three or four days you will not do many things right. You should expect that. It will be up to you to learn quickly. Now, if you will promise yourself never to give up on yourself, you will make it. Good luck."

Major James C. Brennan, the Company Commander, is introduced and he, in turn, introduces the Platoon Commanders (captains) and the company's SNCO cadre consisting of the Company First Sergeant, the Company Gunnery Sergeant, and the Platoon Sergeants and Sergeant Instructors. This is the first glimpse the candidates have of the people who will evaluate them for the next two and one-half months. They are a formidable looking group in their immaculately pressed camouflage uniforms, imposing and unsmiling. All have had successful prior tours training enlisted recruits.

> Then it was just like that scene from *Gladiator*, where Maximus states, "On my word, unleash Hell." As soon as the company commander gave the order for the staff to take charge of their platoons, Hell was indeed unleashed.
>
> E-mail from female PLC to the author

The SNCOs are shouting at the top of their lungs, "Get out! Get out of here! Get out!" They are menacing, moving close to candidates, getting in their faces, violating the personal space that human beings feel belongs to them. There is no personal space here because all space belongs to the SNCOs, who are called "Hats." This nickname is derived from the wide-brimmed campaign hats worn by DIs at the recruit depots. It is a long-held tradition that only DIs and rifle range personnel wear the campaign hat so OCS staff personnel wear standard camouflage covers but are, nevertheless, called Hats. The platoon's senior Hat is generally a gunnery sergeant who holds the title of Platoon Sergeant Instructor (PSI). He is assisted by two Sergeant Instructors (SI), generally staff sergeants, but frequently a junior gunnery sergeant will fill an SI slot. These three Hats are the OCS equivalents of Senior and Assistant Drill Instructors at the enlisted recruit depots. PSIs are identified by the black leather belt they wear; SIs wear green web belts.

Candidates learn quickly that the Hats' looks are not deceiving, and the uneasiness in the eyes of the candidates is understandable. Regardless of how much these young people have heard or read about the Marine training process, it's impossible for them to know just how their emotional and physical limits will be tested by the Hats. It will be some weeks before they see a Hat smile.

The classroom clears in less than 30 seconds, and the candidates are outside in platoon formation, picking up every piece of gear they have stowed on the grass. With campstools over their shoulders, burdened with their newly issued gear and personal luggage, they are ordered to double-time the quarter mile to the drill field. The smart (or lucky) candidates have traveled light, bringing minimal civilian property with them. Some have made the mistake of bringing more than one personal bag.

> It was like a bomb exploded in that classroom when we were introduced to our staff. Like nothing I've ever seen before. I was scared. I've always been neat and

> organized in my life, so when we had to drag all of our belongings onto the parade deck and dump them out for inspection of contraband, then stuff them all back in our bags, I thought I was going to have a nervous breakdown. I didn't know where anything was. Other candidates belongings were mixed up in my own. It was utter chaos.
>
> E-mail from male PLC to the author

A few candidates, on the run to the drill field like overloaded beasts of burden, begin to drop some items. The angry voices of the Hats can be heard across the drill field.

"Jones! You get back here! Pick that up! Why do you have all that stuff?" Jones doesn't respond and the Hat bores in. With his mouth just inches from the candidate's ear, he's inquiring, "Did I ask you a question? Are you a rock, or can you speak?"

Jones stutters, "I—I."

Use of the first person pronoun sends the Hat into orbit. Another Hat, smelling blood, joins him. With one shouting in one ear and a second Hat yelling in the other, the candidate learns that double-teaming isn't limited to the basketball court.

"I? I? There is no 'I' here! You are a candidate and you are speaking to a Sergeant Instructor! You've been here three days and you don't know who I am? Where's your brain?"

"Sergeant Instructor! This candidate won't make that mistake again, Sergeant Instructor!" The Hats aren't finished. The first Hat says menacingly, "Jones, you and I are going to have a lot of fun! A lot of fun! Do you hear me, Jones?"

"Sergeant Instructor! This candidate hears you, Sergeant Instructor!" With disgust the Sergeant Instructor waves his hand. "Get away from me!" Jones sprints to catch his platoon, grasping his belongings tightly.

The five platoons (four male, one female) that make up this company are now in ranks under the afternoon sun with all of their possessions spread out on the drill field's macadam surface. Hats are issuing instructions. From all corners of the drill field there is a constant, "Aye, aye, Sergeant Instructor!" response being shouted by platoons responding to orders or questions.

The first order of business is a search of the candidates' belongings for contraband. "If you have any of the following items in your possession, raise your hand! Any weapon, knife, or scissors. Any prescription medications. Any cameras or tape recorders." As the PSI drones on describing other forbidden items and instructs the platoon to bring the items to him, the other Hats have already begun searching through the personal effects of the candidates. One Hat finds a pair of tiny scissors and gets in the face of an offender who resembles a deer in headlights. "What is this? Didn't you hear the Platoon Sergeant? Why didn't you raise your hand?"

"Sir, I. . . ."

The "there is no I here" lesson starts again.

Candidates will learn to anticipate and move quickly when a Hat gives instructions. The fact is that the candidates won't ever be provided with sufficient time to do anything. This fixation on speed is all about making decisions and acting under the pressure of time. And the candidates are learning that there are no friends, no good guys among the Hats. The staff's job is to confuse and disorient. Candidates must learn to think and act under the pressures of time in an environment characterized by uncertainty and chaos. What the Hats look for are mistakes, lack of military bearing, "civilian" behavior, such as averting the eyes downward, when being questioned, admonished, or instructed. Most important, Hats learn how the candidates respond to this unfamiliar and friendless environment. Is there some sign of weakness, frustration, or surrender emanating from the candidate, some signal that a candidate may break?

Once the search for contraband is concluded, the platoon is ordered to pick up its gear and double-time to the barracks that will be home for the next ten weeks. Another candidate drops an item. This time Company First Sergeant Tim Campbell confronts the young man. After a series of questions, the answers to which seem only to further infuriate the first sergeant, the candidate runs to join his platoon. But, if he was listening, he heard some advice on how you survive at OCS. As the candidate runs off, Campbell yells after him, "You people are unorganized, undisciplined, and you don't know how to help one another!"

At OCS candidates are judged individually, but the cohesiveness of the unit is vital. Candidates are constantly reminded, "Help your buddy." In the ultimate stress and chaos, in combat, Marines instinctively take care of one another. That's why Marines fight. Here at OCS the candidate who doesn't help when his or her buddy is in need won't last the course. Either the Hats will notice or his or her peers will notice, and peer evaluations carry great weight with the Hats.

So it's off to the squad bay where 44 men have now arrived with their civilian and Marine-issue gear. Outside the barracks, PSI Gunnery Sergeant Paul McKenna has lined up the platoon in alphabetical order and sends the candidates up the ladder (not stairs) to Gunnery Sergeant Charles Jackson and Staff Sergeant Tyrone Horton, the platoon SIs. Horton's hissed instructions to each candidate to "take your time" drip with sarcasm as Jackson places two men in front of each double-deck bunk. The squad bay will, over the next few hours, be turned into an orderly, Marine living area as Jackson and Horton teach their people the most basic rules of Marine living. These include mundane subjects such as how or where to

- Make a rack (not a bed)
- Place their extra pair of boots
- Fold their towels and washcloth

- Place their laundry bag
- Align their footlockers.

Of course, in responding to Jackson's orders and instructions, time is of the essence and, as noted, the platoon will never complete any assignment in time to satisfy the Hats.

> The whole platoon was forced to do everything step-by-agonizing-step. Then, not having done it fast enough, we had to do it all over again. I hated the repetition and the constant yelling, but we were kept so busy that there was no time to really ponder how much life sucked. I loved how the instructors counted down our time limit to perform a task. It usually went something like this. "30, 29, 17, 13, 12, 11, 7, 3, 2, 1 . . . you're done!" It confirmed my belief that these guys were too vicious to have ever learned how to count.
>
> E-mail from male PLC to the author

In a time-honored process, Gunnery Sergeant Jackson refers to all government property as if it were his own personal property. Jackson instructs his charges, "You will never sit on *my* rack—never sit on *my* deck—never sit on *my* footlocker." I smile inwardly, recalling one of my platoon mates in 1953 observing, "Darn! I thought taxpayers owned all this stuff and now I learn it all belongs to Corporal Libby!" Instructions are followed by the now familiar, "Do you understand?" To which the appropriate shouted response from the candidates is, "Aye, aye, Sergeant Instructor!" If the response isn't aggressive enough, the candidates are ordered to repeat it, often several times. This "I can't hear you" routine has also been around military organizations for many, many years. The reason, of course, is that clear, easily understood communication in the noise and confusion of combat is very important. Leaders must make themselves heard above the din. Candidates are not told the reason behind this seeming harassment until they are deeper into the course.

At 1800 the platoon is ordered outside, back to the drill field for a boxed dinner. They are first taught how to "dress" ranks (align themselves to the person on their right) and "cover" (stand directly behind) the person in front of them. Then they sit down for a box supper in the late afternoon sun.

PSI Gunnery Sergeant McKenna, a very intense man, addresses the platoon. He launches into the dos and don'ts of chow time at OCS. Candidates sitting on their campstools will sit up straight "unless you have a physical condition that doesn't allow this, which means you aren't qualified to be here." Heels will be together with toes pointed in a 45-degree angle. Chow time is not a social hour. There will be no talking at chow. Juice containers will be placed between the feet. Food will be brought to the mouth, not mouth to the food. They will never speak with food in their mouths.

McKenna tells the platoon, "Eating in the chow hall is a privilege. If you can't follow the procedures I've covered, you will have this privilege taken away.

And daggone, let me tell you. The good Lord blessed us with a beautiful day today. Normally, in January it can really get cold eating your chow down by the Potomac River and that's where you will be if you don't follow these procedures."

McKenna then goes into instructions regarding military customs and courtesy. When candidates encounter *any* OCS staff member this requires a proper, prescribed military greeting. They are to greet every officer appropriately, for example, "Good morning, sir" accompanied by a salute. OCS staff will be addressed by their billet (position within the company), for example Company First Sergeant, Company Gunnery Sergeant, Platoon Sergeant, or Sergeant Instructor. This may sound simple, but during the first hectic days of transition training, candidates will inevitably encounter an SNCO whose billet they can't recall. Or, they will stumble over the correct format of the greeting. This produces a tirade from the offended Hat and some uncomplimentary comments regarding the candidate's intellectual capacity. The candidate is reminded that he'd better not suffer the same memory lapse twice. The word here is, do not make the same mistake twice.

The candidates have been with their platoon staff for five hours. The rest of the evening will be spent doing much of the same as they complete administrative details and receive instruction on the care, cleaning, and arrangement of uniforms, equipment, and personal hygiene items. Before they go to bed, the squad bay must be cleaned and "squared away." At 2200 lights-out occurs. It has been a long, stressful day. The candidates, who have had only boxed meals for the past forty-eight hours, will go to bed tired and a bit hungry. They will get used to this. Welcome to the Marine Corps.

The first day of Transition is structured to be a defining moment for candidates as the civilian world's freedom and pace are stripped away and replaced by structure, stress, and the constant presence of authority which is willing and able to criticize the smallest error. The Hats, from the first minute of Transition, establish the need for speed in everything the candidates do. Through the repetitive process of acknowledging orders with "Aye, aye, Sergeant Instructor," the SIs are moving candidates into the disciplined environment of Marine life and out of their "nasty" civilian habits (as the Hats describe them). Within a few short hours, the SIs have the platoons speaking (shouting is a better descriptor) and acting (with notable and noted exceptions) like Marines.

I made the long walk across the drill field to my car as the sun set on an uncommonly warm day and concluded that the current version of Transition is not all that different from what it was many years ago in terms of the reaction it produces on the part of the candidates. Some previous practices, however, have been drastically altered or eliminated.

The most noticeable to the observer is the absence of profane language on the part of the Hats. The closest any of the staff came to swearing was the use of words like "daggone" or "friggin'" (used as an adjective). The practice of speaking without swearing may, indeed, take candidates away from the familiar environment they left behind on the college campus. Profanity, street language, and such throwaway expressions as "you know?" or the frequent insertion of "like" into sentences, are unfortunately, not uncommon in the young American's world. That language is not spoken here and its absence plays a part in moving candidates out of their comfort zone. This isn't the fraternity or sorority house, dorm, or student union where street idiom may substitute for clearly articulated thought. Here words mean something, and it takes some time for candidates to adjust to this more demanding milieu.

Less blanket criticism appears to be thrown at the platoon. Instructions are generally given to the entire platoon, while criticism and correction are aimed at individuals. The smart candidate will keep his ears and eyes open to corrections not aimed at self and file them away for future reference.

Finally, the DIs of the 1950s didn't double-team candidates as much as they do today. If you messed up, one DI would let you know in uncertain terms. Candidates who emit hints of wilting under pressure are now more apt to be on the receiving end of a two-part corrective lecture, a stream of nonstop questions from two directions, or a combination of both.

A final thought crossed my mind as I drove to my hotel. Anyone who has run large meetings knows how draining it is to be "on stage" for just a few hours. That work produces a unique physical and mental weariness. The Marines assigned to a tour at OCS spend their days rising very early (4 A.M. is common), and they seldom get to bed before midnight. For 18 to 20 hours per day they are on stage, setting the example in dress and demeanor, required to be more alert and responsive than their charges, most of whom are years younger. Family life is certainly affected during these tours because of the time demands placed on the Hats. Theirs is a demanding job, and they perform it selflessly and professionally. At some time in the future, when the candidates review those people who had a significant impact on their lives, they will remember the Campbells, McKennas, Davises, and Hortons with increased appreciation for the job they did. For some candidates, that realization comes early, soon after they return to their campuses or head for their first duty post.

> Each of the instructors and staff at OCS had their own distinct persona. Without a doubt, however, the most interesting was First Sergeant McKenna. He had the word "intensity," all nine letters of it, tattooed across the width of his forearm. The very sight of him or the mere sound of his voice was enough to strike fear into anyone. . . . At the same time he was, without a doubt, the most motivated and motivating Marine I encountered in my time there. When we weren't laid out doing flutter kicks at his behest, he would cite epigrams. "Repeat after me. Today I have given everything I have. Everything I have kept I have lost forever." Or, "One man's actions affect us all." These became part of our candidate mantra.
>
> E-mail from TBS second lieutenant to the author

Day 1 of Transition marks the beginning of a ten-week journey that will screen out every fourth candidate in the company. According to those men and women who have had the OCS experience, these things are clear. Those who make it through the entire OCS process will be in the best physical condition of their lives and will be more mentally acute. They will learn to cope with fear, time pressure, cold, wet, heat, uncertainty, and chaos. They will be changed from the college men and women who entered the Main Gate at Quantico ten weeks earlier. It will be a difficult, but rewarding, road to a Marine commission. The platoon has taken its first step.

4

OCS—Pride, Passion, Professionalism

> And knowing they are disciplined, trained, and conditioned brings pride to men—pride in their own toughness, their own ability; and this pride will hold them true when all else fails.
>
> T. R. Fehrenbach, *This Kind of War,* 1963

> OCS is going well. At times it is very hard and extremely frustrating. But there are also times that are SO motivating that I can't even describe it. You pull energy from places inside yourself that you don't even know exist and put out 250% and it's just an every day thing. I can't believe some of the stuff I've done. I am definitely in the right place. . . . You can't believe how limited we are for time, always moving and having to do six things at once with no time to do it. That's what frustrates me the most. Training is starting to get more intense and hard core. There is no doubt that they are training us for war and pushing us to lead while constantly evaluating us.
>
> E-mail from female PLC to friends and family

The clear, professional manner in which candidate evaluations are conducted at today's Officer Candidates School (OCS) is a departure from the days when OCS was, for the most part, an "officer's bootcamp," a sort of Parris Island for college men. The techniques employed by the OCS staff haven't changed in terms of the school's objectives. Evaluating and screening out candidates who are judged to be unqualified have long been the goals of officer candidate training. What has changed is the formal structure of the evaluation system and the manner in which it is conducted. These are much improved, in terms of objectivity, efficiency, and effectiveness over the practices of the 1950s.

Candidates are provided with very specific instructions regarding their physical fitness program prior to reporting to OCS. The Officer Selection Officers (OSOs) also become heavily involved in preparing candidates by clearly laying out what they should expect when they reach Quantico. In frequent practice sessions the candidates perform against the requirements of the Physical Fitness Test (PFT) which allows the OSOs to measure candidate commitment and progress. The OSOs do not sugarcoat what awaits candidates at OCS. (Older Marines may remember the description of the many amenities offered by the Quantico Marine Base in the literature we received before reporting to OCS in the early 1950s. It described the golf course, tennis courts, swimming pool, and other attractions available on the base. Stories abound about candidates who actually believed that we PLCs would be able to use these facilities at our leisure. Some showed up at OCS with golf clubs and tennis rackets visible in the back seats of their cars and received merciless treatment at the hands of the DIs.)

Now candidates are issued a 100-page *Candidate Regulations* booklet (*Candidate Regulations,* Marine Corps Combat Development Center, rev. April 2001), which provides information and instructions on subjects ranging from Marine Corps terminology to how to write a Peer Evaluation Report to how to stencil skivvies (underwear). "Candidate Regs," as the booklet is called, not only provides basic, day-to-day information on mundane subjects, it also includes sections that cover leadership principles and instructions intended to enhance a candidate's understanding of what OCS expects every day, as well as during tours in a leadership billet.

In the 1950s candidates were provided with the *Guidebook for Marines,* the same book provided to enlisted recruits. This was an excellent publication for the training of enlisted Marines, but it did not provide leadership-focused material for the education of the officer-to-be. The graduate of OCS in the 1950s was simply a more highly educated copy of the basic Marines graduating from the recruit depots. Today the Marines are doing a much better job of providing officer candidates with leadership education and exposure rather than relying totally on The Basic School (TBS) to develop the leadership skills of their newest officers. To be clear, TBS remains the place where the lieutenant masters the skills required to lead Marines; however, the product TBS receives from OCS is much more fundamentally grounded in leadership knowledge and has a proven capacity to lead Marines.

Candidate Regulations provides both the staff and the candidate with an effective tool. It provides the OCS staff with a teaching and reference tool and clearly places responsibility for success squarely on the candidate. Candidates who leave or are disenrolled from the program for any reason would be hard pressed to say that they were unaware of, or uninformed about, OCS regulations and expectations. These are very simply and clearly spelled out for them.

The previous chapter discussed Transition, a two-week period in which candidates have their civilian habits seemingly stripped from their personae. They are immersed in the strenuous everyday life of OCS. When Transition is completed, the Evaluation phase of OCS begins in earnest and continues to the end of the course. As Transition melds into Evaluation, the successful candidates are adjusting to OCS and its demands. First, they understand that they will be evaluated on just about everything they do. They also understand that they will never perform any task so well that the Hats will have no suggestions for improvement. This realization is part of the candidate's maturing process, developing an understanding that, in the final analysis, all people can do is to force themselves to dig down to the very depths of their beings and do their very best—as fast as they can. Then they must learn to let the evaluation chips fall where they may.

The Hats will do everything possible to motivate candidates to raise their personal bars of performance. That's the Hats' job. But it is the individual candidate who must come to terms with the fact that he or she will seldom meet, much less exceed, the Hats' unending stream of demands. They will run farther and faster than they thought themselves capable of and even that won't be good enough. They will learn to endure heat, cold, and wet unimaginable just a few, short weeks earlier and grow stronger in the process, and all the while the Hats will focus on their failings and weaknesses. They will discover that they can force themselves to stay awake when their exhausted bodies cry out for sleep, and then some 30-something-year-old gunnery sergeant will put most of them to shame on a three-mile run. On average, the candidates will put in 90-hour workweeks, but they will become aware that their SIs are working more than 100 hours. Finally, they will learn to cope with the 24-hour-a-day presence of the Hats, who constantly seek and find things that candidates aren't doing fast enough, well enough, or in the prescribed Marine Corps manner. For most candidates, OCS will be the first time since childhood that someone not only closely monitored their daily lives, but insisted that even the most basic routines be completed in a specified fashion.

Finally, it becomes clear very early at OCS that no one is immune from an SI's strongly expressed disappointment in a candidate's performance in some aspect of Marine Corps life. For example, a gifted athlete may find running the obstacle course relatively easy compared to his platoon mates. The OCS staff will insist that the candidate never become satisfied with his performance. An intellectually gifted candidate will likewise be challenged in ways that the average candidate may avoid. Any prior enlisted Marine at OCS will be expected to help lead his peers successfully into the world of the Corps. More will be expected of those who have already experienced Marine life. The OCS staff probes and searches until they find each candidate's strong points, then challenges them to exceed their previously determined performance potential. They do the same with each candidate's weaknesses, and they push and probe until they're satisfied that the candidate will not wilt under pressure.

The 1950s Marine, reviewing the current training schedule at OCS is struck by three facts. First, a number of the subjects being taught today are the same subjects that were taught 45 years ago. Though weapons and technology have changed, the fundamental skills required to become an officer remain the same. Second, it is apparent that some of today's OCS training subjects certainly were not part of candidate training in those bygone years. For one thing, the world has changed dramatically, and the Corps must deal with the same problems, some of reasonably recent vintage, which face American society as a whole. Finally, OCS is more focused on determining the leadership capabilities of candidates and less focused on the old harassment-as-training approach of years past.

One societal issue that candidates bring with them to OCS is the appropriateness of tattoos on an officer's person. (According to OCS staff, about 40 percent of today's candidates arrive with a tattoo.) Medical evaluations conducted in the first two days of a candidate's arrival at OCS include a tattoo check. The OCS position is clear. As one officer told me, "We are not going to pass any candidate through the system who will not provide the proper example for their people. And we do not believe certain types of tattoos set the proper example."

Over the course of the ten-week OCC class are a number of instructional sessions that weren't even on the horizon when the older generation was at OCS. Among these are training or discussion sessions on such subjects as equal opportunity, substance abuse, sexual harassment, homosexuality, moral leadership, and suicide intervention. These subjects underscore the increasingly complex leadership demands that are made of today's young officers.

A review of the ten-week training schedule at OCS is beyond the scope of this work. We will summarize some of the most important aspects of the course.

PHYSICAL FITNESS TRAINING

The Marine Corps takes an almost mystical attitude toward physical conditioning. You never see fat Marines walking around Quantico. What you see are scores of Marines running during lunchtime rather than eating chow. This near obsession with physical conditioning is even more pronounced at OCS, but candidates do not need to skip lunch. Their activities each day will consume whatever caloric content the Corps provides. Many of the officers and SNCOs I met would be classified as physical fitness devotees, if not fanatics.

As we have seen, candidates are expected to arrive at Quantico in excellent physical condition. Those who do not are generally dropped from the program quickly because no remedial time is allotted for getting into shape although the staff will work hard to motivate marginal, but truly committed, candidates to make it over the PFT bar. Over the course of ten weeks the candidates will

- Perform 158 hours of physical training
- Hike 52 miles
- Run 77 miles
- Do 640 pull-ups
- Do 50 rope climbs
- Do 1,350 push-ups.

On the OCS grounds there is a variety of physical fitness courses with which the candidates will become familiar, including the Obstacle Course, the Combat Course, the Endurance Course, the Stamina Course, and the Confidence Course, also known as the "Tarzan Course." (This course is composed of a series of rope obstacles and challenges located high in the trees behind the obstacle course, hence the nickname.)

PHYSICAL FITNESS EVALUATIONS

The objectives of physical training at OCS are detailed in *Candidate Regulations,* and about ten hours of each training week are devoted to physical fitness activities. Candidates receive a physical fitness grade at the conclusion of the ten-week course, derived from their performances in the following events:

- The Combat Readiness Test (CRT) which includes a rope climb, push-ups, fireman's carry (evacuation), advance by fire and maneuver, and a combat run.
- The Physical Fitness Test (PFT) consists of a test for males that includes pull-ups, stomach crunches, and a three-mile run. Female candidates are required to do flexed-arm hangs rather than pull-ups but otherwise are required to do the same exercises as males. Points are earned based on the number of exercises done in a given time as well as their time in the three-mile run. Male candidates will earn a maximum of 300 points if they perform 20 pull-ups, do 100 crunches in two minutes, and run three miles in 18 minutes. Females may earn a perfect score by doing a flexed-arm hang for 70 seconds, performing 100 crunches in two minutes, and running three miles in 21 minutes. All candidates must achieve a minimum of 225 points, regardless of gender or age.
- The Obstacle Course, which is designed to test agility, strength, and endurance.
- The Endurance Course, which combines the full Obstacle Course, a designated run, the Stamina Course, and designated obstacles on the Combat Course. Portions of the event are conducted with combat equipment.

> I am still alive and kicking. Going into week 8 and my body hurts and I am tired and sore, so basically I'm doing fine. Another hard week coming. We're going to do the fun stuff, Tarzan and Confidence Course. For those who don't know much about them, they are big, high obstacles that are SO motivating. We did the obstacle that Pyle gets stuck on in "Full Metal Jacket." The Tarzan Course looks like an Ewok village . . . I passed the Combat Readiness Test and every minute of it sucked. It's a rope climb and 3-mile run with gear and weapon, fireman's carry, pushups from hell and a fire-and-maneuver course. I was convinced I'd fail the stupid thing but ended up doing really well, so that was motivating. It's amazing where you end up pulling this energy from.
>
> We're down to 25 (in our platoon) now and I think we'll graduate between 19 and 23. We're really starting to come together and there are so many awesome women in this platoon.
>
> E-mail from female PLC to friends

In addition to an almost mind-numbing array of physical fitness events and courses, one thing that is different is the emphasis placed on upper body strength at OCS. This isn't news to the candidates because they've been instructed to perform a lot of upper body exercises in preparing for OCS. What brings the point home upon arrival is the appearance of the OCS staff, particularly the SNCOs filling the platoon sergeant and sergeant instructor billets. The Hats can generally be classified as one of two body types: the heavily muscled weight lifter or the lean, greyhound type. It's evident that the gym, which is located close by OCS, gets a lot of use by the Hats.

In the Korean War and the period following, 1950s Marines were trained to become masters of the long, fast march. The Marine Corps, including OCS candidates, didn't run nearly as much as they do today. Yes, we double-timed from place to place, but running against the clock was required only once, in my recollection, and that was at TBS. There, before we were sent to the Fleet Marine Force (FMF), we were required to pass a test that included sit-ups, pull-ups, and a one-mile run (in combat boots, utility trousers, and skivvy shirt) which had to be completed in less than seven minutes. While my "old Corps" classmates may hate to hear this, today's candidates are in better condition than we were. The running requirements alone would tip the scales to today's candidates. This should come as no surprise. This generation of candidates is no tougher, physically, than previous generations, but running is now recognized as the most important aspect of any physical conditioning program, both in and out of the military. Distance running simply wasn't a popular exercise or pastime in the 1950s.

THE COMBAT COURSE

One particularly grueling evolution in physical training is the Combat Course. It combines a number of challenging obstacles and a military objective at its conclusion. A four-person fire team event, it combines a test of the command, control, and security skills of a fire team in the attack with physical challenges and discomfort.

The course starts with the team's negotiating a rope bridge across a gully which leads to several climbing obstacles. Then the team arrives at the "Quigly," named for the man who, in an apparent fit of misanthropy, designed the water hazard. It consists of a long trench; the first segment is 30 yards long, two or three feet deep, and is filled with muddy water. The trench then takes a 90-degree turn and runs another 40 yards. A number of logs are strategically placed in the obstacle which require candidates to crawl under them, squeezing their heads and bodies under both the water and the logs while attempting to keep their weapons dry. While candidates are in the water; the company staff including officers, Hats, and Navy corpsmen keep a sharp eye out for any snakes that might have adopted these waters as their home. It is rumored that the Quigly's designer made this comment about his creation: "After running the Quigly, the candidates should look like they tangled with two constipated pit bulls—and lost!" His objective has been met.

After the Quigly, there are several more climbing obstacles. This is a simulated combat environment, and the candidates' attention to security is part of the evaluation. While negotiating obstacles, the candidates must keep their weapons at the ready. At each obstacle, two team members provide security, front and rear, covering their two teammates as these work their way over, under, or through the obstacles. They then reverse roles.

After making it over the climbing obstacles and another immersion through a chest-deep ditch filled with water, the team comes to the final two obstacles. The candidates are required to crawl uphill in a barbed-wire-covered trench that is kept very slick with mud. They must use their toes to make upward and forward progress, all the while working to keep their weapons out of the sludge that might render them inoperable during the team's assault on the final objective. As candidates sweat their way up the steep, muddy slope on their bellies, a grunt emanates from one of the trenches. A Hat sticks his head over the edge of the obstacle. "Is that you, Jones? Is that you making those noises? Are you whining? You need to get some self-discipline about yourself. You've just given away your position with all that noise."

The final obstacle is another chest-deep lake. The team slides into the water in a skirmish line formation and traverses the 30 or 40 yards to the far side of the lake. On a hill above the lake is a sandbagged bunker where a 7.62MM G240 machine gun is firing blanks, making an ungodly racket. One of the Hats throws an artillery simulator into a nearby pit along with a smoke grenade. This signals the final assault. The fire team sprints up the hill and overruns the bunker with shouts of, "Kill! Kill!"

Once they pass through the objective and form a defensive line around the position, the fire team leader reports to the company gunnery sergeant, advising him that the mission has been accomplished and reports on casualties and prisoners. The gunnery sergeant, in almost all cases, has a few questions and comments about the fire team's execution of the assault on the objective and the acting fire team leader's performance. As is the case with most activities at OCS, a leadership performance evaluation will be placed in the acting fire team leader's file.

The Combat Conditioning Course is a messy business and, according to the staff, it will take candidates two days fully to rid their persons and equipment of the grime and mud they pick up during the exercise. The course is designed to condition candidates to the combined effects of physical exertion and discomfort on the individuals and the team as they work toward successful completion of their mission. Candidates also learn about the difficulties that they and their Marines will experience in maintaining weapons in functioning order under trying conditions.

> Week four is over and I'm short on time but want to say hi! . . . Next week marks the half-way point and it will be hard but I'm ready for it. The stuff we're doing now is getting intense and getting to be fun, too. We ran the Combat Condi-

> tioning Course this morning. Walls and rope bridges and the Quigly. Mud and nasty water and barbed wire. Oh, and snakes! . . . It's getting hot. We are constantly fighting dehydration. We are also learning and applying fire team tactics that are really cool. Next week is our mid-term SULE I [Small Unit Leadership Evaluation] when we go to the field and put it all together. Next week is the 4th of July. I have no concept of time and I'm going to miss the D.C. festivities because I have my tactics exam.
>
> E-mail from female PLC to friends

In the midst of the physical, mental and emotional pressure that is OCS, there is some humor—and sometimes legends are born. Even the OCS Staff occasionally finds humor in the serious business of evaluating candidates.

> My PLC Junior summer . . . was the summer of 2000. This [incident took] place during a 9-mile day hump. During one of our breaks . . . I looked . . . at my bunkmate, Bobo (not his real name). [He was] looking down at his feet and laughing. Seeing as we were . . . exhausted [having completed] 7 of the 9 miles . . . we couldn't understand what he could possibly be laughing at. [We] asked him, what was so amusing?
>
> . . . Still laughing, he turned to us and said, "I've got my boots on the wrong feet!" All of us broke into laughter, which wasn't good . . . because our laughter caught the attention of our not-so-fun-loving sergeant instructors. They came running over and started yelling at him, asking what could possibly be so funny? [When] they heard he had his boots on the wrong feet, they just couldn't believe it. They called over the rest of the staff to see the candidate that had walked 7 miles with his boots on the wrong feet! They weren't mad . . . they were amused. They [began] to ask him questions about how he could have [done this].
>
> He gave the standard answer, "This candidate has no excuse." But the SI's weren't buying that. "Oh, there has to be an excuse for something like this."
>
> [Bobo] replied, "[Thinking back to how the day began] being [awakened] at 0500 and having about two minutes to put our tents away—it was dark and everybody was yelling—I couldn't see!"
>
> With that everybody broke into laughter. I think it was the first time the candidates and the staff laughed together. For the last week and a half, Bobo had all the attention focused on him. Staff from other platoons would come into our squadbay with their shoes on the wrong feet. I remember one Sergeant Instructor yelling at Bobo as we marched to chow, "I just spoke with Colonel Flynn, Bobo . . . He needed me to confirm that there actually was a candidate who humped seven miles with his boots on the wrong feet. We will always remember you Bobo. You may be gone in a week but they will remember you here for 25 years to come!"

And so, the legend of Candidate Bobo was born.

E-mail from male PLC to author

And then, sometimes a sergeant instructor becomes so frustrated with a candidate that his instructive tirades approach Shakespearean levels, witness this vignette.

> We had a guy named Smedley (not his real name) . . . who spoke with a heavy Southern drawl. He would give long, protracted answers when all that [the SI] wanted was a simple, "Yes (or no), Sergeant Instructor."
>
> One day we were marching to class and the SI asked Smedley why he didn't have his binder. [Instead of responding with "no excuse, Sergeant Instructor] Smedley's answer went something like this. "Sergeant Instructor, I was gonna get my binder, but then I broke a shoelace and couldn't find my spare laces because you dumped out my footlocker this morning, so . . . "
>
> The Sergeant Instructor erupted, "Smedley, you could walk the earth for a thousand years, questioning every person you come across . . . you could get in a space ship and search the galaxy, questioning every sentient being you find and you couldn't find anyone who gives less of a shit than I do!"
>
> TBS lieutenant e-mail to the author

ACADEMICS

Academic evaluations, based on the scores attained on written and practical examinations covering basic military subjects, account for 25 percent of a candidate's overall ranking. The passing grade for all subjects is 80 percent. Future officers will spend 600 hours in classroom instruction and practical applications in the following subject areas:

- Small unit tactics
- Land navigation (map reading and compass)
- Weapons
- Marine Corps history
- General military subjects.

Candidate Regulations (p. 2–10) spells out the policy regarding cheating or collusion.

At OCS, as well as anywhere else in the Marine Corps, violations of integrity will not be tolerated. The reputation of the Marine Officer corps is based on the integrity of each officer. Any candidate who observes cheating will immediately report the incident to the duty officer/instructor. Any attempt on the part of a candidate to give, receive, or have in his/her possession, any unauthorized information or material during an examination shall be considered as an integrity violation which constitutes grounds for dismissal from the program. Cheating also consists of any attempt to obtain unauthorized information. Whether or not the information is actually received or used is irrelevant.

LEADERSHIP

The OCS approach to leadership evaluation is also detailed in *Candidate Regulations*.

Officer candidates are *continuously* [OCS emphasis] evaluated by members of the platoon and company staffs. It is not expected that candidates initially possess all of the required leadership traits. By study, instructions and practice, a reasonably intelligent person can become an effective leader.

LEADERSHIP TRAITS

Candidates will be evaluated on fourteen leadership traits:

- Military bearing
- Courage—physical and moral
- Decisiveness
- Dependability
- Endurance
- Enthusiasm
- Initiative
- Integrity
- Judgment
- Justice
- Knowledge
- Loyalty
- Tact
- Unselfishness.

Candidates are rated favorable, unfavorable, or marginal on all fourteen traits whenever they hold a leadership billet. Ratings are provided by both the OCS staff and a candidate's superior, also a candidate. That is, if the candidate is in a Platoon Sergeant's billet, he will receive a leadership evaluation from the OCS staff Platoon Sergeant and from the candidate holding the acting Platoon Commander billet. The OCS staff relies heavily on these peer evaluations as a comparative checkpoint for their own evaluations of candidates. Any candidate who tries "managing up," that is, looking good to the OCS staff while making life miserable for subordinates, won't survive peer evaluations.

MARINE CORPS LEADERSHIP PRINCIPLES

The Marine Corps provides its leaders with eleven principles of leadership. These time-tested principles apply to all leadership positions, from the corporal leading a fire team, to the Commandant of the Marine Corps.

- Be technically and tactically proficient.
- Know yourself and seek self-improvement.
- Know your men and look out for their welfare.
- Keep your men informed.
- Set the example.
- Ensure that the task is understood, supervised, and accomplished.
- Train your men as a team.
- Make sound and timely decisions.
- Develop a sense of responsibility in your subordinates.
- Employ your command in accordance with its capabilities.
- Seek responsibility and take responsibility for your actions.

> Delete at will if you're tired of hearing from me, but some of you are checking to see if I'm still alive. Yup, survived the halfway point, SULE I. It was [a] seven and one-half mile hike and then fire team tactics evaluations. Then we were tested on tactics on the 4th of July. I thought I was going to die several times and it hurt every step of the way, but what a sense of accomplishment and self-satisfaction when I was done! It was an amazing way to spend the Fourth . . . I scored 296 (out of a possible 300) on my Physical Fitness Test, ran a 21:34 3-mile run and I'm happy about that. Still healthy, thank God, and very motivated. I'm tired and sore but that's to be expected. Lots of tests and big hike coming up but I can see the light at the end of the tunnel and want to get there NOW. It's so close I can almost put my hands on it.
>
> E-mail from female PLC to family and friends

Leadership is unquestionably the most important, arguably the most subjective, judgment made about a candidate at OCS. In order to give every candidate a fair evaluation over the course of ten weeks, each will hold from six to eight leadership billets in which he or she will have the opportunity to demonstrate leadership ability. Candidates will demonstrate their leadership in other activities, including,

- Drilling the fire team on the drill field.
- The Leadership Reaction Course, which requires the fire team leader to make a fast assessment of a situation, develop and communicate a plan, then lead execution of the plan.
- Fire Team and Squad in the Offense exercises, which involve leading a unit in the assault of an objective.

- Small Unit Leadership Evaluations I and II, which are the OCS equivalents of the enlisted Marine's "Crucible."

Generally, a candidate will hold a leadership billet for 48 hours. At that point the staff will assign new candidates to fill sixty-four leadership positions, or "billets," required to manage a company made up of four platoons. It is the OCS staff's intent that every candidate receives sufficient exposure in leadership positions so that the staff is confident that their rankings of their people reflect performance reality. Over the course of OCS, candidates will find themselves in several of the following billets in their company (number of billets available are given in parentheses):

- Company Commander (1)
- Company Executive Officer (1)
- Company First Sergeant (1)
- Company Gunnery Sergeant (1)
- Platoon Commander (4)
- Platoon Sergeant (4)
- Platoon Guide (4)
- Squad Leader (12)
- Fire Team Leader (36).

SMALL UNIT LEADERSHIP EVALUATION II (SULE II)

The most demanding, as well as the most heavily weighted, evolution that the candidates will experience at OCS takes place at the end of the ten-week course. Known as SULE II, it is the OCS equivalent of the recruit depots' Crucible, the crowning event of enlisted bootcamp. There are some variations, both in the underlying purpose and the manner in which, the Marine Corps uses this final test for its enlisted personnel and its officers. The following tabulation indicates the requirements of SULE II compared to the enlisted recruits' Crucible.

	SULE II	**Crucible**
Duration of the exercise	60 hours	54 hours
Meals provided	4 MREs	2.5 MREs
Distance covered	48 miles	40 miles
Total sleep allowed	10 hours	8 hours

The difference between the sleep time and number of meals allotted to candidates versus recruits is explained by an OCS staff officer.

> At OCS, we allow more sleep and provide more chow in order to level the playing field between the first candidate evaluated on Day 1 and the last candidate evaluated on Day 2. It would be a significant advantage for the first candidate to be evaluated versus the last if we limited chow and sleep more than we do. Granted, it is still better to go first, but we have reduced, as much as possible, any disadvantage [to the last candidate evaluated] by providing the chow and sleep that we do.

Conversely, the enlisted Crucible is not an evaluated event. It is a rite of passage wherein the Marine Corps Recruit Depots deliver to the Corps basically trained Marines who can respond instantly to orders, who possess self-discipline, and who understand the Marine Corps legacy and ethos. As described by James B. Woulfe (*Into the Crucible: Making Marines for the 21st Century*, 1998, p. ix) the exercise is

> a major fifty-four hour challenge designed to underscore the preceding eleven weeks of recruit training, to test, to the ultimate, the recruits' minds and their bodies, to emphasize the qualities of reliability, loyalty, honesty, resolution, patriotism and teamwork to which they have been subjected in the weeks just past.

Recruits have qualified on the rifle range and have experienced the gas chamber and swimming qualification, among other requirements. OCS doesn't produce basic Marines in the sense that recruit depots do. OCS delivers people who have demonstrated the leadership potential to serve as company grade officers and the aptitude to succeed in follow-on training at TBS.

The Crucible and SULE II are both rites of passage, with slightly different objectives. For the recruit, the Crucible signals his or her full acceptance into the family of Marines. He or she is a finished, albeit basic, product. The Crucible is a nongraded event designed to bring recruits together as a team by their drill instructors in the Crucible's emotional and demanding events.

At OCS, SULE II is the capstone evaluation of leadership and tactical skills, and candidates are under significant pressure to do well. Performance in SULE II will represent 25 percent of the total leadership grade for the ten-week course and 13 percent of the overall grade at OCS and factors in to whether the candidate can, or should, graduate. The event takes place over three days and two nights in which the candidates get little sleep, live on curtailed rations, and experience heightened levels of chaos, confusion, and exhaustion. Throughout the exercise, Corps Values, exemplified by the selfless acts of heroism performed by Marine heroes, are emphasized. In contrast to the enlisted Crucible, the purpose of SULE II is to determine the leadership capability of each candidate.

Over the 60 hours the candidates will

- March or run over 40 miles
- Complete four or five Leadership Reaction Course (LRC) problems

- Carry out at least 12 squad tactical field problems
- Conduct five resupply/infiltration missions
- Sleep less than ten hours
- Eat four meals.

Descriptions of this final testing at OCS are best provided by those who have undergone the experience. SULE II is a relatively recent development at OCS, having been inserted into the program about the same time the Crucible became part of enlisted recruit training. Here are two snapshots of the SULE II experience viewed through the eyes of recent OCS graduates.

> As with most exercises at OCS, the less one participated and the less enthusiastic one was in tackling the challenges, the more painful SULE II became. . . . Our platoon was strong and this made things much less painful than they could have been.

> We returned from a 24-hour liberty at 1600 Sunday afternoon, went to chow, and then hit the rack at 2000. For the most part, the mood was one of excitement and anticipation, rather than one of dread. The lights went on at 0100 and we fell out with full packs for our night hump. . . . This was to be a 10-mile affair and, although not as difficult as the previous 11 and 15-mile humps, it was crazy shuffling along in almost total darkness. The only thing I could see was a faint hint of the white nametape [on the back] of the guy ahead of me. We had to rely more on sound than on sight to stay aligned. . . . I found myself able to take 30 second catnaps here and there during the straighter parts of the hump while keeping my left hand on the pack of the candidate ahead of me. Other candidates had problems, one falling and losing his rifle in the woods. The entire company was halted for a good twenty minutes while the staff doubled back to look for (and find) the weapon. . . . Sleep was definitely at a premium. Any opportunity I had to shut my eyes for any length of time, I took advantage of. Luckily, as I said, we had a good platoon that worked well together. Because of this the squad operations were superb. With few exceptions, we moved quickly and well during each movement and, as a result, generally had about an hour of wait time between each movement. (There were eleven of these over two days, one for each member of the squad.) This wait time equaled sleep time for us candidates. . . .

> The hardest parts were the LRC runs. These consisted of running in fire teams from the top of Fartlek Hill down to the LRC area. There we would complete an LRC exercise and then run back to Fartlek Hill on an elongated route over very hilly terrain. The LRC exercise itself took ten minutes, with around five more minutes of wait time. The kicker was that the entire run, totaling a good six miles, had to be completed in a total of forty minutes or less by the entire fire team, running in full combat gear. I was in a good, motivated fire team and, even in our worst run (we did the six miles four times) we managed to finish with a good four minutes to spare. . . .

Day Three was the worst. Nothing too physically strenuous in its own right, but by then everyone was so beat up that it all hurt. Our day started with a promotion ceremony for the company clerk, who was upped from Lance Corporal to Corporal. Then we humped two miles to a LZ (landing zone) and waited for the choppers to come. While we were there we witnessed another promotion ceremony for the Company Physical Fitness Instructor, SSGT Whobrey who was promoted to Gunnery Sergeant. Finally, the choppers came and whisked us away to TBS. The ride was ten minutes of fun but then we were back on the ground again, preparing to run the TBS "washboard," one-and-a-half miles of steep, hilly terrain, with two 80-pound ammunition crates per squad. When we were done with that, we ran the TBS NATO obstacle course, still with the ammo crates, and I reflected that it would be fun to run if I were more coherent and my legs would stop throbbing.

Everyone was so focused on the NATO course, which we'd been told was our last event, that no one noticed the platoons ahead of us RUNNING away afterwards. For me, this was the killer. I'd given it all I had. But when the NATO course ended I was beat and didn't want to go any further. Still, the staff formed us up into platoon formation, right faced us, and gave the command, "Double time! March!" I was horrified. I started to hobble ahead, putting one leg in front of the other, waving the candidates behind me past. Then I heard Sergeant [name] single me out. "You gotta be shitting me, [name]!" And so, somewhere I found the strength to pick it up. It couldn't have been more than a mile over to TBS but it was one of the longest miles I'd ever run. Finally, we were there, looking nasty as hell, and after a short brief by the CO of TBS, we hit the chow hall. And then, it was all better.

E-mail from male TBS second lieutenant to OSO

After the hike we were split into sticks of twelve people and we began the squad problems. There was a lot of stress at this point because this is what we'd been studying for eight weeks, [for] this moment. . . . I didn't find the physical strain as hard as the mental strain. Some candidates broke the first day out, snapping and yelling at other candidates. There were also quite a few candidates that broke from fatigue. Fourteen or so the first day because of heat exhaustion, not eating properly, and not drinking enough water.

Every third squad problem our fire team was required to run down to the LRC. (Each fire team did this four times.) It was about a ten-minute JOG down the hill to the LRC and a 25–30 minute RUN back up the hill to the control point. . . . The run to and from the LRC was the most difficult physical part of SULE II. On the third run back up the hill my legs started to cramp up. Heat cramps, I guess. What kept me going were family and friends at home. I don't think I could have gone home and felt good about myself knowing that I didn't try my hardest or that I quit halfway through that run. After the first day of squad problems and LRC runs, we began our night patrols. Everyone was dead tired and I just wanted to go to sleep. When they finally let us sleep, I jumped into the hooch and didn't take off my boots or blouse and fell asleep on top of my rifle. It felt

> good at the time but the next morning I woke up with a serious crick in my back and neck from laying [*sic*] on my rifle.
>
> E-mail from male PLC to the author

SULE II is a defining moment for the candidates as well as for the OCS staff. As SULE II unfolds, the Hats, up to this point jealous guardians of the title, "Marine," begin to mentor their troops as the candidates struggle to enter the final doorway that leads to acceptance into the fraternity of the Marine Corps. While continuing to look for any sign of a candidate who might break in the demanding environment of SULE II, the staff offers encouragement. As the exercise moves into its final hours, the Hats are occasionally smiling and offering suggestions, providing motivation to the drained candidates.

All that is left of OCS for this company are the Eagle, Globe, and Anchor Ceremony, a warrior breakfast, the graduation parade, and the Commissioning Ceremony, the final events that will cap ten long, hard weeks of physical, mental, and emotional testing.

Upon completing the run to TBS, each platoon is formed in front of Heywood Hall, home to TBS administration, academic offices, and classrooms. At the entry to Heywood stands a statue of Lt. Col. William G. Leftwich, a Marine hero who was posthumously awarded the Navy Cross for his actions in Vietnam. There, in the shadow of his statue, the 34 members of the 45 who struggled across the parade ground nine weeks ago during Transition, stand vacant-eyed, exhausted, and completely aware of the symbolism of the moment. One candidate, near collapse from dehydration, is supported by two of his platoon mates. Two Navy corpsmen in attendance rush to the candidate and carry him to a vehicle where he is treated.

The Eagle, Globe, and Anchor Ceremony is a solemn moment in which candidates are recognized by their platoon staff as Marines and welcomed into the Corps. First, the platoon commander, a captain, addresses the platoon with a few thoughts about what the last ten weeks were really all about and how the staff views its responsibilities as protectors of the gate to a Marine commission. The ritual really belongs to the Platoon Sergeants and Sergeant Instructors. It is a private and touching occasion, as the Hats move through the ranks, stopping in front of each candidate. What they say to each candidate is private. Exhaustion, combined with the sincere emotions of the moment, frequently bring tears to the eyes of these strong, young people. For a long time the staff has existed, at least in the eyes of the candidates, to make life as difficult as possible, as they forced their people to reach down into unknown places inside themselves for the strength and perseverance required to survive the course.

How the candidates feel about the Eagle, Globe, and Anchor Ceremony is captured in this note, written by a recent OCS graduate.

> It [SULE II] is hard. You're hot, dirty, sweaty, hungry, cranky but when it's all done, you're a goddam Marine. Oh, there's some paperwork required before it's

official, but our Platoon Sergeant told us, "I don't care about the paper work to be done. In my eyes, you are Marines." We had proven ourselves to him and that gave me an unbelievable feeling of happiness in the pit of my stomach, like nothing else I've ever felt. That's something that will stay with a person forever.

Male TBS Second lieutenant

The real work is finished. It's off to the chow hall and the Warrior's Meal at TBS, a meal they will share with the lieutenants who are already in the TBS curriculum. It will be a meal to enjoy. The Hats are nowhere to be seen as the candidates ravenously dig into hamburgers and fries. They have made it.

The graduation parade will be attended by the candidates' families and friends. It is an impressive sight when more than 500 candidates perform the age-old soldier's ceremony of passing in review. This marks their passage into an exclusive organization, exclusive not because of its prejudices or personal likes and dislikes, but exclusive in a way expressed by a recent candidate as a place where "The cowards never showed up. The weak left. Only the committed and the strong remained." I would add that, among those who left, were the "physically injured," those who suffered disenrollment through no lack of strength or commitment.

Since this is an OCC and its members have all graduated from college or are prior enlisted personnel, the graduates will take their oath at a commissioning ceremony in the afternoon. (PLC Senior and NROTC classes receive their commissions after graduation from college.) The officer's oath is a unique creation, spawned from a nation of laws, not men. It does not require allegiance to the Marine Corps or its commandant or any other military organization. No loyalty is sworn to any officer of the U.S. government or to any political party. The oath binds the officer solely to the Constitution of the United States, that unique and revered document which has survived foreign wars, a civil war, and an endless human desire to manipulate its words and meaning. Swearing to abide by the oath is a special and solemn moment.

The Oath of the Marine Officer

I do solemnly swear that I will support and defend the Constitution of the United States of America against all enemies foreign and domestic; that I will bear true faith and allegiance to the same; that I take this obligation freely; without any mental reservation or purpose of evasion; that I will well and faithfully discharge the duties of the office on which I am about to enter, so help me God.

5

OCS—The Gatekeepers

Ductus exemplo (*Lead by example*).

Motto of the Officer Candidates School

It is 0600 on a typically humid summer morning on the banks of the broad Potomac River. The candidates have been marched across the bridge that spans both the main road and railroad tracks that cut through the eastern edge of the Officer Candidates School (OCS) grounds. This will be their first breakfast under the watchful eyes of the Hats. They have been given five hours to sleep and, if they did not use it to sleep, that is their problem. The candidates have been jerked from the civilian world into one that is uncomfortable, demanding, and fast paced. Over the past 16 hours they have had a wealth of rules, regulations, and instructions thrown at them. Their meals have consisted of insubstantial box lunches. If any of them are thinking that meals in the chow hall will provide a respite from the constant stream of questions and corrections that emanate from the Hats they are soon disabused of that thought.

The heretofore simple acts of carrying a food tray, making food choices, and eating are done the Marine Corps way, or offending candidates become targets for the Hats' dyspeptic personalities. Candidates are expected to know the names of the company staff and the billets they occupy within the company's table of organization. If they fail to address a Hat by the proper name and billet, in the prescribed manner, their intelligence and fitness for OCS are challenged. The OCS format for communicating with a superior does not come easily to college students whose formal lead-in to a conversation on campus might be, "Professor, did you want to see me?" In this new life things are more complicated. "I" and "me" have been eliminated from any communication. The format for reporting to a superior takes a bit of thought and practice. An example of proper communication is, "Good morning, Sergeant Instructor, Gunnery Sergeant Jones! Candidate Smith reporting to the Sergeant Instructor as ordered, Sergeant Instructor."

Communication with superiors is to follow this prescribed format from *Candidate Regulations*:

- An appropriate greeting is given.
- The senior is identified by his or her billet within the company, rank, and last name.

- The candidate identifies the requested action.
- The senior is again recognized by the billet he or she holds.

If candidates cannot get it right, if they stumble or stutter, they will repeat it until it is performed correctly. On occasion, candidates have been known to embarrass themselves as a result of unsuccessful efforts to request permission to make a head (toilet) call in the proper format.

Instructions ring out across the chow hall as unfortunate candidates do something the civilian, rather that the Marine Corps, way. Candidates eat without engaging in conversation, and the only sounds heard are the sounds of a mute banquet, punctuated by questions, corrections, and orders emanating from the ubiquitous OCS staff.

In 30 minutes they are to have eaten and be back in formation in front of the chow hall. Company First Sergeant Tim Campbell, a Marine for 19 years, observes his people as they move toward the line where they are to deposit their food trays. He spies a tray that contains unfinished scrambled eggs. The scene that unfolds is typical.

"Jones! What is that on your tray?"

"Company Gunnery Sergeant—" (the candidate doesn't remember Campbell's billet).

"Jones! You've been here for three days and you don't know who I am? What's the matter with you? Are you a rock?"

"Company First Sergeant, this candidate is not a rock!"

"What's that on your tray?"

"Company First Sergeant, this candidate can't finish these eggs."

"Then why did you take them?"

(Hesitating) "Company First Sergeant, this candidate has no excuse."

"Jones, you're going to finish those eggs now. Sit down."

Jones sits down at the table, spitting egg fragments as he answers questions fired at him by Campbell. As Jones completes his task, Campbell leans across the table and says, "Candidate, you don't waste good Marine Corps chow. If you waste chow or anything else the Marine Corps gives you, your Marines will think it's OK for them to waste things. Marines don't waste anything. Do you understand?"

Candidate Jones has learned his lesson while forcing a few ounces of scrambled eggs into his body. "Company First Sergeant, this candidate understands."

The candidate moves swiftly out of the chow hall to the company formation in front of the chow hall. More than one candidate has learned that you do not waste food, and all candidates understand that mealtime will bear no resemblance to life back at school. The ever-present Hats have staked out mealtime as their time, too.

The men and women who carry the responsibility for screening and evaluating officer candidates for the Marine Corps take their responsibilities, both to the Marine Corps and to the candidates they must evaluate, very seriously.

The Marines stand apart from other armed services in their approach to officer candidate training. At Quantico, it is the senior enlisted Marines, the Hats, who play the major role in determining which candidates will become their officers of the future. The commissioned officers at OCS oversee and participate in the training and evaluation processes, but it is the Hats who literally live with the candidates. The Hats are experienced Marines and have all served at least one successful tour as an enlisted recruit drill instructor (DI) prior to assignment to OCS.

For most candidates, their time at Platoon Leaders Class (PLC) (Junior), Naval Reserve Officer Training Corps (NROTC), or Officer Candidates Course (OCC) will be the first time in their lives that they have been observed, guided, corrected, and evaluated in everything they do during the long working days. Most candidates arrive in good physical condition; however, the cumulative effects of the physical and mental forces that affect performance once OCS begins in earnest cannot be anticipated.

OCS has a different objective than the program at the Parris Island or San Diego Recruit Depots. Some have described OCS as an "officers' bootcamp," and in many respects this is accurate. However, the goals of the two programs are not identical. In recruit bootcamp the objective is to instill discipline and instantaneous response to orders and to focus every Marine on the unit's mission with 70-some recruits working as one. At OCS candidates will work in an environment where the major objective is to screen out those who do not or cannot measure up. Officer candidates are taught many of the basic skills required by all Marines, and in addition the staff assesses and works to develop the leadership capabilities of the candidates. Fifty percent of a candidate's rank in the class is based on leadership performance.

The men and women who guard the entryway to a Marine Corps commission perform a vital function for the Marine Corps. Regardless of the academic or athletic credentials that candidates bring to OCS, the gatekeepers will judge whether they are capable of leading Marines in combat.

The OCS staff, officers and enlisted alike, are as diverse in background and education as one would find in a civilian organization. The following interview excerpts provide insights about the people assigned to the important task of producing leaders for tomorrow's Marine Corps. Here they provide their own perspectives about their responsibilities to the nation, the candidates, and the Marine Corps, while providing their thoughts across a range of subjects.

Staff Sergeant Bradley R. Newton is a Sergeant Instructor (SI) in India Company, which is composed of 210 Junior PLCs in their first six weeks of training. Newton, who is from Philadelphia, has spent twelve years in the Corps. He and his wife, a former Marine, have two children. He is a tall, lean, and formidable looking man. SSGT Newton is on temporary assignment at OCS and will return shortly to his permanent duty assignment in the Disbursing Office at Quantico.

Q. Why did you join the Marine Corps?

I joined the Corps for a different reason than most. It wasn't that I thought the Marines were the best organization. If I had stayed in Philadelphia I really don't think I would have made it to my twenty-fifth birthday. I intended to join the Air Force but I saw a Marine recruiter and the way he carried himself and I told myself, "I want to be like that individual."

Q. How did you become a drill instructor?

After various assignments at Cherry Point, Okinawa, Japan and Norfolk in my MOS [Military Occupation Specialty] as a Financial Manager/Disburser, I was assigned to Parris Island in 1994. The dream of any enlisted Marine is to be a DI if, like me, they had a good DI, someone they could look up to while in bootcamp. I had individuals like that. When I returned to Parris Island in 1994 and drove through the front gate I told my wife, "I'm going to end up as a drill instructor," and that happened in 1996.

Q. How do you compare the recruits you trained at Parris Island versus the candidates at OCS?

There is little or no difference. The vast majority of candidates are just like recruits. They have no concept of what the Marine Corps is about. They don't understand the chain of command. They don't understand the position of attention . . . you're teaching them from scratch. But there is one difference that's a shocker to me. At Parris Island the majority of individuals either come from low poverty levels or they're from the upper-middle class or upper class. Here, at OCS, the majority of kids come from the middle class. That was a real shock to me.

Q. Could you explain?

I was one of those who came in from the lower end of the economic scale. I was trying to get away from what I was doing in Philly. [At Parris Island] we also have kids right off the farm. They've never done much in their lives and they want to change that so they join the Marines. Those kids make it. Then the kids come in who've had everything in life. They want to prove something to themselves and their families. They also make it. The kids from the middle class get to Parris Island and they get fed up. They come in [to the DI's office] crying, "I want to leave." But there's no leaving Parris Island. We tell them, "Too bad, but you signed a contract. Now, get back out there and train." But here at OCS, the kids from the middle class, they handle the pressure. I won't say the pressure is more or less here than at Parris Island. There we have different tools we use to mold recruits and bend them to do what we tell them to do. Here it's pretty much self-paced. After a while it's, "OK, if you can't do it, I'll write you up and send you home." The majority of officer candidates try harder if you push them.

Q. Many of these candidates have never been shouted [at], other than by a coach. This is their first experience of somebody getting in their face the way you SI's do. Would you agree?

Yes, sir, wholeheartedly. Our voice and appearance are tools we use—and the way we look at them. We close the distance between them and us. Their comfort zone disappears. They find themselves in a brand new element and you're telling them, "This is my world, not yours. I control everything around you right now," and that's shocking to them.

Q. I've watched as two of you SI's get in the face of a candidate at the same time. Obviously, you're making a point with a candidate. Is this two-on-one tactic something you Hats work out beforehand, among yourselves?

It's a funny thing. It's like a shark that smells blood. A Hat sees a candidate getting ready to break and he wants a piece of it, too, so he jumps in. During Transition, we're breaking them down and that is essential. We're trying to get the candidate to respond even though we know he won't respond correctly. We're going to apply pressure, constant pressure, to see if he breaks or if he handles it.

Q. So your job is to create chaos and stress?

No, I can never create stress. The candidates put stress on themselves. I can create stressful situations. I can cause them to create their own stress but I can't create stress.

Q. You and the other Hats are in the unique position of having a major impact on who will and who won't become an officer of Marines. That's unique to the Marine Corps, isn't it?

Yes, we do. We definitely have an impact. [When I see a candidate that isn't cutting it] I say, "I can't see you leading Marines that I trained. I cannot see it happening. I will not do that injustice to them, to the Marine Corps or to you. You just don't have it.

Q. What is the toughest part of training for candidates?

It's different for each candidate. Some candidates are physically weaker and the physical aspect will be tougher. Most of them are decent students and academics would not be a problem for them if OCS were *only* about academics. But when we incorporate academics, physical training, sleep deprivation and a "no McDonalds" environment their comfort zone disappears. They can no longer sit back, study, relax and do what they want, when they want. It's the totality [of all the OCS pressures] that makes it difficult for them. Some straight A students get here and, with all the other demands, they simply cannot deal with it.

Q. You don't use Incentive Physical Training (IPT) here like you did at Parris Island with recruits, do you? (As an example, IPT is concerned with ordering a recruit to do 25 push-ups for making a mistake.)

No, ITP is a disciplinary tool we don't use here. We will never have the discipline here that we have in a recruit regiment. It wouldn't be a good idea for a staff sergeant to ITP a future lieutenant.

Q. Why not?

Let's say that down the road that staff sergeant ends up in the lieutenant's platoon. What does that lieutenant remember when he's writing out that sergeant's Fitness Report [a performance evaluation used in the Marine Corps]? To me IPT is never personal. It simply tells the recruit, "You did wrong. Get up here and pay for your sins, then go away." Here we must create an environment of professionalism between the staff NCO's and our future officers. They should feel that their staff sergeant is going to be their support, their crutch, when some corporal asks the lieutenant a question he can't answer.

Q. When these PLC's leave here after their first summer of training, what do you want to have accomplished with them?

I want to have given them a taste, just a taste, of the Marine Corps. I want them to know our Core Values. They have to understand responsibility, what the Marine Corps stands for. They learn these things every day, even if it's just observing how the SI's interact with one another. They need to know that we do the right thing when no one is watching. That's what we want them to leave with. If they've learned that then they will want to come back and get the whole act. We've given them half. They have to come back to get the rest of it.

Q. You're eleven years older than most of these candidates. Is there a difference in attitudes toward personal integrity between your generation and this generation?

Blatant things like lying about whether a candidate made it to the top of the rope climb on the obstacle course comes to mind. I'll ask a candidate, who obviously didn't make it to the top, "Did you climb that rope?" and he'll answer, "Yes." I then say, "I was standing here watching. The corpsman here was watching. Did you climb the rope?" He says, "No." I ask, "Why did you lie?" and he'll say, "To stay out of trouble." That could be the difference between this generation and mine. We would just say, "No we didn't make it up there. What you want me to do?" But this generation, it seems they will do anything to succeed. And I worry about that. We simply can't create officers like that because if that attitude ever gets to the top there will be a bunch of dead bodies lying around.

Q. You look like a man who enjoys his job.

You have to enjoy watching fifty-four individuals that come from completely different backgrounds and parts of the country come together and become one.

There's no greater feeling than watching that happen. It's an even bigger kick at Parris Island. You watch eighty-eight new recruits bump into each other when they arrive and then you look at them a week before graduation. It's a phenomenal thing to see. When you watch them march out for drill and you're calling commands and the seventy-seven who are left compete as one. It's then you see how training has changed them. I remember one recruit who was a quitter when he arrived at bootcamp. At the conclusion of training we ran the Crucible and he was in pain from the last station all the way back into the barracks. I watched him put his pack on his back and start crying because of the pain he was in. As his DI, I had to continue to apply the pressure. I told him, "You can quit now if you want to," but he refused to quit. That's the attitude you want to see. He had grown up.

Gunnery Sergeant Paul McKenna, 33 years old, is a 13-year veteran of the Corps. The officers at OCS consider him the most intense of the Hats. McKenna, a native of Burlington, New Jersey, is the youngest of five children and the first in his family to become a Marine. He is the father of twin daughters, age six.

Q. Why did you join the Marine Corps?

After graduation from high school I attended Mercer County Community College for a couple of years, then farted around with odd jobs. The bombing of the barracks in Beirut touched me. We had some local guys from the neighborhood, close friends that were killed in those barracks. I just thought I needed something more challenging in my life so I joined the Corps in 1986 at twenty years old.

Q. When did you realize that you would make a career of the Marine Corps?

Since graduation from bootcamp I wanted to return to the drill field. But the Corps said, "You gotta wait." When we deployed to Somalia in 1992 and got involved in some live stuff, I realized there's a lot more to the Marine Corps than Camp Pendleton or Twenty-nine Palms. At the same time some other opportunities opened up for me. When I got back from Somalia I was riding the high of doing something tangible. It was at that time that I got my orders to the drill field. It was probably at the end of my first tour as a Drill Instructor that I realized, "Hey, this is what I want to do for a living."

Q. What do you want these Junior [first year] PLC's to leave here with?

The focus of my effort is to let them leave here with a positive impression of the Marine Corps. I want them to say, "Hey, not only is this something I want to do, but it's going to be hard. The people I was around, the staff I was around challenged me each and every day and I want to come back for that second challenge."

Q. What's the toughest part of OCS for most candidates?

It's the culture shock of such a regimented environment with people constantly observing you, every second of the day. I look back at my bootcamp and that was the toughest part for me. So, whether recruit or officer candidate, the toughest part is the culture shock.

Q. What's the difference between training recruits and officer candidates?

Everything's spelled out for recruits. They are taken from point A to point B and told exactly what they need, where to go and what to do. Here at OCS, after Transition, candidates must try to figure it out on their own. The staff is there to guide and evaluate them on how well they're doing. The biggest thing is that the candidates are given a lot more autonomy and a vehicle to show their leadership capability.

Q. How do you measure a person's leadership ability? How do you determine who doesn't measure up in leadership? Give me some examples.

You're not looking for someone who is a mirror image of yourself because there are all types of leaders out there. You find young men or women who struggle with being aggressive. They struggle with being vocal, with addressing large groups of people about a common goal. You get people who are too analytical, that look at a problem in too many ways. What we're looking for is a basic company grade officer who is capable of inspiring young men and women. I can see it if they don't have the physical courage to push themselves. Or, we see it in a lack of moral courage when a candidate doesn't have the intestinal fortitude to correct his peers or to make an unpopular decision. I'm partial but I think OCS does a great job in developing different ways in which leadership ability is evaluated.

Q. Some people have the impression that the Marine Corps stamps people out, makes everyone the same. How would you answer that?

Absolutely not and it's a shame that perception is out there. The Corps couldn't be filled with more individuality. Just walk down the hallway here at OCS and you'll see it. The public's perception [may be influenced by the fact] that the Marine Corps prides itself on the team concept. Regardless of our backgrounds and our individuality, we all are focused on the goal and what we must do, collectively, to accomplish that goal. Whether we're training candidates or winning a battle. We've been doing that for two hundred and some odd years now.

Q. One thing that intrigues me is whether people join the Marine Corps because the Core Values—honor, courage and commitment—are values they already possess? Or, do they join because they are seeking these values?

We get both. We get those who come from very structured families with good values. And then we get those from broken homes or, for whatever reason, their values are clouded. The Marine Corps becomes their constant, their light in the storm that never goes out. I guess I had a little of both backgrounds. I grew up in a good family. Mom and Dad loved me but when I got to college I lacked the self-discipline to do the right thing. I found myself involved in a lot of things I shouldn't have been involved in. That constant was what drew me to the Corps and that's what drives me each and every day both here and with my family. I have young Marines that look to me for their example. I think what drives all of us around here, officer and enlisted alike, is that I am not doing this only for myself. More importantly I'm doing it for the people around me and that helps keep your values right.

Q. Can you give me your perspective on the comparative physical demands of OCS and recruit training?

It's tougher here at OCS. It's more demanding, just as it should be. We're talking about future officers, who must walk through a door and have instant credibility with forty or fifty young Marines. They're required to lead them not only mentally and spiritually, but more importantly, physically. As I look back when I was a young Marine, that's the first thing that I looked for in my lieutenant. Could he lead me physically? If he couldn't (and I had some that couldn't) he automatically lost credibility with me. When an officer who couldn't lead physically taught a class it was always in the back of my mind. "Yeah, you might be an expert on the heavy machine gun, but you looked pretty humble at PT [physical training] this morning." It's a shame that we're that judgmental, but we're Marines.

Q. Tell me the purpose of the confusion, uncertainty and chaos that you provide for the candidates here at OCS.

Chaos and uncertainty quickly teach candidates that things change rapidly in combat. OCS is by no means comparable to what happens on the battlefield but chaos and uncertainty forces you to think about and rapidly develop solutions to problems. But candidates need to understand the reason behind certain elements of the confusion and chaos at OCS. Three or four days into training I address the company . . . I might ask a candidate, "Why do we have you sound off as loud as you can, and, if you're not loud enough, we have you do it over again?" They'll answer, "That's for motivation," or for other reasons but not the answer I'm looking for. When I tell them the answer, it's like a light goes on in their heads. I say, "Suppose you're controlling a fire team or squad in a live fire problem. If you cannot give commands in a loud, vigorous manner, controlling your people through an objective, you're liable to cost someone their life." I tell them, "You're not going to develop a loud voice overnight. That comes with straining and training, just like anything else. That's why you're required to sound off every time you're spoken to." When you tell them that, they understand, "OK, there's a purpose behind this. It's not just meant to harass me." After that their volume level goes up.

Q. When you Hats pick up your platoons, the first day of Transition, what is the reason for all the shouting?

It goes back to promoting a chaotic or uncertain environment. We're letting them know that they are giving up a lot of privileges, what they've come to think of as their rights, to come here and join our team. Things are going to be thrown at them from a thousand different directions. As you've seen, picking up all your gear and literally dragging it across the parade deck, going into a new squad bay and starting the breakdown process, says, "Hey, everyone's here to become a basic Marine and you're going to give up your individuality for a short period of time in order for us to evaluate you." And that's done with a lot of intensity and a lot of chaos.

Q. Can you see any difference in the young people coming through OCS today versus your generation?

Absolutely, and I tell the candidates this when I talk to them initially. There's no way I had the wisdom or foresight that they have when I was twenty years old. I was reckless, very careless in my behavior. But to come down here and say, "I want to be a Marine officer," to know that or just to give it a shot, says a lot for these young men and women. My generation wasn't that focused. We figured it out as we went along. But these people have a definite, futuristic look. They say, "This is what I want to do and this is how I want to go about doing it because this might help me down the road." So, yeah, I think they're better in that way than my generation.

Q. Apart from being able to handle the physical demands of OCS, is there a common thread that runs through the backgrounds of successful candidates?

First, the successful ones generally come from a good family. Whether the parents are together or not, he or she comes from a good family with other siblings. And second, they've been exposed to the military, whether it be ROTC or simply reading, they've had some sort of exposure to the military's infrastructure and how [the] military operates.

Q. Let's talk about the emphasis on integrity. Today's Marine Corps is really big on that. I don't recall such a major emphasis on integrity when I was a PLC or even as an officer.

We have the obvious things like somebody not telling the truth to the chain of command. Those matters are dealt with very swiftly, as they should be. That's what I love about the Marine Corps. You know, you shouldn't have to mention integrity. Your word is your word. You shake somebody's hand and you tell them you're going to do something, it's going to get done. I mean those things are priceless. Everybody wants to be treated with integrity and to know that they're going to be treated honestly and fairly. A lot of guys never got that in their community and the Marine Corps offers that to them.

Q. Do you Hats instinctively know, early on, when a class of candidates arrives, which ones aren't going to complete the course?

It's funny you asked that question. During the previous cycle, three of us were talking in the duty hut, discussing the candidates who'd just arrived. We made up a list of ten candidates we believed would not complete the course. This was based on our initial impressions that first day. We wrote the names on a yellow Post-it and placed it on the side of the microwave. Eight weeks later we'd forgotten about it until someone remembered the Post-it was on the microwave. Out of the ten names, nine were gone. For whatever reason, I believe you can identify those that just don't have it. We can do that because we've been in this business for a while and you can look at an individual and just tell whether the right stuff is there.

Q. You don't feel this slants your perspective on those people?

No. There are too many factors in this equation to set somebody up for failure. The colonel is going to look very impartially at every candidate that's leaving. He'll say, "Why is this person a failure in McKenna's eyes and everyone else [says] he's doing well?" We can't have it out for anyone. Too many judges are involved.

Q. How has the Marine Corps changed since you joined thirteen years ago?

I think the Marine Corps has gotten a lot smarter, a lot wiser, a lot thriftier than we were in the 1980s. And it's helped us in the good times, being able to do more with less. Now, as far as the people aspect, we have improved the way we treat individuals. I can just go off my own experience. In the past you didn't have to concern yourself with how you talked to a group of Marines or whether you used profanity or not. But now, profanity is not only not condoned, it isn't accepted. It's not professional. Those are good changes, how we deal with our peers, how we deal with our subordinates. It helps us as individuals. I can tell you a thousand stories about my own gunny. I can't remember him ever praising us or talking to us in a civil tone. We were constantly berated and we only interacted with him when we did something wrong or when he believed we did something wrong. I can't do that. I can't do that and expect to have any credibility with my Marines. We've changed greatly, not only resource-wise, but more in our relationships with our people. And that's a good thing.

Captain Kathleen Yolanda Davis is 29 years old, single, the daughter of a Marine and has been in the Marine Corps for seven years. Captain Davis is the Staff Platoon Commander of a platoon of female PLCs. It is Marine Corps policy to segregate male and female candidates in training. Her platoon is housed in the same barracks as the males of the company but in a separate squad bay. Captain Davis, a person of obvious intelligence, provided some interesting insights about the demands of OCS on female candidates.

Q. When and why did you join the Marine Corps?

I came to OCS the summer of 1992. I was originally a PLC Law candidate and after that summer I attended a year of law school. My parents said, "Law school costs an awful lot of money, so what is your Plan B?" I decided to come on active duty and I've worked on completing my law degree, off-time.

Q. So, your plan is to ultimately get your law degree?

I do. It's something I've started and now I want to finish it. I don't know that I'll ever practice law but I enjoy studying law.

Q. I don't mean to sound sexist but I would think it's tough for a woman to be in the Marine Corps.

Yes sir, and I talk to my girls about that all the time. They're going to have to make some decisions that males aren't going to have to make. It's hard for a mother to get on a ship and leave her kids. That's a tough thing for a mother to do. We try to prepare them for things like that.

Q. What's the most difficult part of OCS for a woman?

It's a close call between the stress and the physical requirements. They're introduced to an environment that they're just not prepared for. When they arrive they have a look that says, "What's going on here? Why is everybody yelling at me?" For the first few weeks they take it personally, being yelled at. The first two weeks of this session I think every candidate that I have came in my office and cried. I assure them that it's not personal, that the SI's are trying to correct mistakes, trying to teach them something. Once candidates get past that stumbling block with all its stress, they tend to do a lot better.

Q. Young people today, not just the females, just don't get yelled at when they're growing up. Maybe a coach yells but it looks like it is a different world for them here.

Yes, it is. In America today we sit people down and counsel them on what they did wrong. In the Marine Corps, because of what we do, we don't have time to go through telling people, "This is what happened, this is what you need to do, and why." We need things to happen right now and my candidates aren't accustomed to that.

Q. How do you look at a candidate's leadership ability? How do you come to the conclusion that this person has it and this other one doesn't have it?

I look for confidence. Some candidates arrive and get yelled at and they start shaking. Then you'll see the candidate that gets yelled at and understands they're being corrected because they've done something wrong or incorrectly. They comprehend what's going on and they fix the problem and never make the same mistake again. And that's how those leaders stand out. They have the confidence to take correction and move on.

Q. Do you see any differences in the women coming through the program now and your class at OCS?

We are a lot alike. When I went through OCS we had the athletes, the girly-girls, the cheerleaders. I see the same dynamics in my platoon out there. They seem to be pretty much the same as my class.

Q. Are there similarities in the backgrounds of the people that are successful here?

Athletes do very well here. You have to understand this. My candidates that aren't physically strong, who struggle with PT are *consumed* by PT. Every day for them starts with, "If I can just get past PT then I'll make it through the day." This distracts them from their billet duties and academic work because all they can think about is, "Don't let me fall out of this three mile run." They suffer in other areas because they are so consumed by the physical fitness aspects.

Q. Are there any similarities in family background in your successful candidates?

No, it's all over the lot. I guess different things drive different people. You read their biographies and understand that these are people from different backgrounds. I have the second, third and fourth ranked candidates in the company in my platoon and that includes the males. These women are motivating individuals, outstanding. They have nothing else in common except for the fact that they are good athletes, all of them. They have leadership ability, they're very calm under pressure and nothing frazzles them, but their backgrounds are totally different. Different motivations drive different people.

Q. One issue I'm trying to understand. Does the Marine Corps draw people who already have the Core Values of courage, honor and commitment? Or, does it draw people who see these values and say, "I have not been exposed to these values and I want them"? Any thoughts on that subject?

I don't know if I can answer that question, but they are all looking for something. I don't know if they're looking to belong or if they're looking for a challenge in life and the good ones find it here. We started out with fifty-two candidates in my platoon and we now have twenty-five. And, for whatever reason, those twenty-five wanted it bad enough. You listen to them talk about the Core Values and being commissioned in the Marine Corps and you think they just had to already have those values when they arrived. They came in with them. I don't believe we could have given them that in ten weeks.

Q. Can you tell, early on, who isn't going to make it through OCS?

Yes, I can tell within the first two weeks. They are obvious because they don't grasp anything. They don't want to grasp anything. They just go through the motions and they hold back the rest of the platoon. My staff and I are very good about getting rid of these people because they water down the platoon. They are de-motivating for the platoon since every other candidate must carry them. You can't afford to let that go on very long.

Q. Tell me about your Sergeant Instructors.

My three staff NCO's are outstanding. They're just terrors who are able to instill discipline while maintaining morale and that's a difficult balance. They are very demanding; they do what is needed. . . . At the end of the course, the candidates write a critique of the course and the staff and every one of them praises the SI's and writes about how great their instructors were. I'm lucky to have such capable people. They make my job easy.

Captain Michael V. Samarov is 29 years old. He was born in Moscow, in the former Soviet Union, the son of a Red Army officer who taught at the Soviet Academy of Armored Forces. His parents, who are Russian Jews, immigrated to the United States in 1976. A graduate of Boston University, Captain Samarov entered the Marine Corps in 1992 through the Naval ROTC program. He has published several articles in the *Marine Corps Gazette*, the professional journal of the Corps. His views on the young people of today, our educational system, and the OCS program are thought provoking.

Q. Why did you join the Marine Corps?

I originally wanted to be a Navy pilot. When I came to Boston U. I met Marines from the South Boston area. And these old Marines took care of us. If we couldn't go home for Thanksgiving, their homes were open to us. If we needed a couple of bucks it was always right there. We couldn't buy dinner [when in South Boston]. That was the first place in America to erect a Vietnam memorial. When I met those men from South Boston I knew I would be misplaced as a Navy pilot and that a Marine infantry officer was really what I wanted to be.

Q. Where have you served prior to coming to OCS?

I was in the Western Pacific with the 1st Battalion, 4th Marines and we deployed all over. The toughest places were the Horn of Africa and the Persian Gulf. Then I did a narcotics deployment to Arizona. . . . In 1995–6 I spent a year on the fence line at Guantanamo Bay, Cuba, first as a platoon commander, then as executive officer of the Rifle Security Company, Leeward. We had about 400 Marines down there and it was an interesting time. We pulled whole families out of the water as the Cuban guards took potshots at them. This was during the migrant crisis of those days. I then went to the Naval Academy and served two years as a Company Officer, essentially in command of 130 midshipmen. After that I attended Amphibious Warfare School, graduated this spring and was assigned as a platoon commander here at OCS.

Q. What's your perspective on this generation of people coming through OCS right now? What are their strengths?

There are a couple [of] things. They seem much more serious about their religious faith than we were. When we were growing up it was unusual to have somebody belong to a Bible study group. I'm Jewish and I grew up in a Catholic neighborhood. The Catholics all went to CCD [Confraternity of Christian Doctrines] class but it was like an Ed Burns movie made a few years ago. The father is having emotional problems and he says, "I want to talk to our priest." His son looks at him and says, "But Dad, you don't even believe in God." The father replies, "That doesn't prevent me from being a good Catholic!" (laughs). That was what I grew up with. You followed the family traditions. Whereas, I think a lot of these folks are very, very serious about God and their faith.

Q. What do you see as their weak points?

They're not as physically tough as we were. I try to sell them on the point that, as an officer, you can't go to sick call because that affects the troops. You know—they get the idea that the boss is sick or the boss is hurt. I have an injured right knee that I've nursed throughout this program. I felt, as an officer, that I couldn't let them see me being tended by the docs because then their own injuries would tend to multiply. One of the things I'm proudest of is that this platoon had the lowest NPQ [not physically qualified] rate in the battalion. We had three candidates who were NPQ'd. One was really broken so he couldn't continue in the program. The other two, if they really wanted it in their heart of hearts, could have continued. That's one difference I see. I think physical toughness is a learned attribute.

Q. Thomas Ricks, in his book, *Making the Corps,* talks about the dangers of the Marine Corps' "estrangement" from the society it is responsible to protect. Any thoughts on that subject?

It's troubling that he writes that. Ricks is a Yale graduate, a very intelligent man. I think what he's referring to, perhaps indirectly, is a danger similar to the estrangement of the German military from the German culture, which occurred after World War I. The Junkers went off in one direction while the rest of Germany experienced the chaotic upheaval that produced Hitler. He was able . . . to co-opt the military to do his bidding. I'm positive that was in the back of Ricks' mind as he wrote his book.

I think what General "Brute" Krulak wrote holds true today. "The American people don't need a Marine Corps. They just want a Marine Corps." There are other people who, theoretically, could do what we do. The reason we exist is because the American people want us. We are the repository of a hard culture and the American people want that somewhere. They want to keep it in society, somewhere under control, under their watchful eye, locked up, but ready whenever it's needed.

Q. I observed a class in which you posed a real-life decision problem. I was surprised that only two out of your platoon of forty-four people arrived at the correct decision. [The problem concerned a Marine who violated orders in order to save the lives of two other Marines. The issue was whether you should punish the Marine who performed a courageous act. The problem was based on an actual situation that occurred at Guantanamo Bay, Cuba. In the actual case the Marine was given a citation for bravery. Forty-two of the PLCs in Samarov's platoon believed the man deserved some sort of punishment.] What is it that led so many candidates down the wrong path? Is it that the candidates believe you're trying to find out how macho or tough they are? Are they trying to come up with the "school solution" rather than follow their own logic and judgment?

Several candidates came to me and said they were trying to give the school solution. But, let me take a step back. The high school education that these people received was sub-par. They were never taught to think on their own, to think for themselves, to come up with their own solutions. I think that has to do with the fact that our teachers, as a whole, are doing the nation a disservice. Even in higher math you have to find your own solutions because there are no forms. There isn't any "here's exactly how you solve this problem" solution supplied. You must use creativity. Further, in analyzing more complicated issues, certainly in arriving at a balanced view of history, young people aren't taught to think critically. For example, we know that the Civil War was about freeing slaves. That's where today's student stops. Obviously, the Civil War was about freeing the slaves, but it was also about a million and one other things. We're not teaching people to think and analyze for themselves. What they're taught goes like this. "Here's your information. Look for the form, plug the form in and boom! Here's your answer coming out the other end." And, young people aren't taught ethics or moral reasoning, either in high school or college. I think these two subjects are most important.

Finally, I find it curious that they don't understand that to be a good leader you have to have an inordinate reservoir of reasoned, not emotional, compassion. That's difficult to teach them. As a leader it's good to be hard—but it's hard to be smart. And you've got to be smart when you're dealing with people. There are few easy, clear-cut solutions with people.

Q. We talked recently about a candidate who received a bad report from his student platoon commander because he dropped out of a march. He wrote a two-page legalistic explanation of why he dropped out. Is that typical? This need to explain rather than just admit to messing up?

I don't know if it's a generational thing or a maturity issue. I have a candidate in this platoon that troubles me. He instinctively cuts corners and the Hats and I work with him over and over again. It's almost like housebreaking a puppy. You rub his nose in it, then he does it again. Why is he like that? Is it generational? Is it because he's seen others do that and get away with it? Is it courtroom dramas on TV where clever lawyers get people off? I don't know, but teaching people to accept responsibility for errors or mistakes is one of the hardest things to teach, in my experience.

Q. What would you change in the OCS program?

One of the things I'd change is this. Our own [OCS staff] preparation needs to be more valuable. I never felt, as a company staff, that we came up with a goal. Precisely, what is it that makes one candidate acceptable to us and what makes another unacceptable? What is the use of the stress we impose? The staff has a general idea but if you asked someone to stand up and explain it, I think they'd have a hard time. As a platoon staff, we came up with answers to these questions as we went along.

Finally, this is a tough assignment for our Hats. They are true professionals in every sense of the word. Most of them are temporarily here and they are working much harder than their peers back in their permanent duty sections are. When they get back, they will be required to catch up on a full summer of work at their old jobs because they've been gone. I think it would be better if we could find a way to staff OCS on a permanent basis.

Colonel George J. Flynn, Commanding Officer, Officer Candidates School, has been a Marine for 24 years. The son of a police officer, Flynn was raised in Rutherford, New Jersey, the younger of two children. He attended parochial elementary and high schools prior to his appointment to the U.S. Naval Academy. He is a 1975 graduate of the academy. A 47-year-old artillery officer, he has a quiet but obvious air of command about him.

In addition to a variety of command and staff assignments in the Marine Corps' artillery regiments, Colonel Flynn's duty stations and assignments have included:

- Attendance at the Command and Staff College at the Naval War College where he graduated with distinction
- Service as Junior Aide-de-Camp to the Commandant of the Marine Corps
- Attendance at the National War College where he graduated with distinction
- Appointment as a Military Fellow at the Council on Foreign Relations
- Heading the Strategic Initiatives Group at Headquarters, Marine Corps

Colonel Flynn holds a Master of Arts Degree in National Security and Strategic Studies from the Naval War College, a Master of Science Degree in National Security and Strategy from the National War College, and a Master of Arts Degree in International Relations from Salve Regina College.

He is married to the former Sally Anne Riordan of Elmwood Park, New Jersey. They have three children, George, Danny and Maureen. Recently, George received his Marine Corps commission from his father upon graduation from Virginia Tech University.

Q. Do you have any military background in the family?

My grandfather was in the Navy in World War I and my father and his brother were in the Navy in World War II.

Q. While at Annapolis, was it always your intent to become a Marine officer?

No, I went with the idea of becoming a doctor.

Q. When did that change?

My senior year two things changed. I was one of sixteen midshipmen at the academy who were pre-med. majors. Eight got into medical school and eight didn't. Guess which group I was in? I'm on a waiting list somewhere, I guess. The other thing that affected my decision was my senior cruise. I decided the Navy wasn't what I wanted to do and I'd had good experiences dealing with Marines at the Academy. On service selection night everybody thought I'd go Navy but I decided I was going into the Marine Corps. And my mother almost fell over when I told her.

Q. You've been the commanding officer at OCS for several months now and have had several companies go through the program. What needs to be changed at OCS?

I don't think we need to put OCS on a major course change right away. I think what you have to do is always make sure that the evaluation process serves the Marine Corps well; that those who are selected, those who pass the test, are the right men and women to become Marine officers. Nothing has changed in the Marine Corps with regard to the high standards that are expected of officers. We haven't changed standards, so there's no need for major change. At the same time, I think our leadership evaluations need to be a bit better. We need to be more feedback oriented, to tell candidates early on why they're not performing in a leadership billet in the way that they should. They need to know, constructively, how to fix that situation, as opposed to just telling them, "You are a lousy candidate platoon commander." We need to tell them why and what they need to do to fix their situation.

We need to work on fairness in evaluation. Evaluations must always be fair for two reasons. First, not everyone has the right to be a Marine officer. But the institution has a responsibility to the people who volunteer to do this, to make sure they get a fair shot. Institutionally, we have to make sure that the Marine Corps gets what it needs and deserves. Making sure that candidates get fair evaluations is important to the institution. The public must perceive us as doing things fairly, doing things the right way. Therefore, all our training must have a purpose and that purpose must be to evaluate.

Q. In judging a candidate, there has to be some subjective evaluation, doesn't there? What if you have a candidate who makes all the right moves but, in your gut, you know you wouldn't put that person in charge of a group of Marines?

That's a key point. The staff at OCS, officers and SNCO's alike, are assigned here, not because they're great drill instructors. I don't want my SNCO's to be drill instructors. And, I don't need captains acting like drill instructors. These men and women are paid for their professional judgement. And their judgement should be seasoned *leadership* judgement, knowing what it takes to be a leader. I think anyone who's been a successful leader gets a gut feeling that this person has it. On the other hand, it's also true they get a gut feeling that this other person doesn't have it. A man or woman can do well physically but, when it comes to leading two other people in performing a task, they don't have a clue about how to get it done. That person shouldn't be in front of a platoon. You have to ask yourself, "Do you want that candidate leading your son or daughter, someone near and dear to you in a dangerous situation?" If you can't answer that question affirmatively, that person shouldn't graduate from here.

Q. I know, from talking with your SNCO's, that they get a pretty quick fix on who will not make it through OCS. Are there checks and balances to ensure that you are not pre-judging someone, that your judgements are not slanted?

As you know, candidates are evaluated in three areas. The academic evaluation is cut and dried. The physical evaluation is a standards-based program and, again, you either pass or fail it. So academics are twenty-five percent and physical fitness is twenty-five percent. Leadership is a different story. It is half your grade. It has some standardized, graded requirements while some other requirements are more subjective. One of the components of leadership evaluation is the candidate's performance in command billets. Peers evaluate a candidate's performance in these billets and the other candidates tend not to pull any punches. If the SNCO evaluations and the peer evaluations are in lock step, that gives you confidence that the judgement is being made correctly, good or bad. Then, the staff platoon commander evaluates each candidate, separately. This officer is looking at a larger group than the SI's so he has a broader perspective. We also have the company commander, the first sergeant and the gunnery sergeant that all provide different perspectives on the candidates. Within the candidates, each billet holder evaluates the other billet holders. The final check and balance is exercised when the officers and SNCO's come to me for disenrollment of a candidate. My philosophy is that when a candidate is disenrolled, whether it be for a category failure or multiple category failures, he must clearly believe, in his own mind, that he failed and was fairly evaluated. Many times I'll put a candidate on probation and set goals he or she must achieve. If the goals are not achieved then there's no question in the candidate's mind that every opportunity to prove himself was provided but that he came up short at the finish line.

Q. When you came into the Marine Corps did you already possess the Core Values—honor, courage, and commitment?

The fact that I went to the Naval Academy in 1971 shows that I was a little out of step with my contemporaries. The military was institutionally affected by Vietnam but the leadership in all the services were, I believe, committed to the values passed on to them by what Tom Brokaw calls *The Greatest Generation*. Growing up in northern New Jersey, with an Irish-Catholic father who was a cop, probably tells you what kind of values I had. His admonishment was this. "If you always tell me the truth, I may not agree with you but I'll always be in your corner." I remember that to this day. If you own up to a mistake you may still get in trouble for being stupid but at least you aren't in trouble for being a liar. Courage? I think, as kids, we were always taught about courage and we picked it up along the way. My dad died when I was seventeen so there had to be commitment. You had to be committed to making something of yourself on your own. It came down to this. "If you want to go to school you need to find your own way to get to school and do your part." Lately, the Marine Corps has publicized the values, but in my heart of hearts, I always believed those values were there from the beginning and we just didn't talk about them in those ways.

One of my early heroes was Jim Webb who wrote *Fields of Fire* and *A Sense of Honor*. I could relate to the latter because I'd gone to Annapolis and understood the importance of honor. And it always seemed to me that when institutions veer off that course, they get in trouble. Does that mean civilian society doesn't have values? No, I just think that the military, especially the Marine Corps, requires us, as individuals to perform well. However, your focus has to be on the team rather than on yourself. In business, in the civilian world, I think the biggest clash is not that they don't have a sense of honor, or courage, or commitment. I think what they have is more self-centered than team-centered. And I think you see that with the way people move from job to job these days.

Q. The Marine Corps consistently meets its recruiting goals and has done so for over five years while the other services have struggled. How do you explain that?

You're an old Marine. No matter what you or I say, you simply can't put it in a box and say, "This is it." There is a Marine mystique. You and I know that exists. And it's because Marines believe they are special, and nobody's going to tell them otherwise. (Test them on this point and you're going to learn why they are special!) I also believe that the American people think Marines are special. They sense it. I think this is what connects it all. The institution is special, but equally important, the individual is special just because he or she is a Marine. So now you have an organization that feels special about itself and individuals who feel special about themselves.

The other services have the same call to duty but they all approach it a bit differently. The Air Force is technology-based and a service that is heavy with officers. That's because the officers do the fighting. In the Corps, from day one, you are taught to take care of your Marines because they're special. The idea is to bring them all back home. I don't think anybody else stresses that as much as we do. Here we invoke the memories of past heroes and tell them, "You can't leave your Marines. If you can't keep up on this conditioning run what makes you think you're going to be able to live up to the standards of those men of the past?" We use the examples of Marine heroes over and over again at OCS. They are examples that the candidates must measure themselves against. We are different. The Army says, "Be all that you can be," the Navy says, "See the world," the Air Force says, "Aim high." The Marine Corps says, "Okay, you want to be a Marine? Prove it."

Q. Is the Marine Corps losing young officers it shouldn't be losing?

Yes and no. Those who end up staying in the Corps see themselves as providing a service, like a doctor, lawyer or clergyman. We have a code of ethics that you must live by. We have a code of conduct you must adhere to. It's a calling. People who approach the Corps as a job will learn that's a mistake. It's not a nine to five job. You are required to take care of your people. In business you take care of your people by training the person who works for you or by remembering Secretary's Day. But here we say, "Here's this Marine. Take care of him. Make sure he's trained and ready to fight. And here's his family and make sure they're taken care of. Make sure he's counseled on what he needs to do to be a good Marine. Also, make sure he's doing the things he needs to do to get promoted, but make sure he gets time off." You need to be able to sense when he's been working extremely long hours and days that it's time to send him home. You need to tell him to spend time with his family so that he stays on an even keel. If an officer comes in with the idea that it's just a job, he'll find out it isn't. If you think it's a resume builder, it's not. But if you come in with the idea to serve, to put yourself in second place behind the organization and we lose you, that's a problem. And, if someone comes in and says I want to do this for three years because I owe the country, that's fine. Because, after they finish their tour, they're never going to let go of that. They're always going to be there, giving something back to the country. And those would be the successful businessmen and others who are also leaders in their community who will always take pride in saying, "I'm an old Marine."

Colonel Flynn was selected for promotion to brigadier general in 2002. He is currently serving as Commanding General, Marine Corps Training Command.

In many ways these five Marines could not be more different. Colonel Flynn, the Annapolis graduate, son of a tough Irish cop whose initial goal was medicine; Staff Sergeant Newton, who chose life in the Marine Corps rather than dying young in the tough Philadelphia streets; Gunnery Sergeant McKenna, the college student in need of direction, who opted for the Corps when friends from the neighborhood were killed in the bombing of the barracks in Lebanon; Captain Davis, an aspiring attorney, daughter of a career Marine; and Captain Samarov, Jewish, born in Russia, cerebral and outspoken. They are as different as the ethnic and racial threads woven into the social fabric of American society. And yet, when one talks with them, they are of one mind when it comes to the Marine Corps. All proudly claim ownership in the institution of which they are a part. How unique and refreshing this is in today's America.

OSO Captain David Parks discusses the PLC program with a student at the Ohio University Job Fair.

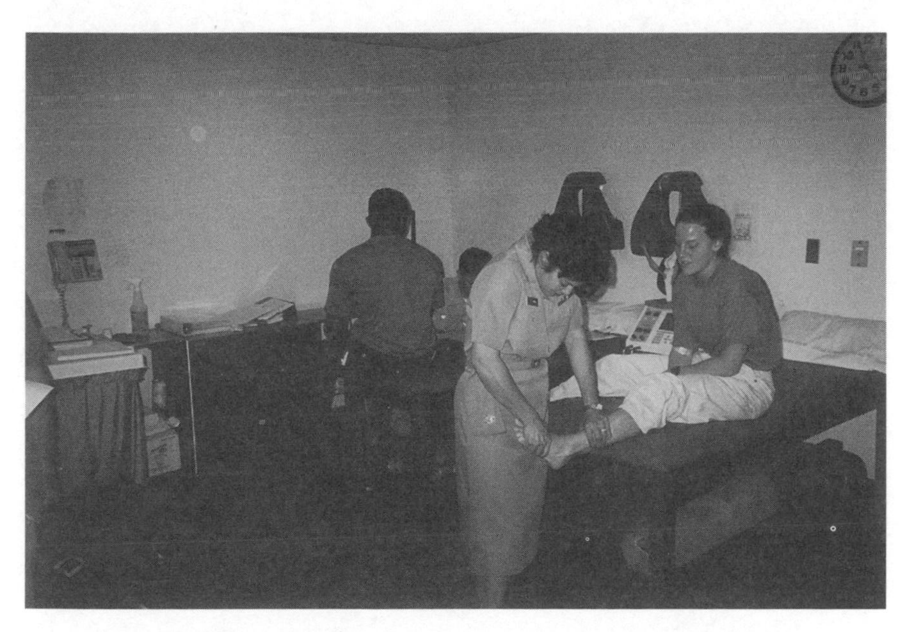

A Navy doctor examines a candidate's ankle for range of motion. Knee, ankle, and foot injuries are the most common causes of medically based disqualification at OCS.

First Sergeant Tim Campbell (left) and Gunnery Sergeant Paul McKenna are demanding and professional senior staff NCOs who turn college students into Marines at OCS.

Transition or "pickup" at OCS. Candidates dump all their belongings on the tarmac outside the barracks during the search for contraband.

A candidate "sounds off" as he turns over his camera, which is classified as "contraband," to his Platoon Sergeant, Gunnery Sergeant Paul McKenna, during Transition at OCS.

Platoon Sergeant, Gunnery Sergeant Paul McKenna (right), and Sergeant Instructor, Gunnery Sergeant Charles Jackson, are not pleased with a candidate's answers during the contraband search.

First Sergeant Tim Campbell questions a candidate about his performance on the obstacle course.

This company prepares for a three-mile run at OCS. Staff officers and staff NCOs (in darker T-shirts) lead the candidates through the course. "Don't ask your people to do anything you are not willing or able to do yourself" is a Marine leadership tenet.

A fire team approaches the final assault on the Combat Course at OCS.

As a fire team crosses chest-deep water on the Combat Course, a Navy corpsman and an OCS staff member keep an eye out for snakes, which can be a problem in coastal Virginia.

A fire-team member traverses a cable at one of the Leadership Reaction Course stations. The leadership demonstrated by the fire-team leader in arriving at a plan and leading his team in executing the plan is more important than actually solving the problem.

As SULE II wears on, the OCS staff begins to mentor its charges, providing motivation and relief from physical strain and exhaustion. Here a Sergeant Instructor shares a smile with his people as they await a helicopter to lift them to TBS and the final events of SULE II.

Exhaustion is evident in the face of this candidate as he forces himself through the NATO obstacle course, near the conclusion of the 60-hour SULE II. A TBS lieutenant (behind candidate) provides motivation and encouragement at each obstacle.

The Eagle, Globe, and Anchor Ceremony. A Sergeant Instructor presents the eagle, globe, and anchor insignia to a candidate. This marks the candidate's acceptance into the brotherhood of the Corps by the OCS staff. It is an emotional moment and tears are not unusual. Female platoons experience the identical rite of passage.

Competition between platoons and companies continues to the end at OCS. The log run is one event at the Field Day that marks the end of OCS training. Field Day is devoted to military and athletic events and skits presented by candidates which poke fun at their officers and Hats.

At the OCS Field Day the barriers between the Hats and candidates are lowered. Here a platoon of female candidates present a skit that mimics the voice and favorite sayings of their Sergeant Instructor.

Presentation of Colors at the Graduation Parade for the 171st OCS Class.

Female OCS candidates pass in review at the 171st OCS Class Graduation Parade. These women have met the same challenges as their male counterparts at OCS.

At a reception held for the candidates' families after the Graduation Parade, Captain Michael Samarov chats with two members of his platoon who will head immediately to TBS.

A newly minted second lieutenant meets with his family after completing SULE II.

This statue of Lieutenant Colonel William G. Leftwich, Jr., stands at the entry to Heywood Hall at TBS. The inscription reads, "Killed in action 18 November 1970—Still remembered for his leadership, tactical skill, bold fighting spirit and unflagging devotion to duty." The Eagle, Globe, and Anchor Ceremony, which marks an officer candidate's acceptance into the Marine Corps, takes place in the shadow of the Leftwich statue.

Learning to live in the mud hasn't changed at TBS over the past 50 years. Here a Squad Automatic Weapon (SAW) crew finishes their fighting hole.

A squad of TBS lieutenants double-time up the road after completing its first live-fire exercise at TBS. Because the terrain is open and fairly level, the exercise has been dubbed the "Squad on the Golf Course FFEX."

(Left to right) The author, 1st Lt. Bob Calamari, 2nd Lt. Ed Cerninka, 2nd Lt. Pete McCloskey and 2nd Lt. Tony Del Priore aboard USS Rockbridge (APA 228) in Mediterranean Sea, 1957. (Photo courtesy of J.M. Keese)

The graduation parade is the culumination of ten challenging weeks at Officer Candidates School. Here, members of the 171st OCS Class file by the reviewing stand.

After the MOUT (Military Operations over Urban Terrain) FEX, a student lieutenant discusses details of urban combat with Captain William Shuell (right) the Primary Instructor for the exercise.

The leading element of a squad-size patrol enters the main square of Hogan's Alley at the FBI Academy during the Urban Patrol Field Exercise. This facility provides students with a realistic urban setting for this training evolution.

The TBS staff works hard to match training to the real-life situations a lieutenant may face in the Fleet Marine Force. Here an officer, playing the role of media reporter, accompanied by the ever-present television camera, questions the patrol leader as the patrol faces a volatile group of demonstrators.

Demonstrators become more aggressive during the Urban Patrol FEX, when the patrol is unable to provide aid for a local citizen who has suffered a heart attack. The enlisted Marines who play the role of demonstrators are provided wide latitude. Violence against the person of a patrol member is about the only activity that is not allowed.

Captain Tim Powledge (center, clipboard in hand), the Primary Instructor for the Platoon War FEX at OCS, a two-day, free-form exercise, covers some details with the Assistant Instructors assigned to the exercise.

Mess Night is a formal dinner with all the trappings, including candelabra. Toasts are raised to the nation, the Commandant, the Corps, and its fallen. It provides a genteel respite from the daily business of studying warfare. It is a night of camaraderie and fellowship. (Photo courtesy of *The Marine Corps Gazette*)

6

TBS—Learning the Trade

> Those which mislike studies or learning in gentlemen, are some fresh water soldiers, who think that in war it is only the body that must bear the brunt of it all.
>
> George Pettie, Preface to *Guazzo's Civile Conversation,* 1581

The forest green Tahoe skimmed along the road through the lush green of the Prince William Forest, which covers much of the 60,000-acre Marine Corps Base at Quantico, Virginia. In the truck were three old Marines who had not met since the day they departed The Basic School (TBS) in February 1957, heading for their first duty stations in the Fleet Marine Force (FMF). We three gathered for a trip down memory lane. Our destination was Camp Upshur, a remote camp located about 15 miles west of the Main Gate of the Quantico Marine Reservation. I spent the summers of 1953 and 1954 as a member of the Platoon Leaders Class (PLC) here at Upshur. Ort Steele was a member of an Officer Candidate Course (OCC) and Jimmy Rosser was a Naval Reserve Officer Training Corps (NROTC) midshipman. They both underwent Officer Candidates School (OCS) training at Mainside, Quantico, but are very familiar with this place. The three of us, along with 554 other 3–56 Basic School classmates, sweated and crammed our way through eight months of Usphur's curriculum, and that is a time one does not forget.

Our lives have been as different as our regional backgrounds. Included in the trio is Major General Orlo K. "Ort" Steele who retired from the Corps in 1990 after 35 years of service and now lives in the same house in which he was raised in the tranquil setting of Grass Valley, California. He spends his spare time hiking the California mountains when he's not traveling or doing consulting work for the Corps. Tall and erect, Steele has the eyes of a man who is very much in charge. Possessing a warm sense of humor and the common touch, he was a respected leader of troops throughout his career. Steele spent 17 of his 35 years in the Corps in direct command, more command time than the average flag officer. His modesty cannot conceal his record and reputation throughout the Corps, even after years of retirement.

Jimmy L. Rosser is a soft-spoken, Southern gentleman from Anniston, Alabama. Six feet four and trim, he has had to deal with some heart problems in the past few months. This hasn't dampened his enthusiasm for a reunion with two guys with whom he shared the Second Platoon, G Company Quonset hut in 1956–1957. After his active duty tour as commander of a reconnaissance platoon, he spent many years as an NFL official. During the week Rosser pursued a career in personnel management with the Burlington Company in Martinsville, Virginia. Retired now he still resides in Martinsville. He and his wife, Sue, have made a special trip to Quantico for this small reunion.

I am a Midwesterner, a native Cincinnatian, and my career at Procter & Gamble spanned 33 years in sales management. Since retiring I have done some consulting and, for a few years, I have written a column for a local community newspaper group. It has been my desire for some time to revisit the Marine Corps part of my life. The wish became a possibility when, a few years ago, I learned that two TBS classmates, Harv Morgan and Cliff Fox, had done the hard work of tracking down most of the 490 surviving members of our class. When I asked them if they would give me permission to use their roster to gather material for this book, they immediately and graciously gave their approval.

With Ort Steele's help I went to Quantico to obtain access to OCS and TBS. Steele introduced me to Brigadier General James C. Conway, President of Marine Corps University, who commands both OCS and TBS. General Conway generously gave me permission for full access to both facilities. We met Colonel George J. Flynn, Commanding Officer of OCS, who encouraged our efforts. Colonel John R. Allen, who has just recently assumed command of TBS, was away from the base, but Steele was scheduled to see the colonel in Washington, D.C., in several weeks and was confident that he would approve our request. It was a productive morning and as we headed for downtown Quantico we drove past scores of Marines in running gear who apparently were spending their lunch break pounding the pavement.

We met Jim and Sue Rosser at the Command Post Restaurant in "Q'town," as the Marines call it. Quantico, a small community situated on the west bank of the Potomac River, is surrounded by the Marine base and is almost totally devoted to selling things Marines consume or wear. The town has changed very little since 1957. We spent our lunch quickly catching up on what had transpired over the four-plus decades since we last met. After an hour or so, Sue Rosser excused herself to make some business calls nearby asking, "Why don't you guys go do your old Marine stuff?" We saw her off and headed for Camp Upshur.

Our route took us past the FBI Academy which was located here in 1972 and occupies 385 acres within the boundaries of the Quantico Marine Base. Here, FBI and Drug Enforcement Agency (DEA) agents are trained as well as other law enforcement personnel in a state-of-the-art facility. The road goes by a variety of firing ranges and landing zones on the way through the seemingly endless piney woods.

The Prince William Forest is an extension of what Civil War historians call the Wilderness, where two major battles were waged. About 25 miles south of here is the place where Confederate General "Stonewall" Jackson was mortally wounded by his own troops at the battle of Chancellorsville, Virginia. A few miles north is Manassas, where the first and second battles of Bull Run were fought. The region is a treasure trove of Civil War history.

After driving for 25 minutes we found the entry road leading to Camp Upshur. As we drove past the old parking lot, now filled with light armored vehicles (LAV), it became apparent that this was no longer the bustling training camp we once knew. It now houses the LAVs used by the Fourth Light Assault Recon Company, a reserve unit, and DEA personnel who are in training. Missing were the salty cadences that once filled the air and set the rhythm of 45 pairs of officer candidate boots digging into the asphalt parade ground or the company streets. There were no sweat-soaked platoons humping down the dusty trail leading from the obstacle course or along the firebreaks. The silver Quonset huts, for the most part, stood silent and unused, in the thick humidity of the July afternoon.

In 1958, a year after our class graduated, TBS was relocated to new, permanent facilities at Camp Barrett. There, lieutenants now live four to a room rather than in platoon squad bays. Upshur, or Silver City as we called it, has fallen into a state of neglect and disrepair. The Quonset huts, with the exception of a few used by the Fourth LAR Company and the DEA, are falling apart, paint peeling and cracking, showing the effects of a half century of Virginia's sultry summers and bone-cold winters.

We searched for the hut that housed our platoon, the Second Platoon, Golf Company, and, in a few minutes, we found it. Because some DEA personnel were living in our old hut, rather than risk breaking and entering into quarters occupied by people carrying loaded weapons, we wandered up the path toward the Officer's Club where we had spent an occasional evening over a cold beer.

The "O Club" is now a crumbling disaster area. A few vestiges of the bar remain, a moldy and mute testimony to the Mess Nights held there. Mess Night, a tradition of long standing in the Marine officer corps, requires dress uniform for an occasion which begins with cocktails and is followed by a formal dinner punctuated by toasts. The event is structured to provide an interlude of gentility, fellowship, and camaraderie in the testosterone-filled lives of people who spend their nights and days learning new and better ways to destroy other people when the nation requires that. Mess Night brought together some of our instructors, company officers, and our guest of honor, Colonel William K. Jones, Commanding Officer, TBS. We lieutenants listened as the older officers recounted their experiences. We discussed our MOS (military occupation specialty) aspirations and hoped-for duty assignment with them. In these relaxed surroundings we learned that these men were, after all, a lot like us. As the evening wore on, we toasted Marine heroes, our country, our Corps, and the Marines who had fallen since 1775 in defense of a society that often quickly forgets the need for its warriors as soon as the danger is past. Mess Night was a special time and the O Club, despite its ramshackle condition, unleashed many memories.

We left the battered shell of the old watering hole and walked toward the chow hall. We recalled some of the names that were important to us: our CO, Colonel Jones who earned a Navy Cross at Tarawa and whose nephew, General James L. Jones, was the 32nd Commandant of the Marine Corps; Colonel Lew Walt, our former CO and another Navy Cross winner, who later became Deputy Commandant of the Marine Corps; Major Joeph R. Fisher, yet again a Navy Cross holder, who taught Offensive Tactics with unduplicated verve, enthusiasm, and humor; Captain James Meyers, our Platoon Commander; and Major Bill Timme, G Company Commander, who could walk the legs off any lieutenant in the Corps. All of these Marines, who are now gone, were members of, as Tom Brokaw has dubbed it, *The Greatest Generation.* We were very fortunate to have known and learned from such men.

We also had some unforgettable classmates. We haven't been able to locate Bob Keane, a prototypical 1950s LA guy whose dream was to become a big-time Hollywood producer. We wondered whether his dreams ever came true. Paige Rogers, now deceased, was one of several Rice University football players in our platoon. Rogers, a handsome, smooth Texan, cut a wide swath through the ranks of the opposite sex who populated the HiHat Lounge and other Marine watering holes in nearby Washington. Manho Hwang, a South Korean Marine in our platoon, could not have weighed 110 pounds, but he could hump a 60-pound pack up and down the firebreaks with the very best of us large, well-fed Americans.

Somewhat reluctantly, we took one last look and returned to the truck. Camp Upshur, though showing its age, was a part of our youth, long past but pleasing to contemplate. Men of our age have a need to return to the past. The places and things we knew in our youth are never the same. And yet, despite the ramshackle condition of this place we called home for a time, this little journey was an affirmation. Separated in time and having traveled dissimilar roads in life, the three of us shared something unique. Certainly it included our bonds as Marines, but it was something more than that. It was the affection and respect that men feel toward those with whom they have shared the fun, adventures, adversities, and stresses of early manhood. Young men seldom express these feelings, but experience and knowledge of our own mortality teach us that such reticence is foolish. The fact is that we do not have forever to rebuild our friendship. It does not matter that only one of us ever heard shots fired in anger. Our diverse lives have been deeply influenced by the people we knew and the things we learned in that camp.

We headed back down the road to Quantico's Main Gate. The truck moved swiftly as we returned from the past to the present. Remembering that place and time and the men with whom we shared those things contributed to a lasting, unbroken bond of brotherhood we share, unaffected by the years. It is good that we did this.

The history of TBS bears little resemblance to that of West Point or Annapolis. West Point was established in 1802 and the Naval Academy in 1845, and an obvious air of permanence surrounds them. The peripatetic wanderings of TBS correspond to the Marine Corps', at times, uncertain history. This incertitude is woven into the history and legends of the Corps. While there has never been a serious challenge to the existence of the U.S. Army or Navy, the Marine Corps has faced a number of challenges to its very existence since its founding in 1775.

Of course, there are major differences between the academies and TBS. The Basic School is responsible for training commissioned officers whereas the service academies prepare their cadets to become officers. In that sense, TBS is something of a graduate course in officership, a place where the Marine Corps takes the unfinished product of OCS and some from the Naval Academy and polishes and refines it, readying it for the responsibilities incumbent on those who must lead Marines. No other service makes such a large post-commissioning investment in its most junior officers prior to their assuming responsibility for even one enlisted service person. In the 1950s many officers were required to serve only two years on active duty. When one considers the fact that fully one-third of that obligation was spent educating the officers before they were entrusted with Marines, the value the Corps places on its Marines becomes clear. Every officer must prove to be fully qualified to lead Marines, and TBS is the proving ground.

In 1891 the School of Application was established at the Marine Barracks in Washington, D.C., and was assigned the task of training recent Naval Academy graduates. In the first of a series of disruptions and dislocations, the class of 1898 was hustled through the course to provide officers for the impending war with Spain, and the school was closed until late in 1900. In 1902 the school was closed when its lieutenants were shipped off to the forces involved in protecting U.S. interests during the Boxer Rebellion in China and to units fighting in the Philippine Insurrection.

After leaving Washington, the school began a series of migrations and name changes. During this period, the school moved to Annapolis, then to Parris Island, to Norfolk, to Quantico where, for a time it was identified as the Marine Officers School, then as the Marine Officers Training School. Finally, in 1922, it was designated The Basic School, or TBS as Marines refer to it. In the 1930s TBS moved to Philadelphia where it remained until World War II. That war placed great pressure on the Corps to turn out large numbers of officers, and TBS lost its identity because men were assigned to combat or support units immediately after undergoing officer candidate training.

In 1946 TBS was reestablished at the Mainside area of Quantico where it remained until 1955. Camp Upshur, a remote location west of Quantico, served as the TBS location until 1958 when Camp Barrett, the current site, was completed. Camp Barrett provides brick-constructed, four-person rooms for its students, a far cry from the days when a platoon of lieutenants was housed in a Quonset hut at Camp Upshur.

It is unique to the Corps that every officer of Marines, since World War II, has passed through this institution at some point. During World War II and the Korean War, enlisted personnel who were given battlefield commissions and who remained in the Corps oftentimes came through TBS after commanding troops during combat. They were required to attend TBS, just like every other officer.

TBS is not nearly as well known by the American people as are the other American military academies. The rigors of West Point and Annapolis have been broadly exposed through movies, books, and the electronic media, but only those who have attended TBS understand its importance to the continued successful evolution of the Marine Corps as a premier fighting force.

Today's TBS resides at Camp Barrett, 5 miles west of the Mainside area of the Quantico Marine Base. Each year between 1,200 and 1,400 second lieutenants are trained in a variety of military subjects with emphasis on the development of sufficient skill and knowledge to operate as infantry platoon commanders. During the 27 weeks of the course, 1,500 hours are devoted to training.

Present in the ranks of a TBS class will be Annapolis graduates, officers who aspire to Pensacola's Naval Flight Training School, law school graduates, prior enlisted personnel, and recent graduates direct from college campuses across the country.

While the training at TBS is heavily focused on the weapons, procedures, and tactics employed by the operating units in the FMF, equal focus is centered on the tangible and intangible elements of leadership. An internal TBS document (*Defining the Institution of The Basic School,* Colonel John R. Allen, 2001) summarizes the criteria used to define a Basic School graduate. While these criteria cover the technical aspects of leadership, the Marine Corps has very clear expectations of its graduates on the intellectual, ethical, and moral fronts. The following excerpt from that document describes the finished human product TBS seeks to produce.

A Marine. An officer who possesses the leadership qualities and character we so value in our Corps. A leader who understands that he or she is a "public figure." An officer who understands the structure, values and philosophy of the Corps with an emphasis on history, tradition, core values, personal standards, professionalism, ethics, self discipline, accountability and responsibility.

A decision-maker. An officer who possesses a bias for decision making, not just in war or during times of crisis but also in peacetime. One who is comfortable with day-to-day decision making in any environment. A leader who can accept the consequences of his or her decision. A problem-solver who can develop innovative solutions.

A communicator. An officer capable of clearly expressing, both orally and in writing, a decision in some appropriate form of order or guidance. A leader who can listen as well as speak.

A warfighter. An officer that possesses a solid foundation in tactics, techniques and procedures and who understands and can apply the principles of maneuver warfare. An individual of both action and intellect. A leader resolute and self-reliant in his/her decisions. A warrior who can apply combined arms and is energetic and insistent in execution with a penchant for boldness and initiative.

A lifelong student of the profession of arms. An officer who possesses a thirst for knowledge and the desire to continue reading and studying long after leaving the schoolhouse.

It may come as a surprise to some just how committed Marine Corps leadership is to the development of intellectual curiosity and capacity in its officers as well as in its enlisted ranks. The conventional wisdom regarding the Marines is that they are indoctrinated to obey orders, without hesitation or without question. The hard life at boot camp or OCS certainly is designed to break down the individual egos of trainees, to sublimate their individual wants and needs to the common good of the organization and its mission. Strict discipline and unquestioning response to orders are fundamental objectives of Marine Corps training. There is nevertheless a difference between blind obedience to orders and the development of a system of war fighting that requires clear and lucid expression of the commander's intent before the subordinate responds, "Aye, aye, sir!" That, among other factors, is what is different about today's Marine Corps and the one in which my classmates and I served.

What is not broadly understood are the demands placed upon officers for adherence, not only to a strict moral and ethical code, but also to a system that requires the officer to demonstrate capacity for exercising initiative and independent, logical thought. This is not a new development in the Corps. Brigadier General J. C. Breckenridge, in a 1934 letter to Colonel J. C. Smith, wrote, "It is my great and constant hope that the Marine Corps will produce some outstanding man [*sic*] for the country."

Such men are somewhere and they may as well be in our classes as anywhere else. I do not want such a person to be hammered down by narrowness and dogmas; to have his mind cramped by compulsory details. It is my constant ambition to see the Marine officers filled with ambition, initiative and originality; and they can get these attributes only by liberality of thought—broad thought—thought that differs from precedent and the compulsory imprint of others. (Lt. Gen. James Carson Breckinridge personal papers; Box 3/Folder 8; Marine Corps University Research Archives, General Alfred M. Gray Marine Corps Research Center, Quantico, Virginia.)

How closely the reality of the culture and environment in the Corps matched with General Breckenridge's vision has varied widely in the intervening six decades. World War II, the Korean War, and the Vietnam War were major spikes on the chart of TBS activity. In wartime the need for speed in pushing officers through the pipeline, in all probablility, put the general's wishes on a back burner. It is far easier to turn out large numbers of officers with a curriculum and a warfare doctrine that doesn't demand much intellectual curiosity on the part of the student. Our generation was sent through a school in which we were provided with "school solutions" to case studies or other exercise problems. We were given an opportunity to solve a problem or come up with a plan, for example, to defend a certain hill. After the exercise was over, we were given a school solution, which meant, "Here's how you do this when you get to the FMF." When you got to the FMF, that was how you were expected to do it. The emphasis wasn't on developing the thinking ability of the lieutenant; it was focused on the assimilation of a large body of information, much of it in a classroom lecture environment. Apart from the opportunity to ask questions at the end of a session, there was little room for innovation that strayed from the school solution.

Today, the TBS instructor staff is less involved in telling lieutenants how to solve a problem or carry out a mission than it is in demanding that the student prove that he or she can develop an independent plan of action under time pressure. Then, the student is required to expose the intellectual process that led him or her to adopt the chosen course of action.

Of course, the lieutenants are well instructed in weapons, tactics, techniques, and procedures. These are the tools of the soldier's trade. What is different from the training of my generation is the need for the independent thought, boldness, and initiative for which General Breckenridge was striving. When the Corps adopted its current doctrine of maneuver warfare, a concept that requires the leader to outthink as well as outfight his enemy, more responsibility for decisions moved down the organizational structure to small-unit commanders. Leaders who require "loading, aiming, cocking, and firing" simply cannot function effectively in the fast-moving scenarios of maneuver warfare. What is required is well-trained and thoughtful leadership at all levels of command because modern combat involves smaller, more widely dispersed formations, which are dictated by the destructive capacity of modern arms.

Another factor impacts this need for small-unit leaders who have the capacity to think as well as act. In the post-Cold War world, the Corps has been called upon to perform duties characterized as military operations other than war (MOOTW). Humanitarian, peacekeeping, and nation-building missions are the creations of a world in which the United States is the sole superpower. To a much greater extent than in the past, even the individual Marine rifleman needs to understand the subtleties and nuances of such operations. The actions initiated by a corporal leading a four-man fire team or a sergeant leading a twelve-man patrol can have serious consequences, politically or in the court of world opinion.

It is true that the TBS curriculum has changed a good deal since the early days of the Cold War. It is certainly true that "this ain't the old Corps." The wide range of learning required of today's lieutenant far outstrips that of years gone by. The broad spectrum of subjects required by today's officer to master before taking command of a unit is impressive. Before getting into the curriculum, it is instructive to review the institution's goals. We have reviewed what the finished TBS product looks and acts like. The question now is how does the school go about producing the sort of officer sought by the Corps?

BASIC SCHOOL INSTRUCTION

Shortly after assuming command of TBS, Colonel John Allen sent his "Commander's Intent Letter" to the officers on The Basic School staff. The letter provides the organization with the leader's vision of what he wants to accomplish and what he expects each element in his command to do in order to achieve that outcome.

Endstate—My vision for the outcomes of The Basic School is contained in our two most important institutional products; the lieutenant and the faculty.

The lieutenant—an officer who understands the rightness of the grave decision to serve America. An officer who has acquired a basic mastery of the art of war as revealed through the precepts of maneuver warfare. An officer who will decide and act with boldness and determination. An officer who understands that character and integrity count for everything in war, and who lives from moment to moment seeking to set for Marines an unblemished example of selflessness, martial prowess, and moral uprightness. An officer who understands that the highest calling is doing one's duty and for whom the words honor, courage, commitment and Semper Fidelis are the touchstones, not just for a military career, but for a lifetime. An officer changed forever.

The faculty—Leaders who understand and appreciate the enormity of the mission undertaken at The Basic School. Leaders who have mastered the art of war along with the craft of teaching. Leaders for whom the lieutenants are a national treasure, young men and women to be nurtured and guided through the journey of their first exposure to officership. Leaders whose sense of history, and their place in it, provides the context for their fascination with the profession of arms and their dedication to this calling. Leaders who depart The Basic School [as] members of that small group of Marine Corps faculty on whose talent the Corps will draw for years to come, and to whom America will turn in moments of emergency, when her finest leaders will bring victory or retrieve defeat.

The commander laid out, in detail, those factors required to reach this end state. Such things as ensuring that lieutenants understand the significance of their commission and the "sheer enormity" of the words "special trust and confidence" which appear on every officer's commission. In the letter he discussed the fact that everything done at TBS is done to prepare the lieutenant mentally, physically, and morally for the crucible of combat. Colonel Allen cited four common threads which "bind the TBS curriculum into a coherent whole" and which "must attend every class, every discussion, every opportunity to speak with and influence our young officers."

Manuever Warfare—This will be the touchstone, embedded in our readings and discussions, as well as in every class, sand table exercise and field exercise. . . . Imposing our will on our opponent's will is our endstate. This fundamental truism is crucial for the young lieutenants' understanding of the essence of warfare and in providing the intellectual basis and the long-term context for the increasingly complex study of the art of war.

Character—The great force multiplier in combat is character, not technology, not numbers, but character. Character is the foundation of decision making in combat. While there may be some debate on the exact definition of character, there can be no doubt what I expect. A man or woman of character is one whose existence rests upon a solid moral foundation. This foundation sustains that officer during the greatest trials, and will provide the crucial moral orientation to decide at the moment of greatest need. . . . A large part of character is integrity. Integrity is that unfailing trait which, above all others, our Marines demand from their officers. Absent integrity, an officer has no moral authority to lead Marines.

Human Factors—Fear, fatigue, and other emotional and physical crises will be central to our study of the art of war. As well, death, dying and killing are the common wages of combat, and impact dramatically on both unit cohesion and the individual Marine. These effects are substantial, are often immediate, and cannot be discounted. We must do every thing in our capacity to equip the lieutenant with a clear understanding of the peculiar nature of human factors and their centrality to battle outcomes.

Teachers and Mentors—We must equip our officers to understand the enormity of their obligation to their Marines as their teachers and mentors. *This applies not only to their understanding of how to impart their knowledge to their Marines, but also to their lifestyles.* We will have been successful in our role at The Basic School if our young officers depart Camp Barrett with the absolute conviction that they must embody the very essence of the warrior/scholar, and that their highest calling is bound up in the obligation of developing their own Marines morally, mentally and physically for combat; just as we did for them.

The newly commissioned second lieutenants arrive at TBS from numerous locations. They will find themselves in a different environment, less structured and more dependent on each individual's assumption of responsibility for success or failure. They have been trained, screened, and evaluated. The OCS staff has concluded that they possess the moral, intellectual, and physical qualities required of an officer of Marines. Each has been determined to possess the leadership potential that will be required for him or her to serve successfully as a company grade officer in the operating forces. Here, at The Basic School, each must prove that the OCS staff was right.

7

TBS—"It's Only Us"

> What makes Marine infantry special? Asking the question that way misses the most fundamental point about the United States Marine Corps. In the Marines, everyone—sergeant, mechanic, cannoneer, supply man, clerk, aviator, cook—is a rifleman first. The entire Corps, all 170,000 or so on the active rolls, plus the reserves, are all infantry. All speak the language of the rifle and bayonet, of muddy boots and long, hot marches. It's never us and them, only us. That is the secret of the Corps.
> Colonel Daniel F. Bolger, U.S. Army *Death Ground: Today's American Infantry in Battle*

Colonel Bolger has captured the essence of the Marine Corps according to The Basic School's mission statement: "To educate newly commissioned or appointed officers in the high standards of professional knowledge, esprit-de-corps, and leadership required to prepare them for duties in the operating forces, with particular emphasis on the duties, responsibilities and warfighting skills required of a rifle platoon commander."

The lieutenants who arrive at The Basic School (TBS) are products of an Officer Candidates School (OCS) that is focused on performance. All have been judged to possess the leadership capacity required to lead Marines. At TBS leadership capacity and potential will be actualized.

After completing five months of TBS the lieutenants are assigned to an entry-level school specializing in the MOS (military occupation specialty) to which they have been assigned. For example, an infantry officer will spend ten weeks in training at the Infantry Officers Course (IOC), located at the Camp Barrett complex, before being assigned to the Fleet Marine Force (FMF). Other entry-level MOS schools range in duration from six weeks to 16 months. The Marines believe that one of their great strengths is the fact that almost every officer of Marines has attended OCS and all have attended TBS. (Naval Academy graduates attend an abbreviated version of OCS.) Lieutenants destined for careers as tankers, combat engineers, motor transport or supply—men and women alike—all share the same TBS experiences. At TBS, the 1,500-hour course of instruction includes the following:

- Instruction in leadership
- Techniques of military instruction

- Marksmanship
- Map reading
- Communications
- Infantry tactics on the small-unit level
- Infantry weapons and supporting arms
- Field engineering
- Marine Corps organization and staff functions
- Drill, command, and ceremonies
- Military law
- Logistics
- Company personnel administration
- Marine Corps history and traditions
- First aid
- Data processing utilization
- Patrolling
- Combat intelligence
- Vertical envelopment operations
- Tank-infantry operations
- Aviation and air support
- Amphibious operations
- Contemporary operations
- Physical training and conditioning techniques.

The rain falls equally on all lieutenants at TBS, whether their future is flying jets or helicopters, trying cases before a court-martial as an attorney, or leading a platoon of infantry. Understanding the rifle platoon commander's life and challenges develops a spirit of teamwork which remains with them throughout their active service tours.

In 1999 TBS returned to the practice of requiring all unmarried lieutenants to live on base at Camp Barrett. The reason for this requirement is spelled out in *Defining the Institution of The Basic School* (2001).

> In establishing a command environment conducive to successfully addressing the rigors of The Basic School learning experience, it has been determined that by living together as a unit (with the exception of married officers), lieutenants learn, capitalize on teamwork and develop a common understanding of the social environment that must exist in all Marine units (i.e., esprit de corps, camaraderie, and family).

Married students may live off base and generally find apartments in neighboring locations such as Stafford, Triangle, Dumfries, or Fredericksburg.

TBS STRUCTURE AND RESPONSIBILITIES

TBS consists of three separate, equal organizations which share ownership and responsibility for establishing a proper environment and administering the curriculum: the Student Company Staff, the Warfighting (Instructor Group) Organization, and the Instructor Battalion.

The Student Company Staff

Students are assigned to a student company, composed of six platoons of from 40 to 42 lieutenants. Platoons are led by a Staff Platoon Commander (SPC), a captain, who reports to a major, the Company Commander.

The Student Company Staff focuses the lieutenants on the "moral dimension of war," developing leaders with "character, intellect, stamina and esprit de corps." The Company Commander and SPCs work to develop leaders who understand the structure, values, and philosophy of the Marine Corps, including the following:

- History and traditions
- Core values
- Personal standards
- Professionalism and ethics
- Self-discipline
- Accountability/responsibility
- Responsibility for lifelong learning and professional growth
- Oral and written communication.

The SPC's responsibilities are defined in the *Guide for Student Companies,* another TBS document. "No single officer will have a more profound and wide-ranging impact on the development of officer students than the SPC."

The success of the Basic Officers Course and the Women's Basic Officer Course in preparing students for duties in the operating forces is dependent upon the leadership skills and teaching abilities of the SPCs assigned to each company. A SPC, by design, will spend the bulk of his/her time training, critiquing, counseling, mentoring and evaluating the students assigned.

The SPC exercises broad influence, including matching student officers with suitable MOSs that will afford them the opportunity to succeed in their first tour of duty. The SPC will play a role in the assignment of leadership grades to each member of the platoon. To be consistent and fair, it is a requirement that grades are based on actual observation of performance during formal garrison and tactical billets and day-to-day platoon and squad activities.

The relationship between the SPC and the students does not at all resemble that of the OCS Sergeant Instructors (SIs) to their candidates. TBS students are commissioned officers, novices but full members in the fraternity of the officer corps. The SPC's task is to guide, counsel, and mentor the young officers who, in turn, must look inside themselves for the motivation to learn, succeed, and grow. The SPC's motivational duty is to provide personally an outstanding example of Marine officership for his or her students.

The Warfighting Organization (Instructor Group)

Warfighting, as the Instructor Group is called, is the center of gravity at TBS. Directed by a lieutenant colonel, it is organized around four sections: Maneuver, Command, Combined Arms, and Professional Development. It focuses its efforts and energies on the art and science of war. It is charged with developing leaders who are capable of making rapid decisions and developing practical, innovative tactical ideas with emphasis on:

- Marine Corps doctrine
- Warfighting
- Combat leadership
- Combined arms
- Unit sustainability
- Techniques and procedures
- Capabilities and limitations of weapons and equipment
- Administration and military law.

Warfighting is the center for maintaining educational excellence, and it is responsible for the quality control of *all* instruction at TBS whether that instruction is handled by Warfighting personnel or instructors from other TBS organizations.

The Instructor Battalion

The Instructor Battalion, the TBS support effort, maintains a cadre of highly trained enlisted combat arms instructors as well as combat service support instructors. These Marines provide resident expertise to support TBS's mission.

THE TBS TOUR

Officers are generally assigned to the TBS staff for a three-year tour of duty. Typically, the first year is spent in Warfighting. The officer must first earn certification as an instructor, then is appointed a full instructor. The year-two assignment is to a Student Company as SPC, or, in the case of a major, as

Company Commander. The final year the officer may be assigned to any number of positions. He or she may return to Warfighting as an instructor, to the CO's staff, to the Instructor Battalion, or return to a Student Company Staff. As one might expect, only those officers with excellent records who come highly recommended by previous commanders are assigned to duty at TBS. The Commanding Officer, TBS, personally approves all officers assigned to the school. They are bright, knowledgeable, and motivated.

TRAINING AT TBS

What follows is a sampler of TBS training evolutions.

FFEX (Field Firing Exercise)

This is unofficially called the "squad on the golf course" exercise by staff and students. (A squad consists of one squad leader and 12 Marines, broken down into three, four-man fire teams, each centering around an M249 Squad Automatic Weapon, or SAW.) This is the first nonstatic, live-fire exercise of the TBS curriculum. Up to this point students have fired their M-16A2 rifles only from stationary firing positions.

The Staff Platoon Commander gives the student squad leader a detailed order. The squad leader is given some time to plan and then issue his or her own order to the squad. The squad does a walk-through over the terrain, then holds a live-fire rehearsal. After this preparation and familiarization, the squad performs the actual exercise. The purpose for the walk-through and rehearsal, of course, is to familiarize the students with the terrain and to ensure they understand safety constraints and considerations in order to prevent accidents. The prime objective of each exercise is to complete it with no accidents or injuries.

The squad's objective is an enemy position located 300 meters in front of the line of departure (LOD). The squad's mission is to prevent the enemy position to its direct front from interfering with the main attack, which (according to the lesson plan) is being simultaneously carried out on the right flank of the squad. Three berms provide cover for the attacking squad. These lie perpendicular to the direction of attack, between the LOD and the objective.

The squad is expected to practice "fire and movement" in its assault. This means that one or two fire teams act as a base of fire. Their job is to lay down aimed, continuous, suppressing fire at the objective while the balance of the squad moves forward in short segments until they have found cover. This element of the squad then becomes part of the base of fire while another fire team moves. White pop-up targets representing enemy automatic weapons are located on the objective. This suppressing fire should be continuous to keep the enemy's heads down and prevent their automatic weapons from firing on the main attack taking place on the right flank.

Typically, the lieutenants' first try during the live-fire rehearsal leaves something to be desired. Suppressing fire tends to be sporadic, and students fail to use the cover provided by the berms to the best advantage, leaving themselves open and vulnerable. Finally, during the rehearsal, the lieutenants tend to exercise poor fire discipline and often run out of ammunition prior to their final assault. An Assistant Instructor advises, "The first time they run through this with live ammo they are all worried about getting shot. The second time they get down to business." That is exactly what happened with the squads I observed. The final execution was much improved as the lieutenants grew more confident of their ability to survive traversing this terrain with 12 other armed and dangerous personnel.

At the conclusion of the exercise, the squad leader reviews the results and the strong and weak points of the execution. He also explains the decisions he made or the actions he took and the thought process he used to arrive at those decisions. After the squad leader, members of the squad may offer their own thoughts as to how the squad might have conducted the exercise differently. As was true of all the exercises I observed over a period of two years, the Staff Platoon Commander and the Primary and Assistant Instructors do not make judgments about the actions of the squad leader, his decisions, or the alternative approaches offered by the squad members. At no time during the exercise is the squad leader or any squad member told what to do by the staff, unless safety is involved. This nonjudgmental, more interactive teaching approach would be foreign to my 3–56 classmates.

Live-Fire Exercise—1956

Compared to a similar live-fire problem from the 1950s, the current version is a significant improvement. We did not have live fire "rehearsals." We were given classroom instruction, and an instructor briefed the student squad leader. Then, we invariably conducted a frontal assault, no matter the objective. The squad leader was then given a "chit" that evaluated his performance. The instructor provided us with a school solution which, he assured us, was "not the only way" to approach the exercise. In reality, however, we were expected to execute assaults accordingly in the future. Generally, there was little interactive discussion or critique by the instructor at the conclusion of the exercise. There was just the judgment rendered by the instructor as to the billet holder's performance.

I recall a Lieutenant Jones (not his real name) in our company who was not doing well at TBS. His academic performance was so poor that he was on the cusp of being ejected from Basic School. Jones was assigned the squad leader's billet for a similar exercise, and the members of the squad, including me, were aware of his precarious situation and wanted him to succeed.

The Tactics Instructor who accompanied our squad on the attack was the legendary Major Joe "Bull" Fisher, a great teacher and an aggressive, tough, and motivating officer who believed that a frontal assault was the only way a unit smaller than a regiment should assault anything. One of the sayings he used to express his position on frontal assaults was, "If you're going to make marmalade, you've got to peel a few oranges." Major Fisher was a man who kept things simple.

Our squad had worked its way, using fire and movement, to a point about three-quarters of the way to our objective when we began to run short of ammunition. The squad members were yelling, "Need more ammo!" and "Bull" Fisher could be heard yelling to Jones above the crack of M-1 and bursts of BAR (Browning Automatic Rifle) fire, "What are you going to do now, lieutenant?" The dauntless Lieutenant Jones considered his squad's situation for just a moment, then made his decision. He shouted to the squad, "Fix bayonets! We're going to kill those bastards!"

Major Fisher went crazy with glee. He could hardly contain himself as we charged through the objective, jabbing and slashing at the imaginary enemy, then setting up defensive positions. On the hike back to the assembly area Major Fisher had nothing but good things to say to Jones who, a short 30 minutes before, was on the brink of personal disaster. He went on to serve his active duty tour. "Bull" Fisher knew a leader with heart, boldness, and initiative when he saw one.

TRAINING FOR TOMORROW

It is conventional wisdom that the American military consistently "trains for the last war." In the 1950s we trained for amphibious warfare because amphibious capability and expertise were the reasons for Marine Corps' existence. Helicopters were just coming into the picture, and there were a thousand theories about how this new technology could best be used by the Corps to fulfill its mission. The truth of the matter was that the one mission the Corps could be 100 percent confident about was amphibious warfare. The amphibious assault had proved successful in beating the Japanese in the Pacific and had been vital in reversing the tide of war in Korea at Inchon.

Within a few years, helicopters were large enough to make them practical for larger-scale operations, and the Marine Corps led the way in developing their use. In the 1950s, however, the 3–56 Class was trained to land on the world's beaches, just as our older brothers and cousins had done in World War II. Our live-fire exercises included an assault on concrete pillboxes, the type found on the islands of the Pacific during World War II.

It does not take the Marine Corps very long to match its training with the realities of conflict. A key strength of the Marine Corps is its ability to innovate and adapt to changing conditions, both military and political. This is truer today than ever before. What follows are some training evolutions that demonstrate the TBS determination to expose lieutenants to an array of situations that they and their Marines must be prepared to deal with in the future.

Offense/Defense Week

In this weeklong exercise, half of the company is assigned to the offense and the other half to the defense. The defense digs in, prepares fighting positions, and conducts security patrols and ambush patrols. The platoons on offense conduct platoon-size attacks, usually two per day, against platoons in defensive positions.

The opposing platoon leaders are provided with intelligence reports that may, or may not, be complete, just as it happens in the real world of conflict. The value of this exercise and others in the TBS curriculum is the introduction of an "opposing will" into the problem. Rather than leading attacks or defenses against imaginary foes, the lieutenant must test his intellect, judgment, and skill against another human being's. That added factor makes a world of difference. Adding even more realism to the exercise is the use of civilians as decoys. On the final day of the exercise, the defense must deal with a chemical attack, using CS (tear) gas.

I joined the platoon in its defensive perimeter on the third day of the exercise. The company had hiked 11 miles out to the area on the first day. By the time I linked up with them, a cold autumn rain had fallen for two days. The defensive positions were mud pits, and the lieutenants, cold and wet, were cleaning their weapons while welcoming the sun that had finally peeked through the early morning clouds.

The SPC for the defense platoon was Captain Tim Bairstow of Thousand Oaks, California. He was in contact over a command frequency with the offensive platoon's SPC. Bairstow knew where the attacking platoon was, relative to his platoon at all times. The student platoon commander, of course, was not provided with this information. The role of Instructors and SPCs is to force the lieutenants in command billets to make their own decisions. They are not expected to always make the right decisions. What is expected is that the lieutenants will use logical processes, based on the information they have gleaned from their patrolling efforts and listening posts, to arrive at a plan of action.

The student platoon commander approached Captain Bairstow and related that he had heard from one of the other defensive platoons that they had been attacked and that the attackers were heading toward his platoon's right flank. The lieutenant was looking for approval to his plan to move a squad from his left flank to supplemental positions on the right in case the attackers tried to penetrate that area. Bairstow explained, "Sometimes you just have to roll the dice and hope you're right." Bairstow told me that seeking approval from the SPCs is not unusual. "I don't give them anything. I tell them to make a decision."

As it turned out, the lieutenant had good instincts. He reinforced his flank, which was where the attack was focused. He used the imperfect intelligence that was available, followed a logical train of thought, and executed his plan, and it worked. The lesson learned was that you do your best to anticipate what your opponent is going to do, prepare for that, and hope that you are right.

This was an impressive, realistic training exercise, as a result of the aforementioned opposing will being inserted into the equation. The critiques conducted at the end of training exercises are vast improvements over those of the 1950s, since they are structured for learning, not judging. It was apparent that student lieutenants are most willing to express their thinking processes to the instructors, SPCs, and fellow lieutenants during these sessions.

Convoy FEX

I was riding shotgun in a five-ton truck on a cold and rainy April day in Virginia. We were second in line in a convoy including two Humvees, two five-ton trucks, a three-ton truck, and an ambulance. This training evolution took place about a month before this company of lieutenants graduates from TBS. The TBS staff officers informed me that the lieutenants were getting a bit "salty" in their attitudes, believing they knew just about all they really needed to know. I was told that this convoy evolution would reawaken their attention.

The objective of the exercise was to move this convoy to its destination to relieve a unit under pressure. One facet of the problem for the student convoy commander to consider was the fact that his vehicles were stretched out along 600 meters of roadway. Maintaining communication and control over a unit with a long axis of 600 meters, front to back, was a new challenge for officers accustomed to controlling units with an east/west orientation, as in the assault of an objective.

During the course of the convoy's journey to its objective, it encountered three aggressor actions: a single sniper firing at the convoy, a booby-trapped obstacle blocking the road, and a full-scale ambush set just short of the convoy's final objective.

The student convoy commander, discussing the exercise during the critique, was not pleased with his performance (neither were the SPCs or Instructors, but, of course, they kept that to themselves). The student commander detailed his own leadership shortcomings.

He admitted that he did not prepare sufficiently for the exercise. He had not developed any contingency plans that told his people what action to take when an obstacle was encountered. This led to delaying the entire convoy when a single sniper took it under fire. Instead of returning fire from the machine gun and moving swiftly through the area, the commander had his troops debark and sweep the flanks of the road.

He lost communication with elements of the convoy because of poor radio discipline and relying too heavily on the radio. Two or three people were trying to talk on the radio at one time when an obstacle was encountered. Then, at one point, he was talking on the radio to a convoy element not more than 50 meters up the road. A quick jog to the front of the convoy would have enabled him to exercise his authority to get things moving.

At the final obstacle, a serious one involving a roadblock and an ambush, the platoon performed well; however, the commander again was located too far from the action to influence its outcome.

These are telling comments from the convoy commander about his own performance; however, before being too critical, one should consider the comments of the Instructors. According to them, this level of performance is not unusual for this exercise. This evolution, near the end of the TBS curriculum, is hindered by the fact that the students do not pay sufficient attention to the classroom instruction or the school handouts; student convoy commanders make the same mistakes, class after class. It was evident from the debriefing that these students got the message that they didn't know everything yet. It was a good learning experience for all hands.

One of the Assistant Instructors made this point to conclude the critique, "We are not looking for the *one* right decision. We want to see a decision that is thought out, not just straight-ahead aggression. We need to be asking ourselves, 'What does the enemy want me to do? How do I avoid doing that and accomplish this mission?' "

In the 1950s The Basic School offered no comparable training in convoy operations.

Urban Patrol FEX

At 0630 on an autumn Sunday morning, I found my way to the Warfighting bullpen, an office space occupied by the instructor cadre in Heywood Hall. I met Captain Keith Parry, the Primary Instructor (PI) for the Urban Patrol Field Exercise (FEX) which had been under way since Saturday morning. Captain Parry, 32, carries an MOS of Ground Intelligence Officer, a relatively new occupational specialty in the Corps. For 22 months prior to his assignment to Quantico, he was the CO of the Scout/Sniper Platoon, First Battalion, Sixth Marines. He was assigned to the Basic School and, upon completion of the Instructor Education Program (IEP), was assigned as the PI for all patrol training.

Parry has responsibility for all aspects of this training evolution. His designation as the PI is not based on seniority or time in grade. TBS assigns instructors on the basis of their experience, expertise in their subject matter, and successful completion of IEP. Parry, like most of the young officers I met, exhibited the common qualities of extremely positive thought coupled with an aggressive, but friendly, demeanor. These captains, most in their mid-to-late twenties, appeared to be excited about the work they do, and they were extremely solicitous of this old Marine.

Captain Parry took me through the written material provided to the assistant instructors (AIs) who will monitor the lieutenants through their patrol exercise. The following excerpt comes from *Urban Patrolling FEX Handout* (Internal Basic School Document, 2000):

PURPOSE: The purpose of the Urban Patrolling FEX is to expose students to patrolling in the urban environment with all of the considerations of an enemy presence, terrain and by-stander population. A squad-sized unit will patrol in an urban environment in order to test the student's ability to make decisions on unfamiliar terrain.

The rotation is set up so that every patrol will experience two decision points, in addition to the patrol on urban terrain. The squad-sized patrol is executing "within its own vacuum"—without the support of other squads or react forces. This vacuum will appear as a higher's [echelon of command] word that "react force is twenty minutes out—deal with the situation as you see fit, etc."

If there is one current officer training evolution that highlights the differences between the training of the 1950s and today, as well as the complexities of the demands made on today's military, it is this training exercise. In 1956 student lieutenants were provided with minimal training in urban area operations.

In today's complex world, our armed forces are increasingly involved in urban missions in which it is most difficult to separate the good guys from the bad guys or the guys who just happen to be in the wrong place at the wrong time. The Urban Patrol FEX tests the student patrol leader's ability to operate in this environment in the littorals of the world. The lieutenant (and corporals and sergeants) must make quick, difficult decisions in chaotic and confusing surroundings. A bad decision made by a small-unit leader can result in Marine and civilian casualties, which, in turn, can have far-reaching political and world opinion consequences.

Urban training is conducted in Hogan's Alley, which is located on the grounds of the FBI Academy. Hogan's Alley is a full-scale replica of a small town, which covers about eight square blocks. It provides a mixture of urban and suburban structures, including a movie theater, motel, drugstore, warehouses, fuel tanks, single dwellings, and apartment buildings. These well-constructed, realistic structures provide a real-life setting compared to the gray concrete structures found in The Basic School's Combat Town where Military Operations Over Urban Terrain (MOUT) training is conducted. I suggested to the captains present that the FBI "obviously has a bigger budget than The Basic School." One responded, "Sir, that's true but it's OK. Many of the FBI agents who work here are former Marines, so they are good to us." The bureau provides the Marines with access to Hogan's Alley on weekends only, reserving it for their own use during weekdays.

Parry's radio crackled and he received the message that the first patrol of the day was approaching the town. The morning sun was warming the streets of Hogan's Alley as the first of nine squad-size patrols debarked from trucks a quarter of a mile from the entrance to the town.

How have the TBS students been prepared for this training evolution? Some background is helpful because preparation for Hogan's Alley exemplifies the preparation required for every FEX in which the lieutenants are involved. They are provided with more information and more restrictions than Marines of an earlier time. Detailed verbal orders are issued the day before the patrol is to occur. In this case, the patrol order was issued on Saturday to all members of the squad. Included in the order were the following elements:

Orientation: Describes the terrain and the towns included in the battalion's area of operations.

Situation: The acronyms SALUTE, DRAW-D, and EMPCOA are used to describe the enemy situation, specifically their capabilities/limitations, the composition of their forces, their disposition on the ground, and likely intentions and possible actions they may take. The acronyms and their definitions are as follows:

SALUTE—The enemy's Size, Activity, Location, Unit (if known), and Equipment

DRAW-D—The enemy's options to Defend, Reinforce, Attack, Withdraw, or Delay

EMPCOA—The Enemy's Most Probable Course of Action.

These acronyms are standard in Operations Orders (Op Orders), and the format is used at all levels of command.

The *Urban Patrol FEX Operations Order* (Internal Basic School Document, 2000) reads as follows:

SALUTE. The local government of the town of Hogan's Alley has deteriorated to the point where it has little control of its civilian population and little ability to enforce any lawful order. Civilians have been spotted looting and fighting amongst themselves. The town also appears to have two separate factions of the Centralia Revolutionary Forces (CRF). [Centralia is the fictional name of the country in which Hogan's Alley is located.]

Ideally, the student patrol leader (SPL) and assistant patrol leader (APL) haven't been advised of their selection and will not be advised until late Saturday afternoon. As a result, all squad members pay close attention during rehearsals and discussions. After the patrol leader is selected, he issues his own patrol order to the members of the squad and conducts a sand-table exercise. (This is a sand replica of the terrain to be covered, and it enables the SPL to point out possible problem areas and make contingency plans.) The squad then conducts a rehearsal over similar terrain.

There are six possible "decision points" along the route, and each patrol will encounter two:

- They may be ordered to set up a *hasty vehicle checkpoint* to search vehicles for contraband or firearms.
- They may encounter a *civil discontent situation* in which food is being looted from stores, and fights between insurgents and "authority figures" are taking place.
- A *sniper* may fire upon the patrol.
- The patrol may be lured into an *ambush* by insurgents.
- A situation may occur in which *insurgent versus civilian* violence is taking place.
- The patrol may come across an *insurgent versus insurgent* confrontation.

The SPL and APL ideally are not supposed to know which decision points their particular patrol will encounter. However, Basic School lieutenants are much like students at any other American institution of higher learning. While they may not know specifically which situations they must contend with, lieutenants that have undergone this training earlier love to talk about their experiences and they do. Furthermore, the Sunday patrols have had an opportunity to discuss what happened to their friends who underwent the evolution on Saturday. That is not supposed to happen but it does, and Captain Parry and his AIs were lieutenants once, too. They do their best to mix up the situations each of Sunday's patrols will face. The SPL is aware of the potential situations his squad will encounter, but not the specific problem he will be required to handle. Regardless, there are elements included in the exercise which complicate matters for the SPL.

Thirty enlisted Marines play roles as insurgents and civilian bystanders, lending reality to the training. They are dressed as Centralian civilians, garbed in anything that suits their whim, doing their best to be a mob, despite their high and tight haircuts. Under the tutelage of a staff noncommissioned officer (SNCO)they make this experience as realistic as possible for the lieutenants. Some of these Marines have served in Bosnia or Somalia and, from personal experience, know how to confuse, anger, and distract the members of the patrol. Physical violence against the students is the only activity that is off limits as these troops get an opportunity to assist in the training of their future leaders. Of course, it is a rare Marine who would not jump at the chance to make a "butterbar's" life difficult, if only for an hour or so. The very serious side of their role is that one day, one of these students may actually lead Marines into a dangerous town, filled with armed and hostile people, and it is in the Marines' best interests to help prepare them for this eventuality.

Included are female Marines who play the role of friendly, curious, or available locals with a penchant for penetrating the patrol's moving perimeter. And what patrol in a world trouble spot would be complete without an aggressive electronic media reporter and his cameraman, who constantly question the patrol's motives and tactics? The reporter (a TBS staff captain) picks the most inopportune times to insert himself into the situation as events unfold that require the patrol leader's thoughtful focus and quick decisions.

Here is a compendium of observations made while observing three patrols carry out their missions.

The patrol advances toward the village down a tree-lined road, unsure of what lies before them. As always, flank security (patrol members scouting out the woods on each side of the road) is important as the patrol clears its way to the village. By radio, the SPL advises the platoon command post (PCP) that the patrol is approaching checkpoint no. 3 on the outskirts of Hogan's Alley. From the Commander's Intent/Concept of Operations advisory, the PL is aware of several facts.

Commander's Intent

The Centralia Revolutionary Force (CRF) controls the population of this town based on manipulation of the people through propaganda, fear, and terror. The commander believes that the source of CRF strength is also its critical area of vulnerability. The commander wrote, "I believe we can disrupt the CRF's precarious control of the populace by active day time patrolling operations, education of the populace and through goodwill campaigns designed to win the hearts and minds of the people. My intent is to isolate the insurgents and the troublemakers from the populace in order to create a secure physical and psychological environment for the re-introduction of local government."

The SPL knows there are armed and dangerous elements in the area. His squad carries sufficient firepower to handle just about any armed confrontation that might confront them. However, destroying an enemy with superior firepower is a last resort here in the highlands of Centralia. The population includes well-intentioned people who simply want an end to this civil strife. There are elected officials who are trying to do their jobs in the face of the criminally violent elements that compose the various factions within the CRF. Finally, there are the goons of the CRF—armed, unhappy with the U.S. presence in their country, and willing to kill Americans, if given the proper opportunity. The SPL's problem will be to control his own instincts and those of his subordinates when situations arise and a decision must be made as to the use of deadly, or nondeadly, force.

Controlling the Marines' actions are the rules of engagement (ROEs) to be followed. ROEs are a relatively new factor influencing modern military operations. They were not even a minor part of 1950s training. Some would argue that ROEs have taken precedence over the needs of military commanders to protect their troops and carry out their missions. Commanders would just as soon live without them, but they are an integral part of military operations in today's world and for the foreseeable future.

These are some of the thoughts running through the mind of the SPL as his formation enters the town. It is not long before it becomes apparent that this town is bedlam. Crowds of civilians are milling about in the streets. When the patrol makes its appearance, the citizens of Hogan's Alley react to their presence in various ways. Some are welcoming and want to shake hands and touch the weapons of the patrol members. Others lurk in doorways, making no attempt to conceal their disdain for these Americans or to hide the weapons they carry. Young women try to enter the patrol formation to get close to the Americans. It is ingrained in the American nature to be friendly, and these lieutenants are the products of American society. Smiles and friendly eyes are, for the most part, the way we Americans meet and greet strangers. However, in the Bosnias, Haitis, and Afghanistans of the world, violence and destruction are daily occurrences, and Americans learn quickly to subordinate the friendlier angels of their nature. The key to survival is watchfulness, awareness, and an obsession with security and patrol integrity. Each member has a sector of responsibility and must cover his or her mates and stay alert to any threat. And so, as the formation moves a block down the street, they are fully engaged, attempting to maintain patrol integrity, warning civilians to stay away. The advice they will be given by Colonel Allen later in the day is "to be professional, but *menacing*." Mobs do not respect smiling, friendly troops.

At this point, the SPL receives a radio message ordering the patrol to establish a hasty vehicle checkpoint. He is told that some vehicles in the area are suspected of carrying arms or contraband and is ordered to search all vehicles and detain the occupants if arms or contraband are found. The checkpoint is set up, and the troops go to work as best they can, considering the fact that the local television reporter and his cameraman have arrived on the scene and are doing their best to be disruptive. The lieutenant is faced with his responsibility to maintain the security of his patrol, to carry out the order he has been given regarding the roadblock and, at the same time, be as cooperative with the media as possible under the circumstances. The reporter's physical presence and constant barrage of questions make this difficult.

Four vehicles arrive at the checkpoint. The first vehicle is clean and is allowed to pass. The second is found to be carrying firearms, and its four occupants are placed under arrest. Two run away, but two are handcuffed after a brief struggle. The remaining two vehicles turn around and flee the scene.

While all this is happening the television cameraman is recording the struggle involving the truck occupants while the reporter is shouting at the SPL and the other patrol members, "What are you doing in our country arresting people? What have these men done?" The SPL does his best to answer the questions calmly and unemotionally, but it's apparent that the reporter is getting on his nerves as he orders one of his Marines to "Keep those people out of the patrol formation." Meanwhile, the crowd has been drawn to the melee involving the truck, and some are screaming, "Americans, go home! Americans, go home!" The patrol leader radios his command post and advises that the vehicle has been secured, checked for booby traps, and confiscated. He is advised to resume his patrol route.

The patrol moves on, entering the commercial part of the town where uniformed men peer from windows and doorways; some are carrying firearms. Since the weapons are not pointed at the Marines, the patrol moves on, keeping an eye on the figures that lurk in the hallways.

They come upon several civilians who are loading military rations and clothing onto a truck. They are being forced to do this at gunpoint and are being kicked and punched by CRF forces. One civilian is being severely kicked and beaten by two insurgents. Upon seeing the patrol approach, the insurgents leap into the truck and drive away. The civilian beating victim is suffering an apparent heart attack in the street. The patrol leader's inclination is to continue along the patrol route without regard for the civilian down on the pavement. The reporter quickly jumps into the formation. He shouts, "That man is having a heart attack! What are you going to do about it?" The SPL responds by radioing the PCP, requesting medical assistance for the injured man. After a few minutes an ambulance arrives, the man is loaded onto the truck, and bystanders show their approval of this humanitarian act. The patrol passes a man who is beating his wife. They ignore this situation and push on toward the far reaches of Hogan's Alley.

At a street corner two insurgents, in uniform and armed, spot the patrol and withdraw down the street out of sight. They reappear in a tree line, shouting threats, obviously intent on stirring up some kind of incident. Several more insurgents are spotted in the tree line. A burst from an automatic weapon comes from the tree line, and the patrol leader quickly orders two fire teams to return fire while the third fire team moves down an alley to flank the insurgents. The Assistant Instructor accompanying the patrol judges that two Marines are wounded as are five insurgents. The flanking fire team clears the tree line, and the patrol leader radios for medical evacuation for the two Marine casualties.

The reporter becomes more intrusive and aggressive as the patrol continues past a large warehouse. He continues to pepper the leader and other patrol members with questions about their presence in his country. By now a group of curious civilians has attached itself to the patrol, following closely in its wake. As the patrol's point man rounds the last corner of the route, the patrol is taken under fire from an apartment building. It is not apparent where the shots are coming from, but it is logical that they must be coming from an open window. There are two open windows in the building.

This requires the SPL again to take fast action. First, he needs to get his patrol and civilian bystanders into covered positions, out of the line of fire. He needs to determine where the sniper is located and decide whether to clear the building with his own troops or call for a reaction force from the PCP. He must also take care of any casualties, both Marine and civilian. All the while, the Assistant Instructor accompanying the patrol is in communication with the sniper who is telling him which Marines and which civilians he's shot from his position in the apartment building. The longer it takes for the PL to make decisions and take action, the more casualties the patrol takes. This lieutenant decides to call for a reaction force from the PCP. When he is advised that a reaction force isn't available, he orders two fire teams to establish a base of fire aiming at the open windows while a third team advances to clear the building.

As soon as the building is cleared, the exercise is concluded. The patrol moves to an area just outside the town to critique the operation. This critique, like the others we observed at TBS, is a positive learning experience for the lieutenants. All are encouraged to offer ideas on how and why, in retrospect, they might change the decisions or actions they took during the exercise. The student patrol leader gets the first opportunity to share his thought processes and the learning he has personally gained. Other lieutenants then give their thoughts. The AI who observed the patrol in action skillfully facilitates the discussion. Several of the lieutenants, prior enlisted Marines, added their ideas and thought processes, based on their experiences in Bosnia.

Later that day, I had the opportunity to discuss my observations with TBS's Commanding Officer, Colonel John R. Allen. When I commented on the TBS critique approach and how that had certainly changed since my days at TBS, he agreed.

> You and I were trained what to think, and what to do, not *how* to think and *how to apply* tactics, techniques and procedures in a situational manner. Today, we recognize that this whole business of maneuver warfare demands that everyone, from top to bottom, be a thinking warrior. We require these [TBS] lieutenants to constantly make decisions. Then we go back and have them decompose those decisions. We ask, "What made you make that decision?" We never say, "You made a good decision or a bad decision." We evaluate decisions based on the consequences. For the young lieutenant that you and I monitored this morning—the one who took so long to take action when his patrol was taken under fire by the sniper—the consequences of his being immobilized in decision-making was that most of his people were killed. The vast majority of his combat power was neutralized by a lone sniper who continued to shoot people because he [the student patrol leader] did not lead his unit properly. He will never make that mistake again. And, when those results emerged during the critique we didn't leave him a broken man. We didn't say, "Look at the consequences of what you did. You made bad decisions." We talked him through his decisions and the end state is that he is more confident and will not make those mistakes again. Importantly, the other lieutenants, the point man, the rifleman, every lieutenant on that patrol, also benefited from the process.

The lieutenants, the products of the training described here, will not forget these experiences. It is a time when every officer is a "grunt," a rifleman, sharing the demands and discomforts of the infantry's life. They are required to make the difficult decisions required of the small-unit leaders who find themselves and their people in flashpoint situations or a firefight. This is not to downplay the obvious fact that every other occupational specialty in the Corps faces their own tough decisions and situations. What is true is that this insistence that every officer be trained as a platoon commander pays off when a beleaguered ground unit calls for artillery or air support. The pilot or the artillery battery commander involved understands the situation on the ground because he or she has been there and has shared that life, if only in a training context. In the Corps, one does not hear about "them and us"; in the Corps, "it's only us."

8

TBS—The Thinking Warrior

> Character and intellect: the two poles of our capacity. One without the other is but halfway to happiness.
>
> Baltasar Gracia, *Oracula Manual*, 1647

Colonel John R. Allen is the Commanding Officer of The Basic School (TBS). Like his nearby counterpart at Officer Candidates School (OCS), Colonel George J. Flynn, he is thoughtful, approachable and candid. Both commands, OCS and TBS, are assigned to officers in whom the Commandant places deep trust. They and their staffs must ensure that a continuous supply of qualified, trained, and motivated officer talent flows to the operating forces.

Colonel Allen, 49, the son of a career Navy officer, was born in Warrenton, Virginia. He spent his elementary and high school years in northern Virginia while his father worked in various assignments in the nation's capitol. He attended the Naval Academy, graduating with the class of 1976. Following commissioning in the Marine Corps he attended TBS and was then assigned to the Second Battalion, 8th Marines where he served, first as a platoon commander and later, as a rifle company commander.

Colonel Allen's assignments have included the following:

- The Marine Barracks, 8th and I Streets, Washington, DC.
- Appointed to the Postgraduate Intelligence Program of the Defense Intelligence College and subsequently as the Marine Corps Fellow to the Center for Strategic and International Studies.
- Served as company commander, later as operations officer, Third Battalion, 4th Marines. He was awarded the Leftwich Leadership Trophy during this tour.
- Served at the U.S. Naval Academy where he received the Wm. P. Clements Award as Military Instructor of the Year in 1990 for his work as political science instructor.
- Assigned to TBS as Director, Infantry Officers Course.
- Named Commandant of the Marine Corps Fellow serving as Special Assistant to the thirtieth Commandant.
- Commanded the Second Battalion, 4th Marines as this unit served in contingency operations in the Caribbean in 1994 and the Balkans in 1995–1996.

- Served as Senior Aide and Military Secretary to the thirty-first Commandant.
- Assumed command of TBS in 1999.

Colonel Allen is a graduate of the National War College. He holds a Master of Arts degree in Government from Georgetown University, a Master of Science degree in Strategic Intelligence from the Defense Intelligence College, and a Master of Science degree in National Security Strategy from the National War College.

He is married to the former Katherine Ann Glickert, a third-generation Marine junior. They have two daughters, Betty and Bobbie.

Our conversation took place on a Sunday afternoon after the Colonel and I had observed a company work through the Urban Patrol FEX at the FBI Academy. His comments regarding today's lieutenants and their training are helpful in illuminating the changes that have taken place in the teaching approaches used at TBS, as the institution responds to the requirements of modern combat, new technology, and the evolving American culture. His views on the current state of the Marine Corps, regarding its equipment needs and ongoing deployments, are most interesting.

Q. Tell me about high school and your decision to attend the Naval Academy.

I went to Flint Hill Preparatory School in Fairfax, Virginia. That school was really an island in a sea of storms in the early '70s. It was a very conservative, private, liberal arts school. The most influential teacher I had was a Royal Marine, Colonel Allen Ferguson Warren. My sense of an officer's duty was communicated to me by Colonel Warren and other good professors. While the Vietnam unrest was going on at high schools all around the country, open insubordination was never a piece of my background. I suppose I grew up immune to that. So going to the Academy was something that came to me as a realization in my junior year and then turned into a real passion in my senior year.

Q. When did you know the Marine Corps would be your career?

It was a day in my sophomore year at Annapolis. While I had wanted to be a Marine for many years, I wasn't absolutely certain. There were many things I liked about the Navy but I had attended a class that morning taught by a Marine and, as the formation faced right to head for chow, I made the decision at that moment.

Q. Just like that? Right face and into the Corps?

That's right. It wasn't a bolt from the blue because I'd thought about it for years. My sense was, if I'm going to do this, I need to commit myself to it and get on with the decision—to make it part of my life, now. And I did, unswervingly.

Q. What are your impressions of the generation of lieutenants that you are training at The Basic School today?

They are very smart. They're in excellent physical condition, relative to your generation or my generation of officers. It is physically far more demanding today. What is different is what I call this generation's distance in time from the "greatest generation." When I went through TBS I would say that 98 percent of us were the sons of men who had served in World War II. Virtually all of us came from families that had experienced the Great Depression. These struggles that our parents faced and overcame defined my generation. We also came with a greater sense of selflessness. Regimentation came more easily because we'd learned about it from our fathers or mothers. Today, many of the lieutenants are separated by a couple of generations from [anyone] who actually ever wore the uniform, much less wore it for a career. They are not as sure about why they want to be a Marine officer as we were. After a short period of time they get excited about the idea, like we did, but the selflessness and regimentation that comes with being a good Marine is something that doesn't come as naturally as these did for us.

Q. How are these young officers similar to your generation? Are there common threads that run through both generations, from your perspective?

On a regular basis I have five or six of the lieutenants over to dinner at my home during the week. What comes through so clearly at these meals is how the lieutenants speak with such expectation for the future. They aren't in this thing for a job. They may have come through the front door of TBS with the idea that, "I want to be a financial manager and this will help me," or "I want to get into politics and I need this on my resume." By the second month of Basic School they're in it for the Marines and it's exciting for me to witness that transition. When I talk with the Basic School staff I tell them that TBS is the "black box" for the Marine Corps. We get this product in the front door of TBS and the product comes out at the other end. The product needs to be about the same as it's always been—an officer who is sharp of mind, in good physical condition, understands selflessness and duty and honor. But the gears in that "black box" are probably going to turn a bit differently today than they did before. So, now we spend a lot of effort and time at the front end getting a hold on their spirits, their souls, to make sure they fully understand the consequences of failure. What are the consequences of failure of the mind, or the body, or character when leading troops? They gravitate to that and the enormity of what they have signed on for comes clear after a few weeks at TBS. This is the thread, this sense of utter selflessness learned by these officers that unites them to my generation—and my generation to yours.

Q. One question intrigues me. In today's America, how does the Corps continue to find the 1,400–1,500 young people each year willing to undergo the trials of OCS and TBS to become officers of Marines? How does the Corps continue to meet its recruiting goals while other services are experiencing real difficulty?

There's an old saying that goes, "A man, in his golden years, will always think ill of himself for never having been a soldier, for never having gone to sea." I believe there's some of that alive today in America. And I think there are many young people that see the military as an honorable profession. They want to be part of this. And, as they look across the landscape of what's available to them, the ones who gravitate to the Marine Corps are not looking for a monetary return. There are enough of them out there who are sufficiently idealistic and, in an abstract way, patriotic, who want to be part of something bigger than themselves.

Q. How has TBS changed in the twenty-five years since you attended?

We were largely trained what to think and what to do, not how to think or how to apply tactics, techniques and procedures in a situational manner. Today, we recognize that this whole business of maneuver warfare demands that, from top to bottom, everyone must be a "thinking warrior." It's not enough to be equipped with four or five procedures that you execute to the best of your ability. Today we teach the procedures but we put a premium on learning how to take what is going on in front of you, place it in the context of what you've learned from history, from classroom time, from the sand table, from all your exercises. You need to make a decision as quickly as you can, communicate the decision to your subordinates and then execute that decision with greater operational speed than your opponent. That's today's TBS. I remember, when I graduated from TBS I was the best-trained Marine rifleman the Corps could have produced, but I wasn't the thinking officer . . . that we need today. I was spring-loaded to do exactly what I was told and nothing but what I was told. Today we spend a lot of time and effort against the intellectual preparation of the lieutenants, for war in general, for command in general and then for tactical execution, specifically. We value tactical excellence, but [it should be] dominated by intellectual agility.

Q. There certainly is a more intellectual feel to TBS these days, compared to my recollections from the '50s. Tell me about the critique approach your instructors use at the conclusion of a training exercise. I was impressed by the free-flowing discussion from all participants and the manner in which the student patrol leader's decisions were analyzed.

Basic School is about making decisions and we put our lieutenants in situations where they are required to make decisions, constantly. We then review and decompose that decision. We ask, "What made you make that decision?" We never say, "You made a good decision or a bad decision." We evaluate the decision based on the consequences. For the young lieutenant that you and I monitored a few minutes ago, the consequences of his hesitation in making a decision was that most of his people were killed. He allowed his combat power to be neutralized by a single sniper who continued to shoot down his people because the lieutenant wasn't leading his unit properly. Now, he'll never make that mistake again. Importantly, the process of the critique didn't leave him a broken man. We didn't tell him that he's an idiot, that he made bad decisions. We allowed him to talk through his decisions. The end state will be an officer with added confidence who won't make the same mistakes again. Every other lieutenant on that patrol also benefited from the critique process—each played a role. That's one piece of our approach, this letting the student talk his way through his thought processes. The other piece is that we do a great deal of free play. We carve out a large chunk of the western portion of Quantico and put one platoon in the north and another in the south. We give the platoon commanders scenarios and let them go at each other. They learn that, in combat, there is always an opposing will out there. With a live "enemy" platoon looking for you, if you make a bad decision you're going to get punished for it [in terms of casualties]. So, there is a great deal of emphasis on decision-making, coupled with these free play exercises. Thinking counts—tactics count—techniques count. They learn quickly that their decisions either result in success or they end up being punished in clear and obvious ways.

Q. There has been a lot of publicity about the number of young officers that are leaving the services. What's your experience here at TBS, considering the fact that you have a number of young captains working for you?

I have one hundred captains here at TBS. At any given time, five or six of them are getting out which means my retention rate is pretty good. When an officer tells me he wants to get out, I bring him or her into my office and ask, "What is it at this moment that causes you to want to get out?" Most of the time the problem is that they have a young wife and kids and just don't want to spend any more time away from them. If, on the other hand, their thinking is fuzzy about why they want to get out, I just tell them, "You're making a bad decision. Both you and the Marine Corps need you to stay in the Corps. You tell me the scenario that I can create for you that will keep you." I learned some would stay if someone simply said, "Don't get out. It's a bad idea. We need you to stay." I've been able to turn several young officers who really needed to stay in the Corps. Some I am unable to turn and, of course, there are some that need to go. We don't have any talent hemorrhage here at TBS. Some do resign and that's the nature of the business. I'm not concerned about any exodus from TBS.

Q. How about the Marine Corps in general? Is it a big problem?

No, I don't think so. I'm not in the recruiting or retention business but here is our current situation. We graduate about 40,000 Marines a year from the recruit depots. About half the Corps is made up of lance corporals or below, so we have a lot of young, robust individuals and we can't keep them all. We also have about 40,000 Marines who leave active duty each year. Our goal is to get about 5,000 first term Marines to re-enlist because we need them to become our life-blood, our long-term Marines—our enlisted leaders. It takes the whole Corps to make our numbers each year, but we make them because of commanders and senior enlisted leaders who work hard to get our best young Marines to stay. We are being challenged to keep our aviators but not nearly as challenged as the Air Force or Navy. Your average Marine aviator will stay because he wants to remain a Marine. He or she wants to fly Marine aircraft for Marines on the ground. A decision to get out usually is a function of unwillingness to pay the price at a personal level with the family, due to these interminable deployments that we're on. It's not usually a matter of money. They are wonderful Marines and Naval Aviators.

Q. Just how stretched is the Corps today?

I'll tell you, we are committed. With the end of the Cold War, the Corps reduced in size at exactly the same time that our nation has been confronted with crisis after crisis, where naval forces were [our country's] first or only responders. Between deployments, exercises, and contingencies, Division Commanders can look out across their divisions and find not one infantry battalion available. That didn't happen 15–20 years ago but it's not uncommon today. Our Corps is committed at many different levels and in many different ways. It has challenged our entire institution from leadership to material readiness to family readiness. It's the nature of a world of chaos—but it's the nature of our Corps that America turns to its Marines over and over again. There's little rest for our Marines, our equipment, for our precious families.

Q. How bad is your budget situation today? Is it affecting your ability to execute your mission to any great extent?

Not really. The Marine Corps does everything it can to take care of a few organizations. The Basic School is one of them. Our responsibility is to be good stewards of the precious dollars the Corps invests here at TBS.

Q. Is a tour of duty on the TBS staff a significant career step for a Marine officer?

Absolutely! Outside of the operating forces, there is almost no fitness report that carries more weight at a promotion board than a successful tour at TBS. By and large, most of the people assigned to The Basic School come to me by personal referral. Manpower has been magnificent in sending TBS those fine officers referred from the operating forces. In the Corps we may have a different philosophy than the other services. We go back to the operating forces and bring our very best officers to our schools to teach. The understanding is that one hand washes the other hand. We must make that kind of investment. So, most of the captains and majors I have here came as a personal referral from a regimental, battalion, group or squadron commander.

Q. We've discussed how the Marine Corps is stretched by its challenges. Are there any other issues you care to discuss?

The other area is in modernization. I'm in no better or worse shape than anybody else in the Corps. My gear is old. My gear is breaking from the high tempo of use. The TBS infrastructure is old, basically designed for a post-World War II mobilization style of instruction. You know—a captain up front, yelling at 250 lieutenants so that he or she can be heard by all. We need to break away from that method of instruction and we're planning on putting the infrastructure under the knife in the next eighteen months or so, re-orienting it to support a more decentralized method of instruction.

Q. Colonel, when I went through Basic School back in the 1950s, we didn't talk about Core Values. Today, that's a major area of emphasis at OCS and here at TBS. Where did this emphasis start, and why?

I'm speculating here. While *Tail Hook* may have been the catalyst for our enumerating a set of core values, Marines have always been wedded to core principles and high moral and ethical standards. [The Tailhook Association was composed of active duty and retired Navy and Marine aviators and defense contractors. The annual meetings were noted for heavy drinking and unseemly behavior on the part of the junior officers in attendance. Following the association's 35th annual meeting, held in Las Vegas in September, 1991, charges of assault were lodged by a junior female Naval officer and an investigation was conducted by the Inspector General, Department of Defense. "Ultimately, the careers of fourteen admirals and almost 300 naval aviators were scuttled or damaged by Tailhook." (*Tailhook '91*, Frontline/PBS Online)] The concepts of honor, courage and commitment are consistent with what we are all about as Marines and, I believe, helped address some of the ethical cracks we may have seen emerging in the late 80s and early '90s. General Krulak, the previous Commandant, had one item on his desk. It was a nameplate that contained one word, "Integrity." Clearly he was a man who believed these things were important and should come naturally to all Marines. But, as far back as a generation ago, General Chapman wrote a great article for the *Marine Corps Gazette* in which he covered a wide spectrum of things from drinking to how you treat fellow Marines, regardless of race or gender, how to conduct yourself on liberty, to name a few activities. His point was, "Marines just don't do that." It was a terrific distillation of all that we stand for as Marines. We all understood what "Marines just don't do that" meant.

Today, in addition to our core values, the current Commandant, General Jones, has initiated something which promises to "put flesh on the bones" of our understanding of core values. The Marine Corps Martial Arts Program will likely do more for our sense of who we are, as ethical warriors, as any training we've carried out in the last 30 years. It builds on our Core Values by emphasizing character development and warfighting knowledge, facilitated through physical training. It will be a very powerful contribution to our Corps from our individual Marines to our warfighting units.

Q. Can you describe the best officer you ever served under?

He was an intellectual, a gentleman. He knew his warfighting business but he was a gentleman in the classic sense of the word. He mastered his profession and the art of war, had great ability to do great harm with those skills. But he consciously, intentionally gentled his nature in ways that made him a paragon of virtue. All of us who were touched by him were changed forever and for the better. He taught me more about being an officer, what truly being an officer is, as opposed to being solely a warrior, than anybody else I ever served under. And he made me very nervous, constantly, about whether I was doing my utmost to be worthy of the right to command Marines. He taught me to always ask myself, "What else can I do for my Marines? What else can I do to get them ready for

> war?" And he did all that with this genuine face of gentlemanly conduct and honor.
>
> Q. If you were to give one piece of advice to lieutenants who are moving out to their first duty station, what would that be?
>
> Your obligation is to prepare yourself, as best you can, intellectually, for the business of going to war. If you know the business of war intuitively, then you'll know the business of war in every other sense. It will drive how you prepare yourself, physically. It will drive how you train your Marines. It will drive how you treat your Marines. It will drive all those things. You must learn the business of war and you must study it as a lifelong devotion. It's your obligation.

This nation bestows upon a very select few the greatest gift of the Republic: the commission of an officer of Marines. While earning the commission may occur in one of several ways, understanding the significance of that commission, and grasping the sheer enormity of the words, "special trust and confidence," which attend this honor, occur only at The Basic School. . . . Ours is an awesome responsibility, where literally the future of our Corps hangs in the balance. (Colonel John R. Allen, "Commander's Intent Letter," July 1999)

In January 2002, Colonel Allen was selected to be the Seventy-ninth Commandant of Midshipmen, United States Naval Academy. He is the first Marine to hold that command in the history of the academy. In January, 2003, he was selected for promotion to brigadier general.

9

Profile of a Lieutenant

We be of one blood, ye and I.

Rudyard Kipling, *The Jungle Book*, 1894

At inception, a fundamental premise of this book was that the Marine Corps leadership experience changes people. This is widely accepted conventional wisdom and, were it possible to question the thousands of men and women who have chosen the path that leads to a commission as an officer of Marines, I suspect most would agree. The 3-56 Class, as well as the lieutenants at The Basic School (TBS) today would tell us that the Corps has changed them in some positive ways. That is borne out in the research we have conducted with both groups. On the other hand, as we studied the responses provided to us by 315 current and former TBS lieutenants, it became clear that this is not the entire story, nor is it the big story.

We will examine the responses we received to questionnaires and provide an interpretation of the data. It is clear that the Corps leadership experience is a demanding human refinement process. Identifying, selecting, and developing a very specific stratum of American society appears to be the key to producing men and women who can successfully lead Marines.

We designed our 100-question survey with the objective of identifying differences and similarities between today's TBS lieutenants and the 3-56 Basic School Class. How do they differ in demographic terms? How do they differ in their attitudes about American society, moral/ethical issues, religion, and personal values? How are they the same? What draws them to the hard life of the Marine Corps when America typically offers myriad opportunities to young, intelligent, ambitious, and aggressive people? Have the dramatic changes that have altered the nation in which my generation grew up, the social and political upheavals of the second half of the twentieth century, produced a human resource pool that is fundamentally dissimilar from the 557 men who entered TBS in June 1956?

The older generation of officers grew up in a world far different from that of the generation born in the late 1970s and early 1980s. Born during the Great Depression, the 3-56 Class viewed life through the prism of World War II. Our America was not physically touched by the war, but every American family experienced the emotions and anguish spurred by an all-out, total war; empty chairs at dinner tables and blue stars posted in front windows reminded us of friends and family who were doing the fighting. We were unrepentant in our unquestioning patriotism. We trusted and believed in American institutions, as well as the moral guidance received at home, in movies, in literature, and at school. In our young lives, the struggles of America, of life in general, involved conflicts between good and evil, and very few issues took on shades of gray.

The generation represented by the new lieutenants of Alpha Company 2000 came into this world in the late 1970s. Typically, their parents were members of the protest generation of the 1960s and early 1970s. American institutions were severely battered during the Vietnam War, and a generation grew up in a society in which a significant segment of society lived by relaxed behavioral and moral codes. We assumed that the two generations would prove to be very dissimilar in terms of their collective social and political attitudes and opinions.

Awareness of the impact of my own Marine Corps experience on my life became clearer to me as I reached my forties. This clarification was not unique to me. Most of us reach a time in our lives when we reassess who we are and where we have been, and we begin to sense our own mortality. At this time we make an effort to better understand, and perhaps improve upon, that person that stares back at us from the mirror. I began to comprehend how much of my worldview, my professional and personal behavior, my business management and leadership style reflected the two most important influences in my early life: my upbringing in a solid, middle-class family and my Marine Corps experience. I wondered if my conclusions about my own value systems and attitudes were perhaps shared by my classmates from the 3-56 Basic School Class.

I served, as did many, only two years on active duty and never heard a shot fired in anger. When I drove through the gate at Camp LeJeune for the last time in June 1958 I never looked back. And yet, the Marine Corps has been an important part of me since 1953 when I entered the Platoon Leaders Class (PLC) program at eighteen. You may take off the uniform and walk away from the Corps, geographically—but you never really *leave* the Corps.

After attending TBS I was assigned as an infantry platoon commander in First Battalion, 2nd Marine Regiment, 2nd Marine Division stationed at Camp LeJeune, North Carolina. My tour included a six-month deployment to the Sixth Fleet in the Mediterranean Sea and a later training deployment to Vieques, Puerto Rico. My initial command was a mortar and rocket platoon. A few months later I was assigned command of a rifle platoon.

I believe I am a realist about my personal experiences in the Corps and my view of it as a human institution. As a lieutenant, I worked with some extremely talented, intelligent, and industrious peers and senior officers. I saw how outstanding officers and noncommissioned officers (NCOs) motivated and trained their people. In a few cases, I witnessed the damaging effect that incompetence or a lack of moral leadership on the part of officers or NCOs can have on a unit. The Marine Corps is, after all, a human organization and is subject to the same failings and weaknesses as any other group of Americans. (It is my opinion, based on observation and discussion, not on a statistical basis, that today's ranks of Marine officers and NCOs no longer contain the numbers of heavy-drinking, dissolute-living Marines who were present in the post-Korean War Marine Corps.)

As platoon commander I made mistakes that, in combat, could have cost Marine casualties, usually because I ignored or neglected to seek my platoon sergeant's input. The heart and soul of the Marine Corps, the keeping place for the professionalism, practical knowledge, traditions, legends and myths of the Corps, reside with the senior staff NCOs. My twenty-two-year-old pride occasionally prevented me from tapping into that resource, and those omissions came back to haunt me. I suspect that I was typical of a reserve lieutenant of the day and, as I reflect on those experiences with what I hope is a measure of objectivity, I was an average, perhaps a bit above average, young officer.

While at TBS I seriously considered making the Marine Corps a career; however, my enthusiasm for Fleet Marine Force (FMF) life waned when I married. I began to find sleeping on the ground in the March rains of North Carolina less appealing than my bed in the Tarawa Terrace married officer's duplex where we lived. With a child on the way I felt a need to improve my financial circumstances, and my chances of doing that in the Corps were nonexistent. People do not get rich serving their country in the armed services. That was true then and remains so today.

Nonetheless, I remain a Marine. It is etched in my soul. I carry a secret tinge of guilt, as do, I suspect, many of my peers. Many of my classmates did tours in Vietnam in the 1960s and 1970s while I enjoyed the security and benefits that accrued to those of us who opted for the greener economic pastures of civilian business. I am sure some readers will think it illogical, perhaps unbalanced, for a man to feel guilt about not serving in that awful conflict. I had all the excuses I needed—a growing family and a career that was well under way. Vietnam was, in the eyes of a significant number of Americans, at best a mistake, at worst a criminal, national disgrace. How could an intelligent man feel guilty at not being a part of that? I think the Marines who read this will understand. Did I want to risk life and limb? Did I want to leave my family? Of course not. Would I feel better when I look into the eyes of classmates and others who did serve in that godforsaken war? Frankly, yes. I am also certain that this feeling is not unique to Marines but is shared by former members of the Rangers, SEALS, airborne and other excellent military units. If there is one thing a Marine requires it is the respect of peers and comrades. Respect is earned while sharing whatever hardships or responsibilities are thrust upon the squad, platoon, or company. If the president and the Congress of the United States send you into high-risk situations, you go, without question, period. That is the oath you take as an officer. How well you handle these situations—how well you lead and care for your Marines—are the measures by which you are judged. I have never been under fire and will forever wonder whether I would have earned that respect. That is just the way it is, whether it is logical or not. At least, that is the way it is with me and, I would wager, with a number of my classmates.

In order to identify and assess the differences and similarities that exist between the lieutenants of Alpha Company 2000 and the 3-56 Class, a survey consisting of 100 questions was completed by both groups of officers. Questionnaires were sent to the 440 surviving members of the 3-56 Class and 156, or 34 percent, responded. A similar survey was made available to the 222 members of Alpha Company 2000, and 157 voluntary responses were received, a response rate of 71 percent. For perspective, the 157 responses from Alpha Company 2000 represent 11 percent of all Marine Corps second lieutenants commissioned in the 2000 fiscal year, which provides a projectable sample. We checked the projectability of the Alpha Company data by comparing it with the Marine Corps Recruiting Command data that covered all the officers receiving commissions during the 2000 fiscal year. These comparisons proved to be quite satisfactory. The questionnaires themselves were tabulated and collated by Directions Research, Inc., of Cincinnati, Ohio.

The questions asked of both the 3-56 Class and Alpha Company 2000 are identical with one exception. The Marine Corps would not permit questions about personal politics or socio-political issues (abortion, for example) to be asked of Alpha Company 2000. Colonel John R. Allen explained this prohibition in an e-mail to the author. "It is important to the country that the Marine Corps remain, and always appear to remain, apolitical in America. Of course, every officer has a right to his or her own political and socio-political opinion, but these should not be portrayed as Marine Corps opinion, or the opinions of a segment of the Corps . . ."

Some explanation of Table 9.1 will be helpful. The key figure here is in the Percent of Total USMC Fiscal Year 2000 Commissions. As the table indicates, 8 percent of the lieutenants commissioned in the fiscal year were females. This performance must be measured against the universe of females in the United States who are eligible to enter the military's officer ranks. These college-

Table 9.1
Demographics—Gender

	% 3-56	% Alpha Co.	% Total USMC FY2000 Commissions*
Male	100%	95%	92%
Female	0**	5	8

*Marine Corps Recruiting Command data
**No data available

educated, age 21–35-year-old women typically represent about 7 percent of all U.S. females. The fact that women represented 8 percent of the Marine Corps' total of newly commissioned second lieutenants puts a favorable light on the Marines' efforts in this area.

The Corps has worked hard to increase the number of women in its commissioned officer ranks, and progress is evident. In 1996 there were 625 women officers on active duty, about 4 percent of the total officer complement. By 1998 that number had grown to 854, representing 5 percent of total officers. Today, women officers represent about 6 percent of its total active duty officers.

OCS is a very challenging test for well-conditioned males, and it is probably even more demanding on their female counterparts. It is a dedicated woman who successfully completes OCS and joins the more than 800 active duty women officers in the Marine Corps. The failure rate among female candidates is almost twice as high as that for men; physical injuries, mainly musculoskeletal, and physical disqualification are the major causes of female candidate attrition. Women must meet rigorous physical fitness standards, although not exactly the same as those for men. All other OCS training is identical, regardless of gender. As is demonstrated from the anecdotes and recollections of female OCS candidates, which have been included in previous chapters, those who do succeed are physically and mentally tough, determined, and have earned every right to wear the eagle, globe, and anchor.

The Basic School of the 1950s was almost exclusively Caucasian, with the exception of several officers of Hispanic descent. (The data in Table 9.2 do not include the ethnicity of foreign officers included within the ranks of the two TBS classes. The 3-56 Class included six officers from the Marine Corps, Republic of Korea. Alpha Company 2000 included several of the 30 foreign officers trained each year at TBS.)

Here again, enrollment results should be measured against the 21–35-year-old, eligible college graduate minority populations in the country. In 1996 these pools of minorities included 7 percent African American, 4 percent Hispanic, and 7 percent Other. Eight percent of all Marine Corps commissions in 1998

Table 9.2
Demographics—Ethnicity

Group	% 3-56	% Alpha Co.	% Total USMC FY2000 Commissions.*
Caucasian	99%	83%	83%
Hispanic	1	9	6
African American	0	6	6
Other	0**	2	5

*Marine Corps Recruiting Command data

went to African Americans, 6 percent to Hispanics, and 4 percent to other minorities. Fiscal year 2000 minorities were below target. The Marine Corps has made progress in increasing the number of minorities within its officer ranks from 5.5 percent in 1996 to 6.0 percent today. The ongoing challenge of selecting minority candidates remains an institutional challenge, as it is for the other armed services.

From Table 9.3, it can be seen that in the 3-56 Class the Northeastern states were overrepresented by +62 percent relative to their proportionate share of the U.S. population. (The region's share of the population of the United States was 25.4 percent, but it supplied 41.2 percent of the 3-56 officer population.) The South (index 98) contributed close to its fair share of officers, while the Midwest (index 69) and West (index 62) regions were heavily underrepresented in the 3-56 group. The Northeast and South supplied over 70 percent of the officers in this class from 56 percent of the U.S. population.

The Northeast and South have traditionally been fertile grounds for Marine recruiting and officer selection. The magnitude of the overrepresentation of the Northeast in 1956 appears to have been an aberration. In Alpha Company 2000, the Northeastern/Southern influence is evident but not to the overwhelming degree seen in the 1956 data. In the most recent TBS group, the Southern region (index 117) provided 41.6 percent of Alpha Company's lieutenants, and the Northeast (index 110) supplied 21.4 percent. Here again, 63 percent of Alpha Company's officers were supplied by areas that held 55 percent of the total U.S. population.

Some of the reasons underlying this geographic skew are speculative; some are supportable. In the East, the streets of New York, Philadelphia, and Boston have historically been prime recruiting areas for the Marine Corps. Ethnic populations of long standing as well as concentrations of the newer waves of immigrants, both European and Hispanic, are probably influences.

Table 9.3
Geographic Source of New Lieutenants—1956 Compared to 2000

(Regional distribution of U.S.population compared to regional distribution in 3-56 Class, Alpha Company and Total FY2000 Marine Commissions)

Division	% U.S Pop. 1956(a)	% of 3-56	Index	% U.S Pop. 2000 (b)	% of Alpha Co.	Index	% total FY00 Comm's.(c)	Index
N'east	25.4%	41.2%	(162)	19.0%	21.4%	(110)	21.7%	(114)
M'west	29.3	20.3	(69)	22.9	20.1	(88)	18.5	(81)
South	30.4	29.2	(96)	35.6	41.6	(117)	39.5	(111)
West	14.9	9.3	(62)	22.5	16.9	(75)	20.3	(90)

(a) Population Estimate 1950–1959; U.S. Census Bureau

(b) 2000 Census; U.S. Census Bureau

(c) FY 2000 Lieutenants Commissioned—Marine Corps Recruiting Command

An associated factor, as we will discuss later, is the significant number of Roman Catholics who are attracted to the Marines. In the Northeastern region, Roman Catholics represent 37 percent of the regional population versus 22 percent nationally so we would expect this to influence that area's disproportionate share of both 3-56 and Alpha Company 2000. It would appear that the overrepresentation detailed in Table 9.3 is a result of a combination of these influences.

The Southern region's contribution to the TBS population is another matter. The region has historically contributed large numbers of military personnel, not only to the Marine Corps, but to the nation's other armed services as well (see Table 9.4). In *The Professional Soldier: A Social and Political Portrait* (1960), Morris Janowitz analyzes this overrepresentation in the top ranks of the military. Although Janowitz's study did not include Marine Corps personnel, his findings are, we believe, transferable to what would be concluded from a similar study of the Corps. "There was every reason to believe that the military would be heavily recruited from nonindustrialized areas—from agricultural communities and small towns," says Janowitz, adding:

First, the experience of the United States should not be very different from that of the nations of Western Europe [whose military leadership is drawn from agrarian regions]. Second, the emphasis on native-born personnel would, in itself, imply an overrepresentation of officers from rural and small town backgrounds, since the foreign-born and second generation concentrates in the metropolitan areas. Third, and most fundamental, there has been an integral association between military institutions and rural society. The out-of-doors existence, the concern with nature, sport, and weapons which is part of rural culture, have a direct carry-over to the requirements of the pre-technological military establishment. But in the final analysis the link between rural social structure and military organization is based on the more central issue of career opportunities. (Janowitz 1960, p. 85)

Table 9.4
Military Leadership, 1950: Regional Background at Time of Birth

(Regional service population percentages indexed to regional white population percentages)

Region	% Army	Index	% Navy	Index	% Air Force	Index	% Caucasian Population
Northeast	23%	(74)	27%	(87)	25%	(81)	31%
North Central	37	(95)	30	(77)	43	(112)	39
South	34	(141)	31	(129)	25	(104)	24
West	6	(100)	12	(200)	7	(117)	6

Note: The armed services were desegrated in 1948. Therefore, no minorities were included in this study since there were no minority flag officers.

Data from *The Professional Soldier* (M. Janowitz 1960)

The modern South, as bustling as its metropolitan areas are, remains to a large extent an agrarian society. In his work, Janowitz analyzed the "elite cadre" of the Army, Navy, and Air Force, a total of 761 major generals (Army and Air Force) and rear admirals (Navy) and determined, among other things, the regional representation within that population in 1950. It was close enough to the 3-56 Class to be comparable. The Southern skew to the three services included in the study is clear.

In the South military service has historically been viewed as an attractive profession. Many of the country's military institutions of higher learning are located in the area, including Virginia Military Institute, the Citadel, the U.S. Naval Academy, and Texas A&M. These institutions typically send a number of officers to the Corps each year.

Further influencing the Southern orientation are the numerous Naval and Marine facilities located in the South. In the 450-mile stretch of Atlantic coastline between Annapolis, Maryland, and Port Royal, South Carolina, one can find the U.S. Naval Academy, Quantico Marine Base, Norfolk and Little River Naval Bases, Parris Island Recruit Training Depot, Beaufort Marine Air Station, Cherry Point Marine Air Station, and Camp LeJeune, home of the Second Marine Division. The U.S. Army and Air Force also maintain a large number of facilities in the South. A young person growing up in that region in all likelihood comes into contact with armed forces facilities and personnel more frequently than those living in the Midwestern or Western areas of the country. One thing is clear: despite the passing of five decades, America's Northeast and South continue to fund the officer population of the Marine Corps in a disproportionate fashion.

Average and above average income families provided the Corps with the majority of its officers in 1956 (58 percent) and continue to do so today (86 percent) (see Table 9.5). It is interesting that so few of Alpha Company officers (16 percent) come from below average and poor economic circumstances, compared to the older group where nearly one in three officers were from lower

Table 9.5
Family Economic Circumstances

"How would you describe your childhood economic circumstances?"

Description	% 3-56	% Alpha Co.
Wealthy	2%	4%
Above average	13	35
Average	45	41
Below average	24	13
Poor	12	3
No answer	4	5

income families. At the same time, these data lend credence to the observations of some senior Marine staff noncommissioned officers (SNCOs) who believe that candidates from the middle class are more likely to make it through OCS than are those from either extreme on the economic ladder.

There is also the fact that the 3-56 Class came from a less prosperous society than Alpha Company 2000. That class was slightly more than a decade removed from the Great Depression, and Table 9.5 reflects that fact.

Alpha Company 2000 is heavily populated with Roman Catholics; 46 percent of the officers indicated this as their religious preference while 40 percent of the 3-56 Class were Catholic (see Table 9.6). The fiscal year 2000 data from Marine Corps Recruiting Command indicates that 38 percent of newly commissioned officers indicated their religious preference as Roman Catholic. Whatever number one chooses, the fact is that the Marine officer corps is heavily Catholic, considering that the Catholic population of the United States is 22 percent. Protestant enrollment was 51 percent in the older generation and has fallen to 44 percent in the more recent class. The number of officers expressing no religious preference remains stable at 8 percent versus 7 percent 1956. Almost 10 percent of the class describes itself as "Christian," a general description that has gained popularity in recent times but was not widely used by the older generation. Some religions are notably absent from the Alpha 2000 list, including the Jewish, Christian Science, and Unitarian faiths. At the

Table 9.6
Religion

"What is your religious preference, if any?"

Religion	% 3-56	% Alpha Co.	%Total FY2000 2nd Lts.*
Roman Catholic	40%	46%	38%
Methodist	14	6	2
Episcopalian	13	1	2
Protestant	11	6	30
No religious preference	7	8	8
Presbyterian	6	3	<
Baptist	5	7	4
Lutheran	0	3	2
Jewish	2	0	1
Society of Friends (Quaker)	1	1	<
Christian	0	14	3
All Others**	2	4	8

*FY 2000 Commissioned Lieutenants Report—Marine Corps Recruiting Command

**Includes Agnostic, Church of Christ, Pentecostal, Zen Buddhism, Christian Science, Unitarian, Congregational, Atheist, Latter-Day Saints and Hindu. All less than .5%.

same time in this younger class, both Zen Buddhism and atheism are represented, two entries that would have been unlikely in 1956.

Several questions naturally arise from these responses. First, why is there such a heavy population of Catholics? The answer to this question is speculative, at best. We posed the question to a number of officers, active and retired, and received these responses.

> My guess is that the strict discipline of a Catholic upbringing and its educational institutions have something to do with it. Can a DI be any more intimidating that a nun when you have not met expected standards of conduct? Probably not. Thus, the transformation into the Marine Corps for Catholics is less of a shock. Then there is the business of conservatism, strong beliefs and values, which I also find to be more consistent among Catholics than my fellow Protestants.
>
> A retired officer

> I think the values [between the church and the Corps] fit. What the formative Catholic education enforces in young people is consistent with the Marine Corps message.
>
> A retired officer

> The attraction of Catholics to the Marine Corps may have a partial explanation in racial or cultural terms. Most Hispanics are Catholic and they are attracted to the Marine Corps in numbers far out of proportion to their representation in the general population. There is a strong draw to "machismo" occupations for Hispanics. Thus, when a young man of Hispanic extraction is considering the military, he is more likely than others to choose the Marine Corps. This might not be a politically correct explanation but one would have a hard time convincing me otherwise.
>
> Active duty captain

Within these opinions and others may be the key to why Catholics flow into the Marine Corps' officer ranks in disproportionate numbers. The simple fact is that the phenomenon exists and neither I, nor anyone with whom I have discussed the subject, has come up with a supportable answer.

Marine officers from both generations come from families that attend religious services more frequently than the average U.S. family. Table 9.7 shows that 80 percent of the 3-56 Class attended religious services on a weekly basis. Sixty-one percent of Alpha Company 2000 were weekly churchgoers; 44 percent of all American families attend services that frequently.

The vast majority of officers from both generations were raised by two-parent families (89 percent in 3-56; 79 percent in Alpha 2000). (Unfortunately, we did not ask the two groups of officers if they were raised by their two "natural" or "original" parents, so the results may be overstated to a degree versus the data on U.S. Families.) (See Table 9.8.) However, even considering that potential overstatement, when one considers that the 1998 University of Chicago survey indicated that only 51 percent of children are being raised by their two original parents, the situation of the two officer groups is atypically high. It is directional evidence that leads us closer to the conclusion that men and women from "old-fashioned" or traditional families apparently are attracted to a structured, traditional culture.

The two generations received remarkably similar discipline, especially considering that 50 years separates them. One would expect that Dr. Spock and other more lenient child-rearing experts would have exerted more influence in reducing the percentage of young people being physically disciplined. That is not the case, at least with the two groups under study (see Table 9.9).

The generations are closely aligned in their assessment of the amount of discipline they received from their parents (see Table 9.10).

Both generations are almost identical in agreeing that the discipline they received played a key role in forming their personal values (see Table 9.11).

Parental example played a greater role in the formation of the values of two groups than did discipline, in the opinion of both groups. Again, the similarity of the results between the two groups is surprising (see Table 9.12).

Table 9.7
Attendance at Religious Services

"How frequently did you attend religious services while growing up?"

Frequency	% 3-56	% Alpha Co.	% of U.S. Families*
Almost never (0-5 times per year)	7%	18%	na
Occasionally (10-20 times per year)	13	17	na
Almost every week	80	61	44
No answer	0	4	na

*1995–1997 World Values Survey; University of Michigan

Table 9.8
Family Background

"Were you raised by two parents, a single father/mother, relatives or others?"

Raised By	% 3-56	% Alpha Co.	% of U.S. Families*
Two parents	89%	79%	51%
Single father	3	3	na
Single mother	6	12	na
Relative	3	2	na
Other	1	2	na

*General Social Survey—1998; National Opinion Research Center; University of Chicago

Table 9.9
Family Background—Discipline

"How were you disciplined while growing up? Physically (e.g., spanking), loss of privileges, or in other ways?"

Method	% 3-56	% Alpha Co.
Physically	72%	69%
Loss of privileges	65	73
Other	19	19
No answer	1	4

Table 9.10
Evaluating Parental Discipline

"How would you describe the discipline you received from your parent(s)? Not enough, about right or too much?"

Description	% 3-56	% Alpha Co.
Not enough	4%	3%
About right	92	87
Too much	3	5
No answer	1	5

Table 9.11
Discipline and Personal Value Formation

"What part did parental discipline play in the formation of your personal values?"

Description	% 3-56	% Alpha Co.
A great deal	64%	61%
Some	28	27
Very little	8	7
No answer	1	5

It is never surprising when a member of the older generation decries the slippage he or she perceives in societal values. What is unusual in this instance is that the younger group's opinion on the subject is so close to that of their older counterparts (see Table 9.13).

The opinions of the 3-56 Class and Alpha Company on the three most important influences on American society's values track very closely. The top

Table 9.12
Family—Parental Example

"What part did parental example play in the formation of your personal values?"

Description	% 3-56	% Alpha Co.
A great deal	80%	79%
Some	13	13
Very little	6	5
No answer	1	5

Table 9.13
Societal Values

"American society's values have declined in my lifetime. Agree or disagree?"

Percent in Agreement	
3-56	Alpha Co.
87%	77%

three influences cited by both groups (family values, morals and the media) were mentioned by 89 percent of 3-56 respondents and 70 percent of Alpha 2000 (see Table 9.14). The older generation of officers cited additional influences more often than the younger, as one would expect.

The 3-56 Class, in retrospect, cites more influences on their personal values than do the members of Alpha Company, which is not surprising as older people spend more time reflecting on such things. The striking numbers from Table 9.15 include the overwhelming percentage of respondents who cited their parents as the biggest influence on their values. The older generation, as one would expect, is far more reflective regarding the influence of God and religion and the Marine Corps on their value systems. The fact that the Marine Corps wasn't named by a larger percentage of the younger group supports my contention that many don't really understand its influence until later life.

Other than parents, the three biggest influences on the values of 3-56 members were teachers, coaches, and religious leaders (priest or pastor) (see Table 9.16). Alpha Company is in agreement with the first two influences cited by their seniors, but the members of Alpha Company apparently have not had the same experiences with their religious leaders as the older generation; only 5 percent named these as strong influences. It appears that friends, family friends, or neighbors have replaced religious leaders in terms of influence with the younger group.

Table 9.14
Societal Values—Influences

"If you agree, what influences have caused this decline in values?"

Influence	Percent of respondents mentioning 3-56	Alpha Co.
Declining family values/parent involvement	33%	31%
Decline of ethical/religious teaching/ moral standards	31	11
Media	25	28
Changes in society	18	3
Government input	15	4
Drugs	11	7
Lack of role models	10	4
Apathy/selfishness	8	10
Lack of respect for authority	8	3
Lack of discipline	8	4
Greed	5	3
Single parent homes	4	3
Crime	0	2
Technology	0	3
Other	7	14

Table 9.15
Main Influences on Personal Values

"Who (or what) has had the biggest influence on your personal value system?"

Influence	% 3-56	% Alpha Co.
Parents/father/mother	56%	67%
God/religion	27	13
Marine Corps	23	8
Family/relatives	15	4
Grandparents	6	4
Myself	3	4
Other	7	7

One measure of a generation is its heroes. Of course, heroes are determined by the times and circumstances in which young people find themselves. To see whom the two classes of lieutenants admired in their formative years and who they look up to today, we asked both to name their past and present heroes (see Table 9.17).

With the exception of sports figures and actors, there is little correlation between the older and younger generations insofar as early heroes are con-

Table 9.16
Other Influence on Personal Values

"Aside from your parents, were there other people who influenced your personal values? Who were they (teachers, coaches, etc.)?"

Influence	Percent of Respondents Mentioning 3-56	Alpha Co.
Teacher	57%	45%
Coach	35	45
Friend/ family friend/ neighbor	12	26
Religious leader (priest, pastor)	25	5
Relative	9	11
Grandparent	6	6
Sibling	1	5
Business leader	3	1

Table 9.17
Childhood Heroes

"Who were your heroes while growing up?"

Heroes	Percent of respondents mentioning 3-56	Alpha Co.
Sports figures	38%	20%
Military leaders/heroes	30	8
Political leaders	21	3
Actors	13	13
Father, mother, parents	11	36
Other family/relatives	6	8
Teachers	3	2
Comic book characters	2	8
God/religious leaders	1	5
None	0	17
Grandparents	0	7
Astronauts	0	4
Other	12	8

cerned. This suggests an avenue of inquiry that might help identify the reasons for such disparity in the responses of the two groups.

The first question is, "What were each generation's options in identifying with military heroes?" Military leaders are the second highest ranked heroes by the 3-56 Class. Their choices during World War II, when they grew up, were manifold. Names like Eisenhower, MacArthur, Patton, as well as every GI, sailor, Marine, or airman who was portrayed on the screens of their local movie theaters were heroes of the times. The members of Alpha Company were, for the most part, born between 1968 and 1973. By age ten, when heroes develop, their generation was far removed from any meaningful military actions that produced heroes about whom the country could agree. The Vietnam War had been closed out in the early 1970s, and America, wanting to forget that disruptive epoch in our history, either forgot or refused to give hero status to a generation of its fighting men and women.

The second question is, "What were the generation's options regarding political leaders in their formative years?" The older generation spent their growing years in an America led by Franklin Roosevelt, Harry Truman, and Dwight Eisenhower. In that time, presidents were considered by America's children to be almost God-like creatures. There was not the familiarity that exists today when politicians' lives are microscopically examined, with each flaw or mistake an occasion for a sound bite, or discussion by a group of talking heads. Under these entirely different circumstances, it is not difficult to determine why only 3 percent of the younger officers cited politicians as heroes.

Alpha Company 2000, on the other hand, appears to have looked for close-to-home heroes, with fathers, mothers, or both parents leading their hero list. As noted, actors, notably John Wayne, fared well with 13 percent of both groups claiming him among their heroes. However, in what may be more telling about this generation's formative years is the fact that 17 percent of the respondents listed "none" when asked about their childhood heroes.

Identifying the older generation's current heroes is a difficult task (see Table 9.18). Political leaders (mostly Ronald Reagan) claimed the votes of 25 percent of the class; military leaders (8 percent), family or relatives (8 percent), and parents (4 percent) trailed far behind. Alpha Company 2000 was much more

Table 9.18
Current Heroes

"Who are your heroes today?"

	Percent of respondents mentioning	
Heroes	3-56	Alpha Co.
Political leaders	25%	10%
Military leaders	8	8
Family/relatives	8	12
Father/mother/parents	4	41
Marines	4	6
John Glenn	3	4
Actors/entertainers	2	5
Grandparents	1	8
God/Jesus Christ	1	6
Warriors	1	1
None	0	19
Other	20	15

forthcoming about their current heroes: parents (41 percent), family or relatives (12 percent), political leaders (10 percent) and military leaders (8 percent) all were mentioned. As with Table 9.17, the second most frequently listed entry, 19 percent, was "none." One can only speculate why a significant number of young men and women would have no heroes at their early stage of adulthood or now. Perhaps this reflects some youthful cynicism resulting from negative images cast by leaders and celebrities on the world screen over the past few years. Or, perhaps they are just more realistic than older generations about "heroes."

We asked respondents to provide us with an importance ranking of a number of leadership principles and personal beliefs to compare the importance of these factors to the newest lieutenants in the Marine Corps and the older group. Respondents ranked items as very important, important, or not important. The objective was to determine the extent to which certain principles and beliefs are common to these two generations of officers, separated in time by almost 50 years (see Table 9.19).

Table 9.19
Leadership Principles and Personal Beliefs

"How important are these to your personal success and fulfillment?"

(Ranking: 1-33 Not Important; 34-66 Important; 67-100 Very Important)

Very Important	3-56	Alpha Co.
Personal integrity	94	97
Keeping commitments, regardless of difficulty	94	88
Providing the proper moral/ethical as well as professional example	91	95
Having a good marriage	89	91
Patriotism	85	88
Take care of the troops, they'll take care of you	85	94
Passing on your values to your children	85	92
Never ask others to do something you're not willing to do yourself	84	89
Marital fidelity	83	93
Being a good listener	82	88
Accepting responsibility for failure as well as success	77	82
Avoiding divorce, particularly if children are involved	74	88
Belief in God or a Higher Power	69	68
Not worrying about who gets credit for success if objective is met	67	48
Important		
Having children	58	46
Regular attendance at church, synagogue or mosque	55	26
Achieving professional success	47	70
Not Important		
A man should be the family "breadwinner"	31	13
Making money	25	15

We ranked the factors according to the rankings assigned based on the 3-56 Class responses. It is a remarkable comparison of the importance placed on certain principles and beliefs by both generations. The most significant differences are those in which one group considers a factor very important and the other group places it in the important ranking. In only three (out of 19) rankings of these principles and beliefs does this ranking difference occur.

First, the 3-56 Class placed "Not worrying about who gets credit for success if objective is met" in the very important rankings (67), but Alpha did not (48). One aspect of today's OCS is the intense pressure to perform individually as a leader. That pressure for individual recognition may be involved in this ranking, since the younger group had just recently graduated from OCS when this survey was completed.

Second, "Regular attendance at church, synagogue or mosque" was ranked important by the 3-56 Class (55). The members of Alpha Company assigned an unimportant rank (26) to this activity. There is little need to discuss how differently the younger and the older generations in America view church attendance. My experience leads me to believe that it is common for young people to view attendance at church as a secondary objective in their lives.

Third, Alpha Company assigned "Achieving professional success" a very important ranking (70); the older generation considered it important (47). Alpha 2000 is at the dawn of their professional lives and this importance ranking is understandable. The older generation feels less strongly about the factor.

The differences here are miniscule. There is a symmetry nothing short of remarkable in these importance rankings, gleaned from two such different groups of people.

The two generations are of one mind on five of the issues with 70 percent or more of the respondents in agreement. The issues range from judging a person's propensity to lie to whether it should be illegal to burn the flag (see Table 9.20).

There are two issues about which there is significant disagreement. The first involves whether the experimental use of drugs is part of growing up in America today. While majorities of both groups disagree with that assertion, a significant minority of Alpha Company (41 percent) agrees that this is the case. Our purpose here is not to determine who is and is not correct. On the other hand, Alpha Company is of today's society and culture to a far greater extent than the 3-56 members are, so we would tend to give weight to their opinions.

The second concerns whether living together before marriage is a good basis for a lasting union. Again, majorities disagree with the statement, but the younger group is evenly split with 48 percent in agreement versus 14 percent of the 3-56 Class.

The data in the tables indicate that 3-56 Basic Class and Alpha Company 2000 are very much alike, despite the fact that one group is in its seventh decade of life while the other is generally in its early twenties. Earlier, we discussed the cultural influences extant in the different Americas in which these

Table 9.20
Opinions on a Wide Range of Subjects

"Do you agree or disagree with the following statements?"

Statement	Percent in Agreement 3-56	Alpha Co.
More than 50% Agreement		
Public schools should teach patriotism, honesty, and moral/ethical behavior.	95%	91%
It is a person's duty to serve his/her country whenever asked.	88	84
Voluntary prayer should be allowed in public schools.	86	87
A person who lies about a small issue will lie about a large one.	80	80
It should be illegal to burn or desecrate the American flag.	76	74
Less than 50% Agreement		
Sexual orientation should not be a barrier to serving in the armed forces.	42	na
Affirmative Action is necessary to assure a level playing field.	25	15
Experimental use of recreational drugs is a part of growing up in America today.	22	41
Children raised in daycare centers are as well adjusted as those raised at home by a parent(s)	16	18
Living together prior to marriage is a good basis for a successful marriage.	14	48
Women should be allowed to serve in ground combat roles.	12	na
In a democracy it is dangerous if the military demands higher standards of conduct than are required in civilian society.	5	3

groups came of age. Given the cultural changes and societal upheavals of the last 50 years, one would expect to see two completely different worldviews in these officers, but we did not. Their demographics, attitudes, opinions, and personal values tracked so closely that it is clear that, in these two groups of respondents, the beliefs and principles that make up the their value systems are not the product of OCS, TBS, or membership in the fraternity of the Marine Corps. Certainly, the values that the Marine Corps treasures and claims for its own—honor, courage, and commitment—are enhanced and elevated to a prominent place in a Marine's life through training and exposure, but they are not established at OCS or TBS.

We conclude that these values are the products primarily of American families and secondarily of neighborhoods and schools where values were taught. This is a departure from a fairly common belief that Marine officers are, in large part, the products of difficult training with its heavy emphasis on discipline and Marine indoctrination. Certainly war fighting and tactical and sharpened leadership skills are results of these factors. The raw materials, however, are already ingrained in the successful candidate when he or she reports to OCS. The Marine officer training process is not the place where fearful, less-than-truthful, and uncommitted young people can "find themselves," contrary to what some might think. Courage, honor, and commitment, though perhaps not fully understood or closely embraced, but nevertheless present in the makeup of a candidate, are prerequisites to a successful completion of the journey to a Marine commission.

We conclude that a segment of American society produces the human raw material that can be molded into an officer of Marines. Those families tend to be fairly conservative in their social attitudes and are grounded in traditional values. The core values of Marine life are, in most officers, simply an extension of values to which the person was exposed within the family and its environs.

To review just how closely the two groups are aligned, let us consider a profile of a second lieutenant, based on our survey results. This profile would have been applicable in the 1950s and is it applicable today.

Placing myself in the position of a Marine Officer Selection Officer, I would use this profile in order to identify the officer candidate applicants who are most likely to successfully complete the difficult path to a Marine Corps commission. (Obviously, this profile would include assurances that the candidate meets the physical fitness and intellectual requirements.)

There is an adage among successful corporate recruiters. "A person is going to do about what he/she has done." In other words, "By the time a person is a junior in college, they have either established a strong leadership record, or they have not and probably will not." The recruiter will save a lot of time by focusing on specific leadership accomplishments, rather than looking for potential. By 20 or 21 years of age, leaders have established their base leadership credentials.

The same principle may be followed when interviewing or screening potential officer candidates. Discussion with an applicant of a representative number of the profile factors on the profile list should enable the recruiter to determine whether the candidate's background, attitudes, and values match up with this profile of previously successful candidates.

In the profile I have excluded two factors, those regarding gender and ethnicity. We have discussed the progress that the Marine Corps is making in the areas of female and minority accessions. The fact that our profile would identify being male and Causcasian as positive qualifying factors is unnecessary and somewhat misleading—misleading since the class of 3-56 contained no females and a miniscule number of minorities. The Marine Corps should and, based on my observations, does exert significant time and energy against its female and minority objective and should continue to do so. Finally, there is no reason why the profile we have developed would not be helpful and applicable in assessing the likelihood of a woman's or a minority's successful completion of OCS. (See Table 9.21.)

The obvious barriers to the acceptance of this profile include the following.

- The author is neither a statistician nor a market research expert. Our approach to the development of this survey and its analysis was to provide respondents with more

Table 9.21
Profile of a Lieutenant

A comparison of the backgrounds, opinions and beliefs of 3-56 Class and Alpha Company 2000

Profile Element	3-56	Alpha 2000
Believe a military organization should demand higher standards of conduct than are required in civilian society	95	97
Believe public schools should teach patriotism, honesty, ethical, moral behavior	95	91
Believe personal integrity is the most important factor in their personal success and fulfillment	91	97
Believe patriotism is very important	91	88
Were raised by two parents	89	79
Believe society's values have declined in their lifetimes	87	77
Believe it is a duty to serve his/her country whenever asked	88	84
Believe voluntary prayer should be allowed in public schools	86	87
Attended church weekly while growing up	80	61
A person who lies about a small issue will lie about a large one	80	80
Parental example played a large role in the formation of personal values	79	79
Were physically disciplined by parents	72	69
Are natives of the Northeast or Southern U.S.	70	63
Parental discipline played large role in the formation of their personal values	64	61
A teacher was a major influence on personal value system	57	45
Parents were biggest influence on value system	56	67
Father, mother or both parents were biggest influence on personal value system	56	67
From average income families	45	41
Are Roman Catholic	40	46
Believe declining family values, lack of parental involvement have lowered society's values	33	31

latitude in terms of qualifying their opinions than a market researcher would permit. I believe some of our more informative and interesting responses were a result of this decision, although it made life difficult for our market research company when tabulation time arrived.

- Of more consequence will be the criticism aimed at the conservative, traditional values and attitudes that emerged from the beliefs and attitudes of both TBS classes. Assertions will be offered that our profile does nothing more than maintain the status quo in the Marine Corps' officer ranks. Past studies of military officers generally and Marine officers specifically indicate that they lean toward social and political conservatism. Some of this criticism is thoughtful and enhances the debate over the role of the military in a democracy. Thomas Ricks (*Making the Corps*, 1997) is one such critic who should not be ignored whether agreeing or disagreeing with his thoughts on the subject. There are others, less thoughtful, who automatically respond negatively to the Marine culture and what they characterize as its estrangement from civilian culture. Perhaps oversimplified, critics of the Marine culture believe that the Corps brings liberally educated (in the political sense) American youth into its training machine and, through indoctrination, strict discipline, and some mysterious, but very effective brainwashing technique, turns these young people into conservative right-wingers who, in their view very likely may be a threat to the republic.

The corrective measures that these critics would apply to the Marine culture are sometimes simplistic and almost always based on little or no experience in military matters or knowledge of its history. "The Marine Corps needs to look more like American society. It needs to act more like American society, the society it is charged with defending. The Marine Corps should become more liberal and less conservative in its values. It should be civilianized."

This line of logic continues, "If only more politically and socially liberal officers could be recruited, then we (the critics) would feel more comfortable about the Corps and its relationship to civilian culture and society." This line of thought regarding the nation's military arises periodically in our country's history, generally when the country faces no immediate threats, and it abates when the military is involved in doing what it is trained to do—fight. The Gulf War provided the briefest of interludes and we do not know how long, if at all, the war on international terrorism will mute the civilianizers. Unpopular wars such as Vietnam, as well as peacekeeping and nation-building deployments, do not count and the military appears to be fair game during those times.

It should be noted that we, as a nation, have been through all this before. Unfortunately, in the post-World War II period, the "civilianizers" of the American Army won their case. The effects of that action during the early days of the Korean conflict were tragic, in terms of the human lives lost due to this move to make our Army more reflective of American society. Theodore R. Fehrenbach, in his book *This Kind of War: A Study in Unpreparedness* (1963), describes the slippery slope we discovered we were on when our civilianized Army was required to do its basic job: to fight in combat. "But the greatest weakness of the American Army [in the early days of the Korean War] was not in its numbers or its weapons, pitiful as they were."

The United States Army, since 1945 had, at the demand of the public, been civilianized. The men in the ranks were enlistees, but these were the new breed of American regular, who, when they took up the soldier, had not even tried to put aside the citizen. They were normal American youth, no better, no worse than the norm, who though they wore the uniform were mentally, morally, and physically unfit for combat, for orders to go out and die. They wore the uniform, but they were still civilians at heart. . . . But Harry Truman, President, had not true legions. He had a citizen Army, backed by civilians who neither understood nor approved the dangerous game. . . . Citizens, unless they hear the clarion call, or the angel's trumpet, are apt to be a rabble in arms. (Fehrenbach 1963, p. 59)

Later, Fehrenbach comments on the Marine Corps which had been spared the civilianizing efforts of the cultural elite of the times.

> Marine human material was not one whit better than that of the human society from which it came. But it had been hammered into form in a different forge, hardened with a different fire. The Marines were the closest thing to legions the nation had. They would follow their colors from the shores of home to the seacoast of Bohemia and fight well either place. (Fehrenbach, 1963, p. 130)

In the United States of America, 285 million strong, 1,400–1,600 new Marine second lieutenants are commissioned each year. When they receive their commission they take an oath that requires allegiance to the Constitution of the United States of America. It is the officer's job to remain apolitical, subject to the civilian government he or she is honor bound to protect.

Regardless, America must always be watchful over its military. We spend extremely large sums of money to fund it, equip it, make it the best in the world. We must keep it under control, a deadly weapon to be brandished only rarely, but with great effect. At the same time, the military must be allowed to develop and maintain a culture that supports and enhances its ability to carry out its obligation to protect our nation and its interests. It should not be subject to whim or to experiments concocted in the social science classrooms of our universities or by the leadership of pressure groups who have their interests, not the nation's, in mind.

It would appear logical that Americans would be more concerned that their Marines are trained, equipped, motivated, and ready to carry out their missions in defense of this country than about the political leanings of its officer ranks. Most Americans are not overly concerned about the religious preference of their physician or car mechanic if that person can heal their body or repair their auto. Should the same principle hold true in a political sense for those who must go in harm's way when the nation calls? Is the political philosophy of a general or major or second lieutenant important if, through skill and training, he can lead his unit to achieve its objective, at the same time doing everything possible to minimize casualties among his Marines? Should a culture be criticized because it holds its members to a standard of conduct that is higher than that required of civilian citizens? Most Americans do not care about the political leanings of officers as long as those officers are guided by, and faithful to, their oath to serve only the Constitution of the nation. That is, after all, how it should be.

10

A Legacy of Honor

> Character is a by-product; it is produced in the great manufacture of daily duty.
>
> Woodrow Wilson

The faded newspaper photo, clipped by my mother from the *Cincinnati Times-Star*, one of the city's two afternoon newspapers of the time, is almost 50 years old now. The caption reads, "Xavier Students Join the Marines." I am in that picture, taken in 1953, with several other young men. Mike Conaton was a teammate of mine when Xavier football teams competed with Boston College, Cincinnati, Miami, Villanova, Marshall, and the Marines from Quantico. Mike, now chairman of the board of the Midland Company, at one time did double duty as the CEO of his company and acting president of Xavier University. Chuck Kirkhoff, another football player in the photo, died in the crash of his Marine jet while on an exercise in the Caribbean in the late 1950s.

Not pictured are two other Xavier students who earned their Marine commissions, Simon Leis and James Schwartz. Leis has served Cincinnati and Hamilton County as county prosecutor, common pleas court judge, and sheriff of Hamilton County for more than 40 years. His well-publicized courtroom combat with Larry Flynt over the sale of *Hustler* magazine in the 1960s was the subject of a Woody Harrelson movie in the late 1990s. James "Dutch" Schwartz, one of my closest college friends and another football player, earned the moniker "Commando" Schwartz while serving in the 6th Marines for his love of night operations. Schwartz managed Dart Industries manufacturing operations for many years before starting his own successful business in the Phoenix area.

When I look at that picture and think about the Marines I have known over the years, I realize that these men are typical. They get involved. They raise fine families. They contribute to their communities. They fight for what they think is right. They may, like Simon Leis, be fighting a holding action against the forces of new age "enlightenment," but they are not just in the contest—they are leading the fight.

What did the men of the 3-56 Basic School Class do with their lives? What was important to them and how did they contribute?

- The average member of the 3-56 Class has 3.3 children and 4.9 grandchildren.
- Only 21 percent of the respondents have been divorced. Even among our older generation, this is a low divorce rate.

The class contributed its share of leadership to the Marine Corps and honorable service to our country.

- Four of its members achieved flag rank.
- 29.9 percent of the class served more than 10 years combined active and reserve service.
- 18.5 percent of the class spent 20 years or more on active duty.
- A number of officers served in Vietnam, and five died in the line of duty.
- Four were awarded the Silver Star for bravery in Vietnam.
- One member completed three tours of duty (39 months) in Vietnam.

The majority of the 3-56 Class returned to civilian life after serving their active duty tours. What did they do with their lives?

- 14.1 percent owned their own business.
- 10.1 percent were involved in college teaching or administration.
- 10.1 percent were involved in high school teaching, coaching, or administration.
- 9.4 percent were judges or attorneys.
- 8.1 percent were company chairmen or presidents.
- 8.1 percent were engineers.
- 8.1 percent were sales or marketing managers at national or regional level.
- 7.4 percent were company vice presidents.
- 5.4 percent were FBI agents or other law enforcement officers.

It is not surprising that these men attacked civilian life with the "out front" philosophy they learned in the Corps. A concentration of leadership achievement is evident here that is seldom found outside the country's better graduate programs, not just in business and law, but also in the education of our young people.

What a person does for a living is just one facet of life. What kind of person, what kind of citizen did these men become? One measure of a person comes from finding out what they are proud of accomplishing. We asked the 3-56 Class, "What are you proudest of in your life?" The answers were, in one respect, remarkably similar. The vast majority placed family, children, or their marriage high on their "proudest of" list. They then listed other accomplishments.

- 74.0 percent family and children
- 53.8 percent personal success

- 34.8 percent serving in the USMC
- 19.8 percent serving the community
- 16.5 percent being a good father/person/husband
- 7.6 percent academic achievements.

These percentages cannot convey the intensity and feeling of some of the answers we received. Here are some excerpts drawn from the responses of 157 men, who are looking at life, and what has been important to them, through the looking glass of almost 70 years.

> Having raised four great children, each of whom is self-sufficient and pursuing an area of their own interest. . . . The love I feel for them and that which I believe they have for me is my greatest achievement.
>
> Richard A. Burns, William Jewell College PLC

> I consider myself an average American citizen who has been blessed with a normal American life. . . . I was raised in a Christian home, received a college education, served my country in the USMC, went to work and earned an adequate living while marrying my wife of 39 years and raising three beautiful children. No honor or achievements that have come my way during this time can replace the feeling of accomplishment I have for living a normal American life.
>
> James M. "Spud" Chandler, Middle Tennessee State University PLC

> My proudest professional accomplishment is raising two fine children, now both adults, who have proven to be people of character, as well as of intelligence and accomplishment. . . . As CBS News Saigon Bureau Chief at the height of the war I was given all of the resources I asked for and complete independence in pursuing the story of the war in a way that I thought portrayed and clarified it for the benefit of our viewers at home. Despite modern revisionism, most journalists, and I was among them, were initially in favor of U.S. intervention in Vietnam. I soured on the war as I saw it become first unwinnable, and then a source of corruption and decay for our armed services.
>
> Edward M. Fouhy, University of Massachusetts PLC

> A truly tremendous wife who blessed me with three loving children. Even were I fortunate to have acquired notoriety in a professional sense, like making Forbes' Billionaire's List, nothing could surpass the family experiences and our growing with our kids into their adult lives.
>
> Tom Regan, Seton Hall PLC

> I'm proudest, by far, of the family Barbara and I have engendered and the grandchildren which have followed. The personal achievements and setbacks pale in comparison. I think I can safely say that at least 30 people will miss me when I go. That ain't all bad!
>
> Peter F. Wegman, Marquette University PLC

> My five children have strong values, are totally without racist, sexist or other damaging attitudes. My 36 years in education—the lives I saved and the people I helped to find themselves and turn their lives into something.
>
> Robert H. McGlynn, SUNY-Brockport PLC

> In my FBI career I received 54 commendations in 22 years, many involving very dangerous situations. I had to use firearms three times against armed felons. My training and experience as a Marine officer helped in planning and leading many raids and dangerous assignments.
>
> John F. McGivney, Iona College PLC

> Raising five children who are basically good, honest, caring human beings and who are all engaged in careers that improve the life and health of other people.
>
> Phil Schweri, Tulane NROTC

> My coaching—103 wins, 61 losses, 8 ties. The players who have been successful and come back to thank me for the help they got in school. If I had to do it all over again, I'd change very little . . . most of all, my wife of 44 years.
>
> James L. Wilson, Redlands University PLC

> The large number of my subordinates (in the Marine Corps) that achieved commissions and the large number that still stay in contact with me.
>
> Chester V. Lynn, Indiana University PLC (deceased)

> Family life with sons who have their feet solidly on the ground. Three years of night school and the Marine Corps assigned me to school for my fourth year. I graduated from the University of Maryland 21 years after I left high school. [Author's note: Wally Fogo joined the Marines during World War II. In his career he served in China, Korea, and Vietnam, a three-war veteran. He earned a field commission in Korea and was already a first lieutenant when he joined the 3-56 Class as it went through Basic School. Wally had already served in two wars and must have shuddered at the antics of us fresh-out-of-college second lieutenants.]
>
> Wally Fogo, received field commission (Korean War)

In the multitude of thoughts on this subject sent to us by the 3-56 Class, the importance of family comes through almost to a man. After that comes the importance placed on service to others and the community. That is how these old Marines have lived their lives. How much of an influence on their lives were the Marine Corps training and their leadership experience? According to my classmates, much of what they are is a result of their Marine leadership experience. I believe that.

Based on what these men have revealed to us in their responses to our survey, they came to the Corps with those values of family and service already in place. The Marine Corps certainly clarified and helped our class articulate those values, but I am convinced they were present the day we entered the Corps.

Do Marines join the Corps in order to be exposed to its value system? Or, do they join because they are looking for an organization that supports a value system they already possess? I am inclined to believe that, in the case of its officers, the Marine Corps attracts men and women whose backgrounds and upbringing are closely attuned to the Marines' Core Values of Honor, Courage, and Commitment.

An important conclusion to be drawn from our study is that this country produces, in every generation, people who possess the desire and ability to set out upon a singularly difficult course. The sole benefit is that of belonging to an exclusive fraternal organization dedicated to the service of the country, and just as dedicated to the welfare of the enlisted personnel who must do the nation's heavy lifting. There are numerous other reasons, too, but it is selfless service to this great land that lies at the heart of it all. The Marine Corps is the most visible and available road for those who come to adulthood searching for a place to prove themselves, searching for a place to serve. The Marine Corps is such a place.

I am proud of my generation of officers of Marines. We were not bloodied like the generations of World War II and the Korean War. Yet one out of five of our class served the nation for 20 years or more, and some died in the line of duty. But, for the most part we were very lucky. Most of the class returned to civilian life and impacted that world through honorable lives, the seeding and cultivation of their families with values for a lifetime, and service to others.

A generation can only meet the challenges that the forces of history and fate place in its path on its journey through this world. For most of the lives of the 3-56 Class, a huge portion of our country's military, intellectual and economic resources were focused on our struggle with the Soviet Union. Ultimately, America's free people, coupling the creativity born of freedom and a grudging willingness to pay the price for victory, brought down the rusted, corrupt systems spawned by anemic collectivism. Once the Berlin Wall fell, America's attention seemed to be diverted to some issues that, today, pale into insignificance given the events that took place one sunny September morning in 2001.

On that day we received the message that our homeland is not immune to the ravages of skillful, determined adversaries. We have known for a long time that this world is a dangerous place. September 11, 2001, brought another fact to light. For the first time since early in our history, Americans cannot assume that they are beyond the reach of malevolent, alien forces, even here on our native soil.

The conflicts in such a world will be misty, shadowy affairs, requiring exceedingly well-trained, disciplined, motivated and morally courageous people. Fortunately for America, we possess such men and women. Some of them are Marines and, when America calls, her Marines will respond. Out front will be a young lieutenant, ready to lead, ready to share the sacrifices and hardships he and his Marines will encounter. He will be the salt of the American earth—one of the best his nation can offer. He'll be one of us.

Epilogue

It is uncomfortable in America to discuss things religious. In the 1950s there were three subjects that were off limits in the wardroom (the officers' dining area aboard a US Navy ship). Discussions about politics, women or religion were not permitted. Since today's wardrooms contain women officers, at least one of these taboos has been eliminated.

We will march ahead, though, believing that Marines, old and current as well as friends of the Corps, will understand the appropriateness of closing a book about the United States Marine Corps with a prayer. After all, it is not Marine marching music that raises the hackles on an old Marine's neck or moistens the eyes. No, it is *The Marine's Hymn*. As I have concluded in this work, the men and women we have observed and studied simply reflect solid, Main Street America. Like most Americans, they lean on a God of their individual choosing. Unlike most Americans, however, these people are in a business in which they expect to face dangerous, life-threatening situations. It would be understandable if, perhaps, they lean on Him more frequently than we civilians do.

The following prayer was offered at a Marine Corps Birthday Ball by a Navy chaplain whose name, unfortunately, is unknown.

O Lord, we have long known that prayer should include confession. Therefore, on behalf of the Marines and their guests gathered here tonight, I confess their sins.

Lord, they're just not in step with today's society. They are unreasonable in clinging to old-fashioned ideas like patriotism, duty, honor, and country. They hold radical ideas, believing that they are their brother's keeper and responsible for the Marine on their flank. They have been seen standing when colors pass, singing the National Anthem at ball games, and drinking toasts to fallen comrades. Not only that, they have been observed standing tall, taking charge and wearing their hair unfashionably short.

They have taken Teddy Roosevelt's and John Kennedy's words too seriously and are overly concerned with what they can do for their service and country instead of what it can do for them. They take the Pledge of Allegiance to heart and believe that their oath is to be honored. And, they know well what the definition of "is" is. Forgive them, Lord, for being stubborn men and women who hold these values as genuine. They are aware of the price of honor and with total command of their spirit, they have been willing to pay that price. After all what more can you expect? They're Marines!

O Lord our God, bless these men and women of ideals, continue to raise up in this nation strong leaders and deliver us from "me first" managers and "don't ask me" followers. Be our honored guest this day, O Lord, and join with us in laughter, good food, good drink, and the telling of tall tales and legends that may occasionally exceed the truth.

We bow our heads to those who were lost in places that had names meaningless until the mud-Marines landed, and in that mud reaffirmed the one legacy that brings all Marines together by the blood and tears shed for service of country and each other. Watch over and keep safe all those who wear this nation's uniform with special attention to their families and loved ones everywhere.

With brandy and cigar in hand, I salute you all through this day and all the following nights and days ahead. God bless you, God bless this great nation—and God bless the United States Marine Corps.

Semper fi and Amen.

Appendix

3-56 OFFICERS BASIC COURSE ROSTER

E (ECHO) COMPANY

Company Commander: Major Autry, Robert L.*
1st Platoon Commander: Captain Smith, George W.
2nd Platoon Commander: Captain Woods, John L.
3rd Platoon Commander: Captain Van Den Elzen, James R.
4th Platoon Commander: 1st Lieutenant Martinelli, Joseph

Aberton, John E.*
Abraham, Louis R.*
Adams, Nolan F.
Adams, Thomas G.
Agnew, Thomas J.
Ahles, Robert J.*
Akeson, Thomas F.*
Alexander, John C.T.
Alexander, Robert L.
Alwan, Harold J.*KIA
Anderson, Neal F.
Anglea, Bert A.*
Arbiter, Jan J.
Arnick, John S.
Aspinall, Carl E.
Atherton, George W.
Atwell, Wayne O.
Austin, Howard B.*
Baggett, Robert L.
Baker, George A., III
Baker, William H.
Banks, Howard D.
Barner, George B.*
Barwick, Hugh B.
Bateman, John H.
Bearce, Denny N.
Becerra, Rafael A., Jr.*
Beck, Peter S.
Becker, Raymond A.
Belin, Carl A., Jr.
Bench, Dan A.
Benson, Richard D.
Bishop, Dan R.*
Blackwell, Clay D.
Blasingame, Ben C.
Blodgett, Stephen W., Jr.
Bloom, Allen E.
Blue, Frank L., III
Bogan, Robert T., Jr.
Bojanowski, Joseph C.
Bowlin, Jerry T.
Brace, William A.
Brandt, Loren A.
Bren, Donald L.
Brennan, Joseph P.
Brennan, William J., III
Bricker, James A.
Brown, Robert B.
Buchanan, Ray E.
Buechlein, Charles A.

Bullen, Dana R., II
Burlison, Bill D.
Burnham, Robert G.
Burns, Jack D.*
Burns, Richard A.
Burns, Robert J.P.
Burrow, Arnold G.
Cady, Richard C., Jr.*
Cahill, Ronald J.*
Calhoon, Richard R.
Calleton, Theodore, E.
Campbell, Bobby A.
Campbell, Jack A.
Campbell, Joseph G., Jr.
Cannon, Floyd E.
Cappa, Arthur P.
Carbonar, Vincent A.*
Cardone, Albert A.
Carlstrom, Bradley J.*
Carney, Robert T.
Carrico, James W.
Cerninka, Edward
Chabysek, Herbert F., Jr.*
Chandler, James M.
Cherrie, Hubert B., II
Ciuba, Charles H.
Clements, Jamie H.
Clevenger, Richard E.
Cody, George L., Jr.*
Coman, Joseph M.
Compton, James L.*
Connors, Jeremiah, P.
Connors, John W.
Conway, Charles G.
Conway, Martin J.
Cook, William E.
Cornell, John S.
Costigan, John V.
Crawford, William G.
Cray, Harold L., Jr.
Creamer, Lex, Jr.
Crossingham, Charles E.
Cummings, Walter D.
Curran, Thomas H.
Curtis, Donald R.
D'Aluisio, Nicholas, J.
Daly, David J.*
Davis, James H.
Day, William O.
De Bus, William J.
De Jarnett, Theron E., Jr.
De Jesu, Oliver J.*
De John, Robert J.
Deep, David P.
Deibler, Harold J.
Del Priore, Anthony W.
Dentz, Edward S.
Depwe, Raymond
Dettle, Christian J.
Devin, Cedric E.
DiSalvo, Joseph A.
Dill, Glenn V.
Dolan, John T.
Donahue, John F.
Donohue, Paul Q.
Donovan, Walter J.
Dowling, Edmund H.
Downes, Sheldon C.
Doyle, Raymond J.
Driscoll, Robert
Duffy, Brian T.
Duffy, John F.
Dumais, Richard A.*
Duncan, John J.
Dunleavy, Anthony J.
Dunn, Frank A., Jr.
Durand, Charles C.*
Dyer, Robert
Eaton, Frank G.
Eckert, Fredereich D.
Edwards, Dean E.
Erber, Lewis A., Jr.*
Facklam, Arnold W., Jr.
Fell, John R., Jr.*
Fistori, Paul D.
Fleming, Neil S.
Flynn, Jackson E.*
Flynn, John J.F.*
Fogo, Wallace E.
Fouhy, Edward, M.
Fox, Clifford G.
Friske, John D.
Fuchs, Frederic K.
Gaido, John J., Jr.*
Galleher, Edward G.
Gargano, Frank W.

Gee, Billie F.
Gerleman, Loren D.
Giampetro, Alex N.*
Gianotti, Jerome R.
Gido, John M.
Giles, William G.
Gillespie, Thomas E., Jr.
Gilmore, James D.
Gobeil, Paul A.*
Goham, James E.
Goldburg, Jay B.
Goldstein, Robert G.
Goodman, John C.
Gorham, Thomas F., Jr.
Griffith, Edward T., Jr.
Heneghan, John J.
Kum, Byong Oak (ROK)*
Lindberg, Charles B.
McCloskey, John P.
McCoy, Herbert A.*
Morris, Donney Z.
Pach, Donald M.
Parsons, Theodore R.
Perry, Donald G.
Peterson, Edward D.R.
Peterson, Lee A.
Phelps, J.W.*
Pyo, Myon Ik (ROK)
Reed, Ronald C.*
Regan, Thomas F.
Rosenstihl, William J.
Schmidt, James M.
Wadsworth, Michael G.
Yezzi, Richard C.

*deceased
KIA killed in action
ROK Republic of Korea Marine Corps

F (FOX) COMPANY

Company Commander: Major Holzbauer, Joseph F.*
1st Platoon Commander: Captain Duncan, William B.
2nd Platoon Commander: Captain Armstrong, Peter F.
3rd Platoon Commander: Captain Dinegar, Wilber W.
4th Platoon Commander: 1st Lieutenant Walsh, James A.*

Bradford, Thomas A., Jr.*
Chung, Woo Yong (ROK)
Grace, Charles B., Jr.
Grana, Lewis J.
Gravely, Marion S., Jr.
Greenwell, Robert S.
Griffing, Terry S.
Griffis, John H.
Gustafson, Bruce A.
Hack, Joseph F.*
Haggerty, Paul B.
Haidinger, Robert N.
Hall, Stephen S.J.
Hampton, Bill R.
Hancock, Thomas W., Jr.
Hankins, Ralph D.*
Hannah, Todd G.
Hargrave, Charles C., II
Hazell, Roger K.*
Herlihy, Horace F.
Hill, David G.
Hillyer, Roger D.
Hodge, Robert A.
Hoffman, Russell E.
Hoiles, Edwin K.
Holcomb, Donald D.
Hollis, Claude H., Jr.
Holmberg, Donald E.
Hoover, William G.*
Horton, John H., Jr.
Hurlburt, Victor C.
Hurney, Francis C.*
Hutchins, George M.
Huther, William H.
Jackson, W. David
Jaczko, Eugene S., Jr.*
Janovy, David L.
Jewell, Robert H., Jr.
Johnston, Jerry T.
Jones, David M.*

Jones, Paul D.
Jones, Stanley B.
Jordano, Pete C.
Kallerges, Leonidas J.
Kane, Matthew J.
Kazmierczak, Eugene J.
Keese, John M., IV
Kenworthy, Richard J.*
Kernan, William W.*
Kerr, Jack R.
Kesser, Gilbert R.
Kilcarr, John E.
King, David W.
King, Paul D., Jr.
Kingree, Ben, III
Kirsch, William W.
Knight, Frank P.
Korbakes, Chris A.
Kotrba, Robert H.
Krauss, Walter J., Jr.*KIA
Krebs, William L., Jr.*
Krug, Richard L.
Kuttner, Ludwig G.
La Bonte, Jovite, Jr.
LaValle, Gerald J.
Landauer, Charles D.
Landry, Robert H.
Lang, Ronald E.
Lawhorn, John L.
Lawless, Donald M.
Lay, Bobby A.
Leary, David N.
Lee, Alex
Lethin, Ronald R.
Liebman, John R.
Liebmann, J.G., III
Lietz, John B.
Long, William B.
Longobardi, Robert F.
Lower, Frederick J., Jr.
Lowrie, James F.
Lynch, Thomas K.
Lynn, Chester V.*
MacFarlane, John L.*
MacIntosh, Landis
Maciag, George E.
Mahon, Cornelius P.
Maiocco, Joseph F., Jr.
Messersmith, Frank L.
Mancini, Benedict V.
Marckx, John E.
Marean, David F.
Marino, Frank P., Jr.*
Markley, William J.
Marlar, Richard L.
Marshall, John T.
Marston, Martin M., Jr.
Martin, James M.
Martin, Joel A.*
Martin, Robert S., Jr.
Martini, John J.
Massey, James L.
Maurer, Robert T.
Mauro, Anthony
Mavretic, Josephus L.
Maxwell, Robert S.
Mayes, Francis B.
Mazzoni, Donald R.
McCaffrey, Richard
McCall, Curtis S.
McCarthy, Joseph E.
McClave, James G.
McClay, James J., Jr.
McClung, Conrad O.
McCoy, Merle C.
McDaniel, Clarence E.
McDavid, James E., III
McDermott, Paul M.
McDonald, Bradley G.
McDowell, John D.
McEwan, John M.*
McFadden, John F.
McGivney, John F.
McGlynn, Robert H.
McGrath, William J.
McGuire, Dennis A.
McGuire, James E.
McLaughlin, Daniel V.
McLoone, Richard J.
McMann, James A.*
McMillin, John W.
McNair, Wylie D.
Meeth, John C., Jr.*
Meiners, Joseph B., Jr.*
Mejia, Robert P.
Merrigan, Francis G.

Messenger, Roy P.
Mikkelson, Donald D.
Miley, George P.
Miller, David P.
Miller, Michael
Mlodzik, Donald R.
Mooney, Robert F.
Moore, John M.*
Moore, Robert S.*LOD
Moreton, James C.
Morgan, Harvey J.
Moriarty, Neil F.*
Morris, Marvin
Mulcahy, Robert D.
Muller, Richard H.
Mulrooney, Michael J.*
Murphy, Donald G.
Murphy, Joseph T.
Muse, George P.
Musilli, John A.
Muzio, Joseph N.
Nash, James J.
Newman, Dewey L.
Newton, Carl W.
Nichols, Charles W.
Nichols, Donald L.
Niemeier, John F.
Nolan, William F.
Orio, Carl D.
Osborne, William B.*
Ous, Frederick E.
Patane, Robert J.
Peters, James B., III
Powers, Robert F.
Riordon, Robert R.
Roach, James L.
Sandlin, Ray L.
Sellitto, James G.
Siano, James J.
Springett, William J.
Stephens, Hugh W.
Stephenson, Glenn, Jr.
Stoutt, Bradley A.
Stukey, Francis E.
Swartwood, Theodore M.
Trotter, Richard P.
Vernay, Vincent A.
Waldorf, Richard J.
Watts, John S.
Yeu, Hyun Soo (ROK)*

*deceased
KIA killed in action
ROK Republic of Korea Marine Corps
LOD died in line of duty

G (GOLF) COMPANY

Company Commander: Major Timme, William G.*
1st Platoon Commander: Captain Oltermann, John J.
2nd Platoon Commander: Captain Meyers, James F.*
3rd Platoon Commander: Captain Rice, William H.
4th Platoon Commander: 1st Lieutenant McElheny, Ralph A.

Beazell, John C.
Berendzen, Robert H.
Borjeson, Richard A.
Bozovich, Stanley
Brines, Milo D.
Broderick, John W.
Bucci, Manfredo M.*
Buhler, Jay D.
Burke, John J., Jr.
Cantello, Albert A.
Cheadle, William G.
Chitjian, Markar
Comer, Richard A.
Cox, Gerald L.*
Curry, Allen M.*
Ebberts, Ronald A.
Farmer, Lawrence
Fentriss, James F.
Gates, Delivan W., Jr.
Harrison, Robert A.
Hwang, Man Ho (ROK)
James, Reed H.

Janis, Leopold
Keane, Robert M.
Kelly, John G.*
Kim, Hi Wuk (ROK)
Kisselle, Charles T.
Lawr, William T., Jr.
Licata, Peter J.*
Lohr, James B.
Lohr, Jimmy L.
Lucas, Richard A.
Meserve, Richard C.*
Millington, Seth F.
Moore, Edward C.
Moran, Donald M.*
Noll, Richard A.*
Norman, Ronald E.
Norwood, Alan A.*
O'Brien, Richard A.
O'Brien, Robert L.
O'Callahan, Juan C.
O'Keefe, Arthur J.
O'Rear, Charles W., Jr.
O'Shea, Donald J.*
O'Toole, Patrick E.
Ogden, Don J.
Ortman, Herman W.
Parke, Charles F.*
Petrarca, Emidio D.*
Phillips, Reed, Jr.
Pickering, Cyrenius C.
Pikoulas, Donald G.
Pilato, Louis A.
Pitts, Frank D.
Place, Roy E.
Poche, Adolph J., Jr.
Porter, Leonard E.
Porter, Robert R.,
Prestia, Philip J.
Prevost, Donald D.
Pyburn, Dwain I.
Quinn, John P., Jr.
Rachfalski, Vincent J.
Radoycich, Mischa R.*
Raines, Henry R.
Raitt, George D.
Rams, Edward F.
Rayburn, Edward A.
Redding, Billy B.
Regan, Frank C., Jr.
Reis, Thomas M.
Reno, James T.
Richardson, Samuel B., Jr.
Rieger, Clement J.
Riggs, Adrian L.
Riley, George R.*
Roberts, Donald G.
Robertson, Robert S.
Roche, John L.*
Rogers, Thurlo P.*
Rohloff, Carl A.*
Rosser, Jimmy L.
Rossing, Philip S.
Rourk, John W., Jr.
Roush, John G.
Rowe, Lawrence C.
Ruppert, Jack
Ryan, Thomas J.
Safford, Robert O.
Sailer, Frank J.*
Sales, Edwin D.
Sales, James B.
Salvati, Ralph J.
Sanders, Joe P.
Schaffer, William A.
Schneider, John F.*
Schneider, William L.
Schweri, Philip A.
Scott, Alton A.*
Scotto, Vincent J.
Sergeant, Robert A.
Shearer, John W.
Sheridan, Lawrence D.
Sheridan, Robert F.
Sheridan, William L.
Siragusa, Frank T.
Skelton, Charles A.
Smith, Alexander P.
Smith, Charles L.
Smith, Kenneth L.
Smith, Roy A.
Sneddon, Alexander R.
Sonnen, Charles J., II
Spaete, Robert P.
Spence, Dale W.
Stankus, Donald P.
Stannard, Robert A.

Stark, Homer M.
Stauffer, Robert M.
Steele, Andrew M.
Steele, Orlo K.
Steely, Carl V.
Stith, Edward E.
Strain, Walter L.
Straub, Peter B.
Strawther, Dexter, III
Stultz, Richard N.
Sumner, Thomas B., Jr.
Swanson, Carl R.
Szafranski, Leonard J., Jr.
Szott, John A.
Talamantez, Henry S.
Thomas, Calhoun, Jr.*
Thomas, Landon, Jr.
Thompson, Jack C.
Thompson, Milton S.
Thrash, Robert E.
Toben, Theodore J., Jr.
Tobin, Richard J.
Tomaszkiewicz, Mitchell
Tonini, Franklin J.
Toomey, Thomas E.
Torpie, Richard J.P.
Townley, Edward F., Jr.
Trask, Orville L.
True, Robert H.
Tuton, Garland W.
Valente, Edwin E.
Vigiano, Dominic R.
Vogelsinger, Bruce E.
Vogelsinger, Roger J.
Von Glahn, Jack F.
Wade, Carey J.D., Jr.*
Walker, Charles A.
Walker, Rinaldo A.
Walsh, Donald E.*
Wean, William E.
Weaner, John W.
Week, Thurlow
Wegmann, Peter F.
Weinhofer, Ludwig J.
Weinlader, James R.
Welch, Richard M.
Whaley, William M.
Whirty, Robert F.
Whitton, Frank H.
Wilkerson, Melvin, Jr.*
Williams, James P.*LOD
Williams, John C., III
Wilson, Donald G.
Wilson, James L.
Wilson, Samuel H.*
Wingo, Taylor*
Winoski, Walter M.*
Winsor, Fred L.
Winter, Herman W.*
Witthoft, David G.
Wohlrab, James J.
Wood, Charles D., III
Worrell, James A.
Worthy, David B.
Wray, Ronald N.
Wright, Donald E.
Wright, Grover C., Jr.
Zimdahl, Robert L.
Zimmerman, John A.

*deceased
KIA killed in action
ROK Republic of Korea Marine Corps
LOD died in line of duty

Glossary of Marine Corps Terminology

AI: Assistant Instructor at The Basic School
Aye, aye, Sir/Ma'am: I have heard and understand instructions and will carry them out
Billet: A position, job; generally in reference to a candidate at OCS or a lieutenant at TBS
Bulkhead: Wall
Bunk: Bed (also called a rack)
Cattle Car: A covered trailer, used to carry troops
Chit: A written note (either an evaluation or authorization)
Chow: Food
CO: Commanding Officer
Deck: Platform or floor
Detail: A special task or a number of people who perform a special task
DI: Drill Instructor—Parris Island or San Diego Recruit Depots
Field Day: Cleanup of the assigned area of a barracks or classroom
FEX: Field exercise
FFEX: Field firing exercise
FMF: Fleet Marine Force
Gear: Equipment or belongings
GI Can: A large metal rubbish can or wastebasket
Gunny: Gunnery Sergeant (GYSGT)
Hatch: Door or doorway opening in the deck or overhead
Head: Toilet
HQMC: Headquarters, Marine Corps
IOC: Infantry Officers Course
Irish pennant: Any strap or piece of equipment flapping in the breeze
LOD: Line of departure
MCP: Meritorious Commissioning Program
MECEP: Marine Enlisted Commissioning Education Program
MOOTW: Military operations other than war
MOS: Military Occupation Specialty
Nasty: Replaces a universe of profane terms formerly used to describe un-Marinelike gear or personnel
NCO: Non-commissioned officer: corporal or sergeant

NROTC: Naval Reserve Officer Training Corps
OCC: Officer Candidate Course
OCS: Officer Candidates School—encompasses training of all candidates, including PLC, OCC, NROTC
Overhead: Ceiling
PCP: Platoon command post
PI: Primary Instructor at TBS
PLC: Platoon Leaders Course
Pogey Bait: Candy, sweets, snack food
ROE: Rules of engagement
SI: Sergeant Instructor: SNCO responsible for training OCS candidates
Sliming: Any unmilitary posture or manner of walking
SNCO: Staff non-commissioned officer: SSGT, GYSGT, FSGT
SOP: Standard operating procedure
SSGT: Staff sergeant
SULE: Small Unit Leadership Evaluation
Squadbay: Wing of a building where Marines are quartered or housed
Square Away: Arrange things in an orderly manner
TBS: The Basic School

Selected Bibliography

BOOKS

Bowden, Mark. *Blackhawk Down: A Story of Modern War*. Penguin Books, 2000.
Clancy, Tom. *Marine: A Guided Tour of a Marine Expeditionary Unit*. Berkley Books, 1996.
Ehrhart, W. D. *Vietnam-Perkasie: A Combat Marine Memoir*. University of Massachusetts Press, 1983.
Fehrenbach, T. R. *This Kind of War: A Study in Unpreparedness*. Macmillan, 1963.
Hooker, Richard D., ed. *Maneuver Warfare: An Anthology*. Presidio, 1993.
Janowitz, Morris. *The Professional Soldier: A Social and Political Portrait*. Free Press, 1960.
Keegan, John. *The Face of Battle*. Viking Press, 1976.
———. *A History of Warfare*. Vintage Books, 1993.
Laffin, John. *Jackboot: A History of the German Soldier 1713–1945*. Barnes and Noble, 1995.
Lind, William S. *The Maneuver Warfare Handbook*. Westview Press, 1984.
Miller, Zell. *Corps Values*. Longstreet Press, 1996.
Moskin, J. Robert. *The U.S. Marine Corps Story*. Little, Brown and Company, 1992.
Poole, H. J. *The Last Hundred Yards: The NCO's Contribution to Warfare*. Posterity Press, 1994.
———. *One More Bridge to Cross: Lowering the Cost of War*. Posterity Press, 1999.
Ricks, Thomas E. *Making the Corps*. Scribner, 1997.
Sajer, Guy. *The Forgotten Soldier*. Harper and Row, 1971.
Simmons, Edward Howard, ed.-in-chief, and J. Robert Moskin, ed. *The Marines*. Hugh Lauter Levin Associates, 1998.
Smith, George W. *The Siege at Hue*. Ballantine, 1999.
Stevens, John C. III. *Court-Martial at Parris Island: The Ribbon Creek Incident*. Naval Institute Press, 1999.
Warr, Nicholas. *Phase Line Green: The Battle for Hue* 1968; reprint Ballantine, 1997.
Weigley, Russell F. *The American Way of War: A History of United States Military Strategy and Policy*. Indiana University Press, 1977.
Wolfe, James B. *Into the Crucible: Making Marines for the 21st Century*. Presidio, 1998.

INTERNAL BASIC SCHOOL PUBLICATIONS

Allen, Col. John R. *Commander's Intent Letter*, 1999.
Anderson, Lt. Col. Phil. *Defining the Institution of The Basic School*, 2001.

INTERNAL OFFICER CANDIDATES SCHOOL PUBLICATIONS

Candidate Regulations. Marine Corps Combat Development Center, 2001.

Index

About the Author

JACK RUPPERT is Director of Ruppert Associates of Cincinati, Ohio.